picaflor

finding home in south america

JESSICA TALBOT

PICAFLOR PRESS

Talbot, Jessica (Helen).
www.jessicatalbot.net
Picaflor: *Finding Home in South America.*

First edition
ISBN 978-987-33-4772-6

Catalogued in Argentina, 07/04/2014
Legal deposit made in accordance with law 11.723

Cover painting 'Picaflor nest' Copyright © Fern Petrie, 2014.
www.fernpetrie.com
Cover and text design by Osvaldo Plaza Torrado.
Author photo by Jo Bayliss

Author's Note

Throughout the process of writing this book its title was Hummingbird. Then one day Picaflor, the South American Spanish name for these amazing tiny birds, slipped neatly into its place.

This is a true story about real events and people. Some names and identifying details have been changed to preserve anonymity and some people and events have been omitted, where the omission doesn't affect the authenticity of the story. Many events took place years ago; for this reason, some parts of the story have been reimagined, while always staying as close to the truth as possible.

Given that my family can be readily identified, I have tried to preserve their privacy as much as possible by occasionally using imagery and metaphors instead of describing actual events and family history in detail. I think it's more important to give a clear impression of how things felt rather than exactly what they were.

Finally, even though I'm a psychologist I have purposely avoided using psychological terminology in the book. My intention has always been to write a warm, human story about overcoming a painful past and creating a brighter future.

*For my beautiful son, whose smiling eyes
always bring me home*

*"I long, as every human being,
to be at home wherever I find myself."*

Maya Angelou

Prologue

THE BITTERSWEET SCENT of coffee lingers as I sip the last of the *cortado*. A laptop hums in front of me on a low wooden table. My back starts to protest but I can't stop typing. The words are flowing easily today, as if they have been calling out to be etched on white, to be seen. I'm talking to you silently as I write. I feel the end of the story is near.

Hi Daniel,

I've been thinking about you lately. It's been a while since the last time I sat still and tried to communicate with you. My little boy is almost two now—just starting to string together his first words. He walks with slightly bowed legs, one foot turned in at the toe, like me. He has the cheekiest grin. I still can't believe I'm a mother. I catch myself staring at him sometimes, feeling such a flood of emotion, as if it's the first time I'm seeing him, as if he appeared by magic.

When I relax and focus like this I can see your smiling face—its wide boyish grin. The hairs on my arm are standing up, tingling like minuscule lightning rods. Maybe you're here, listening.

You know, there was a time when I thought this chance, to be a mother, would pass me by. I'm so grateful it didn't. It's the most incredible feeling—cuddling my son, burying my nose in the soft curve of his neck, touching those little fingers, watching him learn and grow. It's ten times harder than I thought it would be but a hundred times more amazing.

I'm writing a book, too. That's my other baby. I had this consuming urge to set it all down, to tell a painful life story that ends with a new beginning. I was so broken when I flew to Peru all those years ago, hoping to find joy again. I know I'm not the only one to feel weighed down by the heaviness of lost hope and the desire to disappear.

You're part of the story. I took the memory of you with me on my grand adventure. I imagined you so clearly all those times I tried to talk to you. I hope you were there, in some way—listening and watching. It was a bumpy ride, but it knocked me back into my skin. I needed all of it.

I do feel your presence. Over the years I have come to believe that your light didn't just fade out. That comforts me. I made a special place for you in this story because I wanted to keep your spark alive. Not to hold me back, but to remember. It's what the Māori people do. They tell stories about the past in order to keep their ancestors and loved ones near.

I do miss my homeland sometimes: the green hills and mountains, the transparency of the people and soft rhythm of life. But this Kiwi girl had to fly far, searching for the right place to land. I found it here in Buenos Aires, of all places. I don't feel alone anymore. I feel loved. I have a new family and a new country, a crazy, confusing and incredible country. I call her 'Argy,' my infuriating but wonderful friend. You can't help but feel alive here. I'm content. Well, not all the time, but more than enough. I'm enjoying today and looking forward to tomorrow. I hardly ever used to feel like that.

So I'm home. I found home. I fit snugly into my own shoes, and around my hearth sit some wonderful people. I also feel the stronger, nearer presence of those who should always have been there. We are closer now than we have ever been, even though they live far away. I saved a place for them. And then there's you, and Granddad and Nana and friends that have gone. When I'm really calm, I have moments when I can sense you all, hovering in the air above, alive like the pure white sparks of a fire…

Hey, I have to go. I can hear the back door opening. My boys are home from dad and son time. They went to the plaza to play and give me space to write. I can feel the last lines germinating; there's an itching in my fingertips.

Oh, here we go… the shattering of silence. I can hear them laughing about something.

Goodbye, Daniel.

Part One
Flight

One

BRIGHT RED DROPLETS FORM, break and then weep into each other. A tissue wipes them away. There's a buzzing, rattling sound as the machine's needle digs into flesh, ploughing in the ink. It's muggy in the small room above a busy restaurant. I smell garlic mingling with the metallic odour of blood. I look up at the tattooist's face. He's concentrating hard; translucent drops of sweat fall, catch in his eyebrows and trickle down his nose. His hand seems shaky. I wonder if he's high. Cusco is known for its coke.

It feels as if a sharp knife is being drawn slowly along my skin. It's excruciating, but oddly calming at the same time. I ride a surge of endorphins as they well up to dull the sting. I understand why they do it now, the girls and boys at the clinic where I worked, 'the cutters'. They want relief. They wait to be soothed by the gentle waves of our body's natural painkillers. Some cut because they crave a point of pain in the sea of overwhelming angst. Others do it to feel something, anything. They seek pain in order to confirm that they exist.

Is that what I'm doing? Is this crazy?

No, I tell myself. It's the opposite. I'm doing this to mark the end of numbness. It's been two months since I landed. Two months in this dusty country, where the light shines differently. I'm aware my feelings are unravelling still; they are no longer knotted together with sadness. I can differentiate one from another. Through the blur, I can sense colour coming back.

It's done. Now I have a mark to remember the moment.

I get up too fast; mist forms in front of my eyes and my legs shake.

'*¿Estás bien?*' the roguish tattooist asks.

'*Sí*, I'm okay.'

I sit down.

As if making a statement, he takes the needle out of the tattoo gun, wraps it up and throws it in the sharps bin. I feel nauseous looking at the bloodied tissues. I always had a fear of needles: it probably saved me. I take a breath and get up again.

'*¿Te gusta*? You like it?' He gestures to my arm.

'*Sí, sí, gracias*. I love it.'

He keeps looking intently at me. His eyelashes are long and curled—a boy in a man's body. I rustle around in my overstuffed bag for soles. He looks pleased when I peel off a few layers of notes to pay him.

As I walk out the room I wonder just how much he overcharged the pale-faced, wild-haired foreign girl. I feel like a kid who has just done something rash, even naughty.

On the way down the passage I look at my forearm and inspect the lines of the little hummingbird. It's covered in a thin plastic sheet, which is already blotched red and blue-grey from the blood and ink.

Cusco under my skin, I think, smiling.

When I emerge onto the street the bright sunlight slaps me. I blink, momentarily disorientated. After sucking in a deep breath, I open my eyes fully. I stand for a minute in the large square, Plaza de Armas, the hub of Cusco. It's hard not to be awed by the history. This is a powerful city, a place of ideas and bloody wars, worship and innovation. It was once the capital of the Inca Empire, which at its height stretched from Ecuador and Colombia down the continent to the north of Argentina and Chile. The very air seems to ripple with something mystical.

A friend back in Melbourne told me, 'You don't just see Cusco. You *feel* it.'

She is right.

Slowly and deliberately I scan a full arch of the plaza, taking it in: the ornate Spanish colonial-style churches, the mansions and darkly stunning Cathedral of Santo Domingo. I stare at the cathedral. The two towers of its façade rise up, ominous, against an intense blue sky. A massive arched doorway leads to its cavernous interior. When I visited I found it frightening, full of spirit but icy cold. Now I feel a familiar knot twisting. I have mixed feelings about churches, and even more about this one. It was constructed on the foundations of an Incan temple, an attempt by the Catholic church to obliterate—to wipe away centuries of belief with a hostile gesture of domination.

I try to imagine what the temple must have been like. Its name was *Kiswarkancha*. I love how it sounds: *kis- war- kan- cha*. Kiss and war. Beautiful and potent. I can almost feel the Incan spirit rising up through the foundations, stubbornly keeping vigil. The present infused with the past.

I turn, and then smile when I see my favourite fountain, an elaborate double-tiered circular structure adorned with horn-blowing mermen that sits proudly in the middle of the plaza. I have an urge to go and sit on its rim and drag my fingers through the water, but instead I head towards home.

Home, I think, shaking my head in disbelief. It actually does feel like home, too; as if I could stay here. I know this place. I know its curves and secret nooks and cobbled streets. It is a nest in the sky, sheltered and protected by the surrounding Andes mountains. At 3,400 metres above sea level, it whips your breath away. My lungs struggled for oxygen the first days here, now they have adjusted to the thin air; my legs have found new strength from exploring the narrow, brutally sheer alleys.

I start up the hill towards San Blas, a pretty, tourist-friendly neighbourhood. Each step takes effort but I feel light, alive. Perhaps it's oxygen-deprived delirium, but I don't care. I hike towards my room, my nest within a nest.

The streets are lined with Quechua women selling their artisan products, earthy-toned spices and seasonal vegetables. They dress in traditional clothing, vibrantly coloured and intricately patterned: layers upon layers of calf-length skirts called *polleras* swing out from their hips, cardigans on top, sandals made from recycled car tires on their dusty, travel-worn feet. Colourful woven cloths hang over their shoulders and are knotted at the front. Their long black hair is tied into a pair of plaits and always topped with a hat—sometimes bowler-shaped, sometimes a more elaborate cloth construction. There are splashes of bright red and orange, purple and pink, green and yellow: an artist's palette. I feel as if I'm ambling through a giant three-dimensional painting, a sensation intensified by the contrast of the colours against the whitewashed or grey stone walls, and the natural stillness of the people. Time seems to pass over them. They remain unchanged, faces passive and watchful. I'm fascinated by the babies strapped so firmly to their mothers' backs. They never seem to cry.

As I walk, I continue my daily search for fluffy friends. I have already collected eighteen different intricately knitted finger puppets but I can't help seeking more. They lie prone in rows, on mats or small tables, begging me to take them home. There are llamas, cows, birds, tigers, snakes, monkeys, butterflies, cats and dogs and a myriad of other animals and figurines. *But I have you, already*, I say to myself as I pass them, the disappointment growing. *I'll stop at twenty*, I think, only half believing it. Ostensibly I'm collecting them for future play-therapy sessions; the psychologist in me is never far away.

Jess, get home, it's late. I berate myself for losing the rhythm of the climb. My thighs burn as I power up the steep concrete steps that run alongside the alleys. Battered taxis race by, moaning and squealing with effort, spitting out toxic black fumes. I block my nose, my eyes sting.

When I arrive at San Blas plaza I stop again. Above me the sky is swept clean of clouds. Below, rolling out in tiers, are thousands of orange-brown tiled roofs, topping whitewashed adobe brick buildings. In my mind the streets become streams cutting through hard mud on their way into the valley's basin. The view is man-made, but somehow seems organic, as if the city belongs there. I stand, mesmerised, thinking of Daniel.

I wish you could have seen this.

A gust of wind pushes a crumpled wrapper along the cobbled street. It skitters and rasps, skids and tumbles, and then it stops in front of me. For a long second it sits perfectly still, and then it leaps into the air and is blown away down the alley. A chill shivers up my spine. *Is that you?*

I walk the last block to my hostel, scale the rickety stairs at the back of a central courtyard and enter my cosy low-ceilinged room, with its exposed wooden beams. From a small barred window I have a partial view over the rooftops and the dry grass and shrub-covered mountains. The wooden bed with its bright woven bedspread, beckons me. I flop down, spread-eagled, letting out an involuntary huff of breath.

I stare at the ceiling. Unable to relax, I sit up and look again at the tattoo under its plastic skin. I'm dying to peel back the protective film, but I remember the tattooist saying something about *mañana*—tomorrow. I can wait.

Picaflor, that's what they call a hummingbird here: a snacker, nibbler, pecker of flowers. Is that what I am? A restless searcher of sweet nectar?

As I trace the outline of my hummingbird, I wonder if it's tacky, getting a famous Peruvian emblem from the Nazca Lines inked into my right forearm. A twinge nips at me. I haven't been to see the mysterious geoglyphs: huge figures and forms scratched by an ancient culture into the surface of the arid plateaus. Intense curiosity about them wasn't enough to overcome an odd reluctance to leave Cusco, even for a day or two.

I brush the thoughts aside.

Since my first day here I have been inexplicably drawn to the stylised hummingbird design—its wings stretched in flight, the long thin beak pointing purposefully into the sky. It—*she*—is everywhere, woven into the bright cloths and tapestries, painted on walls and pottery, reproduced in silver jewellery. I want to take her back with me, a permanent reminder that I could start again, and make new stories. She would be a sign, a lifelong reminder of freedom and movement.

I notice that my *picaflor*'s long beak is a little wonky. Perhaps he *was* high. I wonder what my colleagues, patients and their parents will think. It's not as hidden as I had thought it would be. Was this a dumb thing to do?

Stop! I say out loud. No second guessing.

I wanted this.

I cross my legs under me and lean my back against the wall, with a pillow hugged to my chest for protection. I wonder if my mind is unravelling along with my feelings. Here I am marking myself with tattoos and speaking to the spirits of the dead.

Perhaps I am looking for something magical because I feel lost, because I want more meaning; because I want to believe some radiant light exists beyond what we think we know about the world.

My mind pushes aside spiritual things, but it can only push so far. There are tiny grains stubbornly sprouting in corners; grains of ideas and feelings and hopes about things that may exist, but can't yet be seen, or quantified or measured. I bat around ideas of the soul, of life after death, of atoms and energy. My tired neurons burn as I start to think about fate, the future and the nature of time.

Then, once again, the words of a prediction splash white against the blackboard of my mind.

For years I tried to erase these words, but they resisted, persistently turning up every now and again to tease me. In the end I followed them, and they led me here—to this room in the high hills of Cusco.

I was twenty-two when I first heard them. On a holiday break from university, a school friend took me—dragged me—to see a well-known psychic in my home town on the west coast of New Zealand's North Island. I told myself that I was just accompanying her. After the hour-long session in the neat, crystal-filled leaf-green house, I felt stunned. The serene blonde wavy-haired psychic told me things she couldn't have known. I couldn't rid myself of the sensation that she had just read aloud something yet unwritten.

'You will find the love of your life aged thirty-two or thirty-three,' she said, meeting my gaze.

I cursed her, inwardly. Eleven years is a long time when you're twenty-two. But I didn't forget her words. After every relationship failure or loss, I would remember them. In a strange way it gave me comfort. Okay, I thought, not yet, but love will come.

She also said, at the very end of the session, 'You will live in South America.'

'South America! Really?'

'Yes, South America,' she repeated, as if there was nothing remotely odd about it.

At the time I dismissed it. Us Kiwis don't live in South America. We go to the UK. We move to Australia, Europe maybe, or perhaps the US. Not South America. Her words were filed away in the drawer of my mind marked, 'Things I don't really believe in but am holding onto for later clarification.'

When I turned thirty-two, a few months before I arrived in Cusco, her words woke up hope in me—a streetlight's glow at the end of a gloomy alley. I was getting close. Maybe she had seen something; maybe she had received a peep through a loop in time. I hoped she was right about finding love, and if I believed that part of what she'd told me, even the tiniest bit, why not give her other prediction, about South America, a mulling over?

At that time I was barely living. I was walking robotically one step, two steps, and then another step, in a slow zombie stagger. I didn't recognise myself anymore. I felt like an empty shell and a fraud. I blotted out any emotion that dared work its way to the surface. I marked time, coffee cup to coffee cup, glass of wine to glass of wine. Bad boy in bar to bad boy in bar.

One day I said, *Enough. Move, now!*

With nothing else to grab onto, I decided to investigate the psychic's destination: the mysterious continent of South America. I came up with other reasons for the adventure so that the whole idea appeared less mad. I told myself I had always wanted to learn another language. Spanish, with its passion, its poetry of words, seemed like a good choice. Then there was the incentive—the fantasy—of Latin men.

I chose Peru because it seemed exotic and wild and mystical. Then I found a reason to go for longer than a holiday: a programme working with street children in Trujillo (a fairly large city on the coast, some eight hours from the capital, Lima). I planned to volunteer for a couple of months and then travel to Cusco and the sacred valley at the end of my trip. The Melbourne mental health clinic where I worked gave me three months' leave. I think they sensed how close I was to the edge, toes curled over, ready to jump somewhere dark.

The psychic's words of ten years before were the needle of a compass. I decided to follow it.

When I tire of thinking, I extract myself from the bed and search for my thin blue traveller's towel, buried under my mess of clothes. I flick it open. Disappointment grabs at me; looking at it makes me feel strangely exposed, and I'm not yet naked. My body craves a real fluffy towel that wraps snug, cocooning me.

I take a shower in the tiny bathroom, my arm awkwardly hanging outside. It smells musty in the enclosed space but appears clean enough. I wear flip-flops just in case. I don't open my mouth for fear of nasty waterborne bugs and amoebas making a home in my intestines. As the water runs in glistening streams down my body, I scrub away the bone dry and powder fine dust that coats everything in Peru. It seems to cling to the particles of air, giving a misty appearance to everything.

Clean skin.

Dressed and restless, I head off towards a den-like, art-filled café, a popular haunt, which sits on a narrow street above the hypnotic cascade of a waterfall fountain in San Blas plaza. I hope there will be someone I know there; I want company. It's early still. As the light fades, the cold starts to invade my bones. I hug myself. *Ouch*. I forget—the tattoo's still so raw.

I dip my head and walk through the low-framed blue door. Music is playing quietly. I hear the sound of a pan flute haunting the air. I spot Amy, a new friend. She's from Melbourne, where I have lived for seven years. A month before I left town a mutual friend put us in touch because we were both planning a trip to Peru. Over caffè lattes we clicked, like friends from some other lifetime—and then, to our surprise, discovered we were booked on the same flight.

I see her sitting alone in the corner, a glass of wine on the table, nearly empty. Her hands rest in her lap, her face is immobile. She's leaning her head back against the wall and looking into nothing, or maybe into herself, into her memories. She reminds me of a fragile china doll, with her porcelain skin, huge green eyes and delicate mouth—sweet, but also wise.

I start towards her, carefully inching up my sleeve, ready to show off my new mark. She doesn't look up. As I get closer I'm struck by the sadness hovering around her. It's not the right time; I roll my sleeve down.

'Amy,' I say softly.

She takes a second to come back to this world. 'Oh, Jess. Sorry. How are you?'

'I'm good. What about you? You seem far away.'

'You caught me in a moment.'

'I know those moments.'

She shifts her weight and motions for me to sit.

'I need a glass of wine,' I tell her. 'Do you want another one?'

She nods.

I go to the bar and order from the tall girl at the counter. I'm momentarily stunned by her bright red hair and translucent skin. I wonder where she's from. She smiles wryly at me as she pours two huge glasses.

'Do you want to talk about it?' I ask Amy as I sit down next to her.

She looks around the bar, which is practically empty. She stares into her glass, as if she wishes it were a crystal ball. She breathes in. 'You know I told you I was feeling a bit lost and I came here to have some time to think? Well, there's more to it than that.' She pauses for a long time, and then pushing the words out, she says, 'My marriage is falling apart.'

I pause, conflicted, not willing to play therapist. 'And—' I say, to spur her on.

As the tale unravels, I stay quiet. She keeps rubbing her forehead, as if she's trying to rub the pain away. Her hands involuntarily rise and then fall into her lap. She seems shocked, in disbelief at where she has found herself. 'This is not me,' she repeats, while picking at her nail beds.

After a long pause she looks up and says, 'Jessy, I don't want to go home yet.'

'I'm not exactly ecstatic about going back, either.'

'Enough of me. You haven't told me why you're doing this,' she says, looking right at me. 'Well, the real reasons.' Her face relaxes. 'Your turn. Please, I need a break from thinking about this thing.'

'Are you sure?'

'Yes. I'm okay, really.'

I take a swig of wine and a deep breath. 'Three years ago I lost someone I loved very much. Daniel.' I stop, wonder whether to tell her the rest. 'He committed suicide.'

Amy's eyes widen. I see her mouth move, but she says nothing.

'It nearly killed me. I'm having trouble shaking it off. It's like I have this heavy… grief coat on.'

'I'm so sorry, Jess, that's horrible.'

'Yeah, it was horrible, painful. It was—still is—confusing. We weren't really together at the time, although that didn't change how I felt.'

Her brow creases. 'But you had been a couple?'

'We were together for about two years and then we broke up. We started to see each other again, tentatively, just before he died.'

'What was he like?'

I close my eyes and picture Daniel. 'He was lovely, beautiful and intensely sensitive. You know, one of those people who are so bright but hurt too much—feel too much. I think he attached himself to people he thought would take the pain away. I took on that role too easily.'

'He was depressed?'

'For most of his life. Then he started using drugs, looking for a reprieve. I didn't know about that when we met. He hid it well and I didn't want to see it. He tried rehab over and over, and therapy. It was a war. At the beginning I was determined to fight alongside him. I thought if I loved him enough—'

'You could save him.'

'Yes, so naïve, I know.' I look down at my fingers.

Amy touches my hand, encouraging me to continue.

'One day I realised I wasn't helping him and was ignoring my own stuff. It was hurting us both. So I left him. A year later he was clean, had a Master's degree in his hand, and I thought I could go back. I was still in love with him.' My mind races and I take some long gulps—a too familiar habit—from another full glass of wine.

'What happened?'

I wonder whether I can tell her. I decide I need to. He died two weeks after he turned twenty-eight. His birthday was the last time I saw him. I remember, in the car on the way there I felt so hopeful about us. And then I saw his face. He wasn't okay. I'm sure he saw in my eyes how disappointed I was. He looked lost in the dark. I couldn't hug him properly. I gave him a cold half-hug. We fought about some really stupid thing and the plan to watch a movie was "postponed". When I left I gave him a kiss and a warmer hug, but I was still holding back. I wish…' I trail off. Why hadn't I hugged him properly, why hadn't I given a little more in that moment? That last moment.

'Are you okay, Jess?' The concern in Amy's voice pulls me back into the present.

I nod. I am nearly done. 'As I drove away I glanced back and saw him standing there, in his favourite jeans and an old red T-shirt, on the crest of the hill—it's my final image of him.' I catch a flash of this image now and have to grit my teeth to stop tears. 'He looked so sad; his arms limp at his sides. I cried the whole way home. I nearly crashed the car.'

'I'm so sorry, Jess.' Amy's eyes are shining, wet.

'You know something strange? I felt it, when he went. I was at Cirque du Soleil that night. Something was lingering around me and I couldn't stop thinking of Daniel. Then tears started pouring out of me, like a tap had been turned on. It was so weird. It didn't exactly fit with the clowns running around on stage.'

I press my hand against my chest and continue. 'I felt this terrible tugging sensation, like a piece of me was being ripped out. The next day I rang his house. His sister answered and told me what had happened. I'll never forget it: she had this really strange robotic voice… I didn't believe her at first.'

My face is running with tears and my throat constricts. 'He died watching the sunset in one of his favourite parks.'

'God, Jess, I'm so sorry.' Amy starts crying, too.

Neither of us speaks for a long time. Eventually we compose ourselves. We listen to the music, which has been turned up. More and more people come into the café. My eyes hover over each person who enters. They are mostly *gringos*—foreigners—like us, but there are some locals, too.

'Amy, I don't want to be alone. I'm constantly struggling against this feeling that I'll never find anyone to be with.'

'Don't let Daniel's death close you down,' she tells me, firmly.

'I've been contemplating getting a cat,' I say, deadpan, my shoulders sagging. Amy is giggling. I feel a tiny bit better. 'I picture myself with a cat or three and a bottle of wine in hand. It's like a recurring nightmare.'

'I can't quite see you as a mad old cat lady.'

'Thanks. Here's to stepping off that path fast.' I raise my glass and drown the last drops.

'Well, this is a start.' She waves her hand around the bar. 'Being here.'

'I'm really glad you're here, too. It doesn't feel like a coincidence that we were on the same plane.'

'I know what you mean.'

'I'm also delighted that we're equally screwed up!'

Amy laughs, and I decide the moment has come to show her my tattoo. I slowly pull up my sleeve. 'Look what I did!'

'I love it. It's a hummingbird, right? Did you do it today?'

'Yeah, it's still weeping a little. I wanted to mark this time, because it's been… I don't know, transformative. I feel different.'

'So then, Miss Jess, you've got the tattoo; now, how about a little fling with a Latin lover?' She smiles, her eyebrows raised.

'Sounds fabulous.' I grin back at her. 'But they're a bit on the short side. Plus, I can't string two words together in Spanish.'

'Who needs to talk?'

Later that night, I sit on my bed in the dark. It squeaks with every movement. The glow of the moon filters through the thick bars of the small window. Long shards of light land at my feet as if they are trying to catch hold of me. I pull the flat scratchy pillow to my chest again, take a breath and try to talk to Daniel.

Hi Daniel,

I'm here. Are you? I thought I felt you for a second today but now I don't know why I'm talking to you. Maybe I'm trying to conjure a thread to connect us. I'm imagining you sitting in front of me, your long legs crossed. Your face has that open curious look you get when you are listening intently, the child in you so visible, always a minute away from being distracted.

I have things to tell you.

I've missed talking to you, feeling the warmth of your skin. Since you died, living has been tough. You left a big hole. There have been other losses, too. A friend died of cancer recently after a long illness. You remember that Mum was fighting cancer when you and I were together? You were so overwhelmed yourself, perhaps you don't recall. At the time I was desperate to help you; I couldn't focus on anything else. Mum's okay now, but it's been confusing. It was a massive battle, and I wasn't there enough—more than a thousand miles away, and not just physically.

For a long time I felt as if I was choking on a scream. As I tried to suffocate it, it suffocated me.

Everything was so grey. There were moments when I dreamed of following you, moments when I wanted nothingness. I was sleeping my life away, hibernating, like you used to. It's strange, the memories that stay close to the surface. I still have a perfectly clear image of your 'cocooning'. You would roll yourself up on the floor in that mossy-green down bedspread, just the top of your head peeking out. The blinds were always down, a heater on full. It was such a bizarre sight: you enveloped in a huge green chrysalis.

When I arrived at your house, just after the first time you tried to leave this world, I found you cocooned. I called out to you; you unwrapped. With eyes still closed you beckoned me in. In a low rough voice you said, 'Jessy, come lie with me' and you rolled me up with you. I remember you were naked, except for underwear, your skin warm and soft. I melted into you, and then I couldn't breathe and asked you to let me out. You unrolled, set me free, and then rolled up again without a word. It was so hard to see you like that. You would stay like that for days, so vulnerable, your bare belly protected from the outside world by soft green down. I get it: the need to block out the world, hide from it but I don't want that anymore.

So I jumped. I boarded a plane and flew to Peru. A strange thing to do, perhaps, but it was a good choice. I was working with street kids when I first arrived here. They taught me a lot. Their lives are so tough, but they still smile at the smallest things. You've never seen such excitement over a banana, a game of football, a colourful tray of paint.

They would have loved you. Children always did.

I'm in Cusco now, in the mountains. I wish you could have seen this city. It hurts me to think you never had the chance to travel to all the places that fascinated you. There is something special about this place. It buries itself in your soul. I wonder sometimes if things would have been different if you had seen more of the world.

I hope that by talking to you I'm taking you with me—a quiet witness to all this. Maybe I'm also trying to find a way to let you go.

I've been using this time to think. Things make more sense now. You know how I described my dad as a ghost, not really there? Well, I think I was like that too, growing up—a sad, quiet ghost of a child. I'm starting to think that maybe, in some way, I need to give her the voice she didn't have back then.

You had a little boy in you, too. He was always there, peeping out. I have a vivid memory of a picture of you: you were about six or seven. There was a smile on your face in that photo, but something was wrong with it. It looked more like a grimace. The first time I saw it, I felt the enormous angst living in that 'little you'. Your eyes already contained pain, and fear. It made me want to cry. It was a photo your parents had on display. Did they not see it—see you? The aching started young for you, as it did for me.

Sometimes I think I catch a glimpse of you, in the form or face of a stranger. The fact that you are gone still feels surreal. I tried to make sense of it back then, make it real that you were never coming back. I went to the place where you parked, where you left. I sat in my car, in the same spot. As I watched the sun drop away slowly behind the trees, I tried to feel you, to slip into your skin, to see briefly through your eyes. My mind took a snapshot of the last image you saw before your eyes closed forever. But I struggled to imagine your thoughts. Were they angry, sad, were you saying your goodbyes? Did you think of me? Did you prick a vein one last time to ease the ride?

I wish—I don't know—so many things.

There's no going back. I know that.

For a long time now you have been the only one in my heart, but I need to find a place for some new people, for new love. This is not about forgetting you. I'm just tucking you away, in a quieter place.

I still miss you, but I'm okay.

Goodnight, Daniel.

As I say these last words into the silence, I suddenly feel self-conscious. I hold the pillow tighter to my chest. It doesn't stop the ache. And yet, somehow, having my one-way conversation brings relief. I feel lighter. As I settle down under the woven bedspread, I can hear the yapping of Cusco's wild dogs in the distance. I drag the heavy covers up over my ears to block out the sound and combat the chill from the mountain air.

Two

The eerie atmosphere that hovers in Cusco's valleys seems to attract people who are searching; maybe it even draws people here. Everyone I meet is struggling with something. Protective layers slip off, defences come down fast. There's a freedom that comes from knowing our time together will be brief. I make friends easily in this nest city, my home of three weeks. I surround myself with characters, people who are quirky and interesting, smart and sensitive.

Many of these Cusco characters come here for a few days on their epic backpacking journey through South America, and then fall in love and stay. I name them, the ones that don't look like they are leaving anytime soon, *long-term temporaries*. Everyone has a story. Some are running away from something or someone, others are avoiding the next stage in their life, or taking a break before making an important decision. For some it's time-out, a place to rest and reflect. Others are nomads and spend their lives making long-term temporary homes all over the globe. Some come to grieve a loss. Some remain here for love, or for the idea of it. A few stay—sometimes consciously, sometimes not—for easy access to their drug of choice, cocaine. The more I talk to people, the more I realise so many are drifting, like little white parachuted dandelion seeds in the wind.

I wake the day after my session with Amy and my conversation with Daniel, to the light of the morning pressing on my eyelids. I look around the tiny loft room and realise I want to stay here for a while, or longer. I fear going back to my old life. I fear I will climb back into my old familiar skin and sleepwalk again.

I lie in bed and smile as I think of the visitor who's arriving tomorrow, my friend Elle. She emailed me a few weeks ago.

Jessy,
Surprise, I'm coming to visit you. I have a week off. I've always wanted to see Machu Picchu. So I thought, why not? See you soon. Will send details of my flight asap.
Love, Elle.

It's so Elle, a *quick* visit to Peru!

I can't wait. I'm itching to show her my Cusco. I want to tell her everything that I've been thinking since I got here and to be calmed by her sparse but perceptive words.

I picture her. She is curled up in a cosy old-lady armchair, bright gold hair highlighted against the faded pattern of the headrest, a leather skirt barely covering inches of her shapely thighs, legs tipped with red high heels and her hands busy with a crochet hook and a colourful ball of wool.

Elle blew through my front door and into my life with a whoosh of sparkling vitality. We lived together for a couple of years in Melbourne as flatmates (or *flitmates*, as she would say, to tease my thick Kiwi accent) in a hundred-year-old crumbling Victorian mansion. The house had a name; it, she, was called 'Avalon', and she reminded me of an elegant wealthy old dame, now weary and a touch senile. Elle brought vitality to the house, as well as to me; she brightened its last years with music. After many respites from death row demolition, we knew before we left, Avalon's time was running out.

Elle is a chameleon. In the daytime she wears a neat pressed suit and writes the weather forecast for a national news channel. At weekends she dominates the stage as a singer in two very different bands. Sometimes she's adorned in black shiny gothic outfits, at other times it's a spangled techno ensemble. Her cosy bedroom is filled with musical gear and soft toys and flowery prints. The hard lines of keyboards and speakers and microphone stands make for a strange contrast with the feminine curves of her bedhead, the pretty pillows and curtains and teddy bears. She's fifteen years older than me but giggles like a child and dates men barely half her age. Her face is fresh, full of curiosity. In the time we lived together my face wore many more emotional years than hers, not so much tucked into lines but in the dry, pale dullness. In Cusco my skin shines; a light has come back on.

I collect people like Elle. I always search for the rare and precious ones, and I hope I'm interesting enough for them to want to collect me back. I aim to collect and keep them for life.

The following day, I go to meet her at the airport. I find her face in the swarming crowd. Something's different. Her dark brown hair confuses me, but then her hair has a tendency to change colour like the seasons, and span the rainbow: pink, platinum blonde, golden, purple, red, baby blue. After a long flight from Melbourne and a night in Lima, tiredness pulls at the skin around her eyes, yet her fire shines through.

'Welcome, you're going to love it here!' I say, my voice muffled by her newly coloured hair as she crushes me in a bear hug.

'Of course, I'm so excited,' she tells me, her voice full of energy, already looking around in search of curiosities.

The altitude takes its toll on her the first day, so we relax in the café above the waterfall and catch up on gossip while sipping *mate de coca* (coca-leaf) tea.

I can feel my mind clearing. The world is vivid. It's probably partly the tea, but I am sure it's also Elle's influence.

She is peering over the rooftops. She's already in love with Cusco. 'Bummer, I should have come for longer,' she says, as we watch the early morning sunlight illuminate the hills around us.

'It's so like you, a week-long trip to South America.'

'Only had one week off,' she sighs.

'I'm really happy you're here.'

She smiles. 'Me too. Hey, how was the volunteering? The kids?'

'Great. Hard. Sad sometimes. I ended up leaving a bit earlier than I'd planned to.' I can picture their faces and my guilt stings.

'I think five weeks is a pretty good stint. It's good you left. You need this time for you,' she says, simply.

'They gave me so much more than I gave them.'

'What do you mean?'

'At first I tried to teach them English, but I was useless. A class of thirty kids is a totally different scenario from one child contained in a small office.'

Elle laughs.

'So they moved me to the art class. They behave better there. It was so amazing watching them play and create.'

I remember their faces, lit up, wide awake as they made their little gems; splashing colours around, using fingers, brushes and sponges. I remember waiting for this moment, a kind of glow, which would emerge when they discovered some new mix of colour, when a form jumped out at them, when something unexpected happened on the page.

'It woke me up. I don't know…' My voice trails off. Elle waits. 'I realised I'd stopped being joyful.'

'You've been sad for a long time, Jess.'

'Too long. Those kids have so little, but they made me remember to—' So many words mash together, my mouth opens, but nothing comes out.

'What?'

'Live.'

We both fall silent. I feel embarrassed, exposed.

Our second coffee arrives with a huge piece of layered spongy cake, a colourful Peruvian delight that melts over tongues and infuses bodies with sugar.

My fork slips through the layers. 'I wonder sometimes if we really helped them.'

'I'm sure you did, Jess,' says Elle. Her face is content as she rides a sugar high.

'It's just— there was an eight-year-old girl, very pretty, with almond-shaped eyes and proud cheekbones. Everybody loved her. She was the centre of attention, always smiling shyly when we hugged her. But then, when she didn't think anyone was watching, a cloud would drift over her face. It was as if she was taking a rest from performing. She looked so lost.'

Elle nods but doesn't say anything.

'I've been thinking a lot about her. She saw so many volunteers come and go. I know she became very attached to some of them, and then they walked away after a month, three months, even six. I think she started playing a role, hiding her real self. She became what we wanted her to be. I know no one did it on purpose but I wonder if we were actually damaging her more by giving so much, but nothing long-term. She was closing down to block out each new loss.'

'God, the shrink in you is never on holiday! Okay, I get what you're saying, but don't dwell there.'

'That look in her eyes was one of the reasons I left Trujillo early.

Sorry, Elle. I know, I think too much.'

'No problem, mate.' She changes the subject. 'Hey, how's the Spanish going?'

'Oh God, now that is depressing!' She laughs and I smile but my cheeks burn; I am embarrassed just thinking about this. 'I don't have an ear for it at all. I speak like a drunken two-year-old and I don't understand anything.'

'I'm sure it's not that bad.'

'No really, it is. Listen to this. One day in Trujillo I was out with a group of volunteers, Peruvians and foreigners, searching the streets for kids. One of the locals, this lovely girl called Luz came up and said to me, "*¿Cómo estás, Jessy?* How are you?" I said, "*Estoy muy casada.*" I thought I was saying, I'm very tired, what I actually said was I'm very married.'

Elle raises her eyebrows. 'Very married as opposed to what? Quite married?'

'Wait, it gets worse. Everyone was killing themselves laughing as Luz corrected me; it was totally mortifying. I was determined to try again, so I said, "*Estoy tan embarazada.*" Luz couldn't even speak after that, she was laughing so hard. "What now? What did I say?" "You said, I'm so *pregnant*, not I'm so *embarrassed*." Very married and so pregnant. So yes, I'm a bit useless.'

Elle is doing her best to look sympathetic, but it comes out as a smirk. 'Oh babe, I see what you mean.'

'*Basta*, enough of my bumbling, what shall we do with this time?'

'As much as possible.' I get out a well-thumbed guidebook. 'Machu Picchu, of course,' Elle continues. It's always been one of my dreams to go.'

We sit huddled together as I prise the reluctant pages apart. They are rippled and ridged from a previous soaking, like a topographic map. The task takes patience but sitting here, somehow I feel we have all the time in the world to plan something wonderful.

Day one of our trip is spent rummaging through the traditional Peruvian delights and handicrafts at the famous Andean market in Pisac. The crowds are thick. Our heads brush past bright colours of woven cloth that hang above us. There's music filtering through the corridors and voices in many languages. We get bustled about. We are kids running the halls of a giant toy warehouse, over-stimulated and spoilt for choice.

'These are beautiful,' says Elle, pointing to some Andean pottery.

The sign says they are from the Moche people. Their earthy tones and bold forms depict faces, figures, demons, felines, birds and monkeys. Behind them sit some eye-opening designs demonstrating rather graphic sexual positions. We both go a little rosy when we spot them, smirks thinly veiled as we attempt to direct each other's attention to particularly *interesting* pieces.

'Apparently they weren't shy about sex,' I whisper to her. 'Well, at least before the Catholics arrived.'

Towards the end of the day we stumble across a tiny store with some stunning pieces on display. They are reproductions, made to look old. As we pore over them, wondering if we should open our purses, the store owner waves us over. In Spanglish he tells us he has some 'special stuff' out back that might interest us. 'Come with me, come with me,' he insists.

We look at each other, a touch wary. The last time we travelled together, in Thailand, we ended up being chased down the street by a tiny bone-thin guy with bird's-nest hair and a huge shiny knife. But curiosity gets the better of us. We are two, and he's shrunken and well seasoned. He pushes back a heavy dust-caked curtain and we squeeze through a tight entrance to a tiny room behind the store.

A low-watt lamp is the only light. It takes a minute for our eyes to adjust and our heart rates to calm down. Then we look around. We are surrounded by real, ancient artefacts—probably robbed from graves and archaeological sites.

'We can't buy these things,' whispers Elle into my ear.

I nod.

'No, no money for *hermosas cosas*, beautiful things,' I say to him.

'Cheap, very very old. I give good deal, pretty girls,' he says, animated.

I had been warned about this back in Cusco and was aware that if we did buy something, we might face serious trouble at customs on the way home. It could also be a scam: the rustle of an opening wallet like an alarm that draws a 'policeman' to us. We would have to bribe them royally to extract ourselves.

'No, no *gracias*,' I say, as we rapidly escape back into the light of the market. We don't look back.

'That's sad,' says Elle.

'I know. I hate to see those artefacts decaying back there.'

A day later Elle and I arrive at our true destination—Machu Picchu. On the short and winding bus ride from the tourist town Aguas Calientes to the site, I summarise out loud from our guidebook.

'Okay, so it was built more than five hundred years ago. They're not sure what it was used for but it was probably a royal Inca estate and religious retreat. It's thought that the site was active for about a hundred years. Then the people disappeared.'

I stop; my eyes are blurring and my stomach gripes from the sharp turns.

'What happened?'

'Theories range from infighting as the Inca Empire began to disintegrate to everyone dying from smallpox and other introduced diseases. Once deserted, it sat forgotten in the jungle for hundreds of years until 1911 when an American historian stumbled upon it.'

'Whatever happened, it must have been a pretty miserable way to go for such a proud civilisation,' Elle says, looking out the window.

'An American hippy in Cusco told me that the site sits on a mystical energy line and the Inca people became so wise they just vibrated away to a higher plane of existence. I prefer his version.'

'Me too.'

The moment we arrive, Elle leaps off the bus, her hair splaying out behind her. She's wide-eyed and jittery.

'Gee, you really are excited about this, aren't you?' I say, surprised by the dramatic change in her demeanour.

She powers off. I have to trot, on my stiff legs, to catch up with her.

Uniformed ushers manoeuvre us—like contented cows—through metal security gates.

'Wow,' says Elle, as the site opens out in front of us.

It looks surreal, yet somehow familiar. I have seen it so many times in postcards. Terraces of grass and stone walls rise up in layers; some are bare, others contain the remains of structures. The site is split in the middle by a wide central grassed area. Huayna Picchu ('young peak' in Quechua) stands guard over the site like a huge sentinel.

The air is fresh but feels heavy with activity, as if atoms are clashing together around us. Wispy clouds stretching across a powder-blue sky add to the wonder. I feel energised with each breath but strangely calm at the same time. *Am I just imagining this?* I look over at Elle and see she has the same expression of calmness settling over her features. She looks younger.

Then my brain fires up with slightly fretful analysis. The whole site is dotted with colourful points of people. It's as if some giant playful creature had risen at dawn, scaled Huayna Picchu and then thrown packets of oversized M&Ms all over it. Japanese tourists with three expensive cameras dangling around their necks scurry around—seeing the site through their lenses, desperate to 'capture' it and take it away. Then there are the German and Dutch in their practical clothes, with determined faces. Of course there are hoards of North Americans ticking 'MP—Peru' off their bucket lists. The younger ones stride around in caps and jeans, the older couples circulate more slowly in bright and matching tracksuits. Elle and I are just part of a marauding pack. The thought makes me uncomfortably aware of my big feet tramping around, my finger clicking away, taking photos. It feels sacrilegious.

'Someone told me the government plans to close the site down,' I tell Elle.

'Why?'

'The sheer numbers of tourists are damaging it, wearing it away.'

'That's bloody sad. Good we can see it now,' she says, distractedly.

'I can't help thinking part of the magic is lost when people come.'

Elle's attention is absorbed ahead of her, she's not listening.

I suddenly imagine a feeding frenzy. I see ants. It's as if there are luscious dabs of honey in remarkable corners of the world, and then the swarm comes.

'Hey, Jess, chill. Just enjoy it.'

I hate my face, it shows everything.

'I am, I am. Come on, let's follow them,' I say, pointing to a large tour group.

For a while we tag along behind them, trying to catch some words while also staying inconspicuous. We don't pull it off. Feeling the sideways looks, we detach from the group, content to let our minds imagine. Hours are spent wandering and marvelling. I try to picture the people who lived here, their clothes and their customs. I imagine their gold adornments shimmering in the sunlight, their strong cheekbones and piercing eyes, their elaborate rituals to the gods.

The remains of the walls are so beautifully constructed from cut granite rocks that I can't resist tracing the lines and the joins with my fingers. No two quarried blocks are alike and they are so carefully fitted together, without any type of mortar, that it sends my mind wondering. I think about the skilled Inca builder sanding off the sharper edges of a large stone and then finding another that would fit its angles perfectly. So perfectly that nothing could slip between them. Hundreds of years of sun and rain have left barely a mark on some walls; not even earthquakes have dislodged the stones from one another.

Some hours later Elle and I finally tire of our exploration and find a spot of our own, hidden away. We lie on our backs in the grass. A calm clarity settles over me but I can't stop thinking about those stones, their surfaces snug against each other. I wonder if we too have a matching someone. It might not be a perfect match initially, but with time and patience, we rub together and smooth out the jagged edges until we fit together neatly. Perhaps some of us aren't meant to join: our edges are just wrong. We stick together for a while and then one big bump breaks us apart.

I peep over at Elle. Her face is half-covered by her very Aussie, khaki green full-brimmed hat.

'Elle, do you believe in soulmates?'

She moves slightly. I sense she has opened her eyes and then closed them again.

'No, not really. I think there are many people who can touch our lives at different times.'

'I guess I think that, too.'

'I've had a few special loves, and I'm sure there will be more,' she adds.

'I imagined, for a brief moment, that Daniel was my soulmate. It sounds so silly now.'

'He *was* special, Jess, but he took a lot from you,' she says.

'I really did love him, as painful as it was, as messed up as it was. Now I don't believe one person is enough.'

I think again about the stone walls of the site. There are so many stones in every wall, from foundation blocks to crowning details. *More than one*, I say to myself.

'You always need more than one,' she agrees, as if reading my thought.

'Losing the one you think is "the one" is pretty devastating.'

There's a long silence, then she says, 'After Daniel died you had this haunted, lost look in your eyes. I thought maybe you would never come back.'

'I was lost, still am a bit. But this trip has helped. I feel better. Hopeful.'

'You do seem different—in a good way,' she says, looking briefly over at me.

There's another long pause as we drift into our own thoughts, but there's one more thing on my mind.

'Elle, I want so badly to be a mother one day, it almost hurts. It pulls. Did you ever want kids?' I ask tentatively, nervous about raising the topic.

'Truly, Jess, I've never felt that need. I don't feel I'm missing anything,' she says, firmly.

'Your music is your baby. It's your grand love.' I am relieved that I haven't touched a nerve.

'You're right. It's what I live for. I can't imagine my life without it.'

'I've always envied that. I'd like to find that kind of passion. You look so alive when you play, it's amazing to watch.'

'You will. Just don't stop looking. And hey, I'm sure you'll get to be a mum, too. Don't stress so much, you have time.'

Her words reassure me. I lie back in the grass and look again at the sky. I feel my very bones relaxing. A big sigh releases something and new air replaces it.

I look over at Elle. She's in her own world; maybe she's dreaming of music. A surge of warmth fills my chest. I realise she is a sturdy stone in my wobbly wall.

We take the train back to Cusco. I love the swaying, bumping, hypnotic rumblings of trains. I wonder if the movement brings us back to riding in our mothers' bellies as they waddled around, the fluids whooshing, sounds muffled.

Elle has her head pressed between the seat and window, using her hat to block out the fading sun. It's peaceful. Her eyes are closed.

I find myself thinking of Daniel, of a scene that has been played over and over in my head. It's a scene I keep trying to make sense of, a scene that articulates both the wonders and pain of being with him, of loving him. The memory reel is so well-played that it even has a name.

The wreath episode

On a crisp spring day we went for a long walk in a park near his house in Melbourne's eastern suburbs. The afternoon sun was touching everything in a way that made the world shimmer with life. A light wind gently massaged the grass and breathed life into the new spring leaves. Curious sounds echoed in the air around us, as if children were playing Chinese whispers, secrets distorting and morphing from little mouths with each telling. The blue above was bluer, the spring greens more intense. It was surreal at the time, even more so as a memory.

For many weeks things had been going well. I allowed hope to fill me. As the pollen was thick in the air, I sneezed three times. He laughed. We held hands tightly as we dragged our feet through the long damp grass, stopping every few strides to kiss. Then we sat, bodies pressed close, as if we wanted to merge into each other.

'Things are good now, Jess,' he said.

'You're good now.'

'Yeah, I'm good.'

'We have a chance, right?'

'Yes, we do.'

Suddenly he stood up, lightly kissed my forehead and said, 'Wait here. I have a surprise for you.'

'Okay,' I said. 'Don't go far.'

I watched him spring away down the hill.

I sat basking in the moment, soaking in the rays of afternoon sun. I waited, patiently at first. Then time passed by. Half an hour, an hour—the late sun was now barely visible. I became worried. When I was about to go in search of him, I saw him in the distance emerging from some trees. It's all okay, I thought, putting away the nagging doubts.

In no time he was standing in front of me with a hand-woven wreath of leaves and flowers, still fresh and moist in his hands. He placed it ceremoniously on my head.

'Jessy, I love you. Let's get married,' he said, smiling wide.

Stunned, I stammered, 'Okay.'

We kissed. I felt the muggy, cold sweat on his face. I didn't want to look at him; I didn't want to know. But I couldn't help myself. Scanning his clear blue eyes, I saw what I dreaded: the pin-prick pupils. He was high and he knew I knew. Neither of us spoke. I sucked in my anger.

My thoughts run on as the countryside streams by. Maybe if I had loved him more, been a better, wiser person he wouldn't… *No, don't; don't do this again.* I shake the thoughts away.

I know there was nothing I could have done. He was too sensitive for this world, the moments without pain were too few. We were like rock climbers, scaling a rough wall, attached to the rock face and each other with ropes, cams and metal loops, hoping they would prevent us from falling. We relied on each other, strained against each other, and then he cut the rope. He fell and I almost fell, too. Then, for months, years, I hung there mid-wall.

I think now, as I stare, only half-focused, out the window, that when he cut the rope he freed me.

When the train pulls into the station and scrapes to a shuddering halt I look over at Elle as she extracts herself from sleep. 'Are we here?' she asks.

'Yes, we're here.'

I smile at her. A long sleep-crease on her face marks where it pressed into her hat and a clump of hair extends out in a ragged ball from her temple.

She laughs. 'That bad?'

'No, you look smashing.'

'Liar.'

'Love you, babe,' says Elle over her shoulder as I wave goodbye to her at the airport the following day. I can still feel her warm hug pressing in on my skin.

'You too,' I call out as she melds with the crowds trailing through the gate.

I wipe away quiet tears and then I start the hike home.

Three weeks to go. Make the most of them.

On the walk back I feel a strange sensation, like a glinting in my peripheral vision. When I move my head, it moves too. It's not clear yet, but something is there. If I just keep going I will catch up with it.

Three

LITTLE FLAKES OF SKIN peel off around the edges of my tattoo. Some are translucent, others flecked with colour. I blow onto my arm and they lift off and float away, tiny feathers in the wind. It's itchy, but I try not to pick.

She's settling in, I tell myself.

Tonight is a big night. It's Saturday and there is a dance party in an old adobe brick warehouse in the centre of town—and supposedly it is the place to be. I have a posse to go with. Amy has been persuaded to put her dancing shoes on. Then there's Jen, a dark-haired wild-child Sydney-sider, with a presence that attracts attention. Darkness surrounds her today; confusion and anger radiate from her. An intense month-long tryst with an attractive, jealous and aggressive Peruvian guy had ended dramatically only days before. We ride the waves with her as she puffs up with fury and then deflates with pain, every few minutes. Chrissie, another Aussie volunteer, is never far from her side, her calmness and warmth containing the flames. I feel a connection with Chrissie—she's been wearing a leaden grief-coat, too. The sudden loss of her mother the year before is still visible in her face but a little light is glowing there now, as Cusco works its magic.

'I'm excited about tonight,' I say to Amy as I battle with my hair, an untameable mop that's starting to form into ragged little ropes. I stand behind her in the small bathroom, trying to catch a glimpse of myself in the mirror. Despairing at my hair, I pull it back into a high ponytail.

Amy's putting the last touches of eyeliner around her big green eyes.

'Yeah, me too. It's going to be fun. I need this,' she says.

We give up the mirror and move into Amy's bedroom.

'I hope he doesn't turn up,' says Jen, who is sitting on the bed, back against the wall, an over-full wine glass in hand threatening to spill.

'Don't fret, Jen, we'll be there,' says Chrissie.

'Asshole,' she says loudly.

'I'll kick him where it hurts,' I say, giving a lively demonstration of a highly uncoordinated kick.

Amy and Chrissie laugh. Jen frowns and she shakes her head at me.

The party is in full swing when we arrive. Techno music fills the cavern-like space and bounces off four large columns. The bass vibrates through the wooden floors, tingling into my feet. We are thrown one way and another by waves of people; heads are moving in rhythm, shoulders sway with the melody. Mood lighting and cosy sofas in darker corners stimulate both excitement and nervousness. The place is bursting with locals—tight skirts and shirts press around curves and muscles. The tiny girls flick back dark silken hair and totter around on high heels; the boys have their hair slicked back and wear trendy jeans and US brand footwear. There are a number of slick boys from Lima lurking in corners. Boisterous Aussies, tipsy Brits and chatty Americans mingle with other foreigners, all dressed in the best threads they could salvage from backpacks. Many pairs of eyes scan the room. There's heat in the air: everyone's out for a good night, a good catch.

Time amplifies and constricts as a few toxically strong *Cuba libres*— rum and cokes—play with my senses. When the DJ changes, the beat softens, clearing the dance floor as the crowd dissipates into corners.

In the middle of the floor, flooded in a hazy light, is a man dancing alone in his own space—absorbed completely in the music. His red singlet top is cut low at the armpits and neck, exposing a firm, bronzed body. He's tall. The lights bring out his high cheekbones and handsome jawline. His face is peaceful, his eyes closed. He has no hair at all on his head. The beautifully shaped bare dome and his Buddhist-like aura attract me in a way I can't quite understand. The pull towards him is tidal; it's as if I feel the sucking of the sea under my feet. It tugs at me. With the tugging comes a sharp pang and an overwhelming sensation of reliving a moment. For a brief second I see Daniel there in the light, the night we met. The memory and the present moment overlap and interchange, sending my heart into a painful dance. I close my eyes and open them again. Daniel is gone and the man becomes clear again, real. My heart finds a slower rhythm. I feel each breath enter and leave my body.

I can't stop watching him. I want him to see me but I'm terrified he will. I try to get closer but there's an invisible barrier around him. It feels wrong to invade it. I stand transfixed as the dance goes on around me. As my fear loosens, my legs start to move forward.

Someone grabs my arm.

'Hey, Jess, we're going to Mama Africa to meet the others,' says Amy.

'Can't we stay a little longer?' I beg loudly into her ear.

'No, they're waiting, *vamos*,' she says, her arm at my hip, pulling me.

'You can't stay here alone,' says Jen, seeing my reluctance.

I take one last look behind me. He doesn't look up. His hands are playing with imaginary clouds of sound.

Maybe he never saw me.

I whisper a goodbye as the three girls manoeuvre me through the crowd and out the door.

Mama Africa is crazy and packed to its beams. I feel as if I'm in a boat. I can't find my feet, the rhythm has gone. I'm fixed to the spot, just standing and circling.

He's just a guy at a party, I berate myself, trying to shake off the image of him.

The girls are doing their own thing. I see Jen has her eye on a suave looking English lad. Chrissie is following her around, hopelessly attempting to tame her. Amy is out of sight.

When daylight starts to filter through the windows the barmen usher us towards the door. The wave of people is moving me along with it. I get knocked around and lose sight of all the girls. I look up to see where my tired body is being pushed, and there, ten inches from my face, is his face, smiling at me.

My heart threatens to stop, and then it attempts to leap right out of my body through my open mouth. Questions race through my mind. Has he come in search of me? Or is this luck? Something else?

A thought forms in the muddle. *He's smiling at me.*

We're pushed close together by the crowd. I can feel him, touch him. His hand finds my waist. It takes all my strength not to fall, there and then, on his lovely full lips.

'*Hola*,' he says, smiling broadly, like he's happy he found me.

'*Hola,*' I return. '*¿De dónde eres*? Where are you from?

'*Soy de Argentina.*'

I remember what fellow travellers have told me about Argentines—too good looking.

It's impossible to talk as we keep being shoved closer, our bodies pinned together, damp now with sweat and desire. Neither of us pull away.

Without saying anything, we leave and find ourselves in the main plaza. The sun's glow is visible over the mountains. We sit on the steps outside the club, legs pressed close, hands softly touching each other's curves. As the sun slips into day we kiss for the first time. A warm flash surges through me. Sensations of pressure, of taste, of heat, morph into feelings of passion, of connection. The intensity is painful and beautiful. I feel like crying.

When we stop we are frozen, looking at each other.

'What's your name?' I ask.

'Francisco, but just call me Paco,' he says, his soft mouth teased into a shy smile.

I am entranced by the way his lips push the words out. 'I'm Jessica.'

I swallow the words, as Kiwis do. I see he's concentrating hard to hear me.

'Jessy,' he says.

It sounds familiar, coming from him.

'Hey, you have a tattoo,' he says, looking at my arm.

'Yes, it's very new.'

I show him.

'I like it. It's from *las líneas de Nacza*, no?'

'Yes, a hummingbird.'

I press her against his warm, damp back as we walk towards San Blas.

As the sun illuminates all the dark corners of the deserted alleys, we arrive at my rooftop nest. There I am awakened from a deep sleep and the hibernating parts of me come shuddering back to life.

We spend the next day together, wandering around Cusco. As he only arrived the day before I can enjoy my role as the knowledgeable guide.

Sitting close together on a high shrub-covered hill overlooking the city, we try to understand each other, to thread a connection.

'Your English is good. Where did you learn it?' I ask.

'In primary school. Only for three years. I love movies and music in

English, so I learn more that way.'

'You speak really well,' I say, a little too enthusiastically.

'Me, really?' He looks away, turning red. 'I was the best in class,' he continues bashfully.

'Your teacher did a great job.'

He goes a deeper shade of red.

I wonder why.

'How do you say, you like a lot someone?'

'Oh, you had a crush on her?'

'A crush, yes, a big crush. She was blonde, very pretty, big—' He motions with his hands.

'Breasted,' I say, laughing, thinking *bosomed* (as my Nana liked to say).

'I worked hard to please her, be the top of the class,' he adds, eyes cast down.

I can't help but picture a little boy with wide brown eyes, so chuffed that he had his teacher's full attention. I wordlessly thank that big-breasted blonde English teacher.

Paco tells me he's twenty-five.

What am I doing with someone seven years younger?

He fills me in on his journey so far. He left his home in Buenos Aires two weeks before with a plan to travel up to Mexico over the next year, surfing all the good beaches along the way.

'I try to discover me, what I want to do.'

'A journey of self-discovery,' I clarify.

'Sí, self-discovery. You too?'

'Yes, me too.'

We laugh.

It turns out that our motivations are pretty much identical: grief and a need to search. He had lost his much-loved older brother five years before.

'He died in a car accident,' he tells me.

'I'm so sorry,' I say and then add, '*Lo siento.*' I feel it.

'One minute he was there, so full of life, and then in *un momento terrible*, he was gone—all the air sucked out.'

'How old was he?'

'He was twenty-five when he died.'

'Like you now,' I say.

'Yes. It's only me now. I feel like I have to make a good life,' he explains, his eyes red-rimmed.

'You want to make them proud, your parents.'

'Yes, but I fail. I don't know what to do with my life. I study, but nothing is right,' he says. His distress breaks through as the English words catch in his mouth.

I watch beside him as quiet tears run their course down his face. My heart wrenches, but it's beautiful. Daniel cried like that. I push the thought aside.

Paco roughly wipes the tears with a fist and turns his head away from me. I have my hand on his back, so I can feel his shuddering breaths calming as we sit in silence.

Then he tells me of another more recent loss. Only months before, he had broken off with his girlfriend of four years. More layers of sadness, but I feel his anger, too. I want to know about her, but I stop myself from asking.

'*Siento perdido*,' he says.

'I know that feeling. I feel lost, too,' I say.

Then I tell him about Daniel. His expressions move in empathy with my words; his eyes never leave my face. They become wetter and more earnest as I start to lose my voice. I feel my hand enclosed in his.

When we are both emptied we sit quietly together for a long time, each preoccupied with our own thoughts as we stare down at Cusco.

A familiar itch works its way to the surface. *Maybe I can help him with this pain.*

I can see he's not as damaged as Daniel, but his words betray a similar sensitivity to the world, to the injustice of fate. I recognise the searching in his eyes.

Three days later, our last night comes too quickly. I can't hold him in Cusco, his feet are already yearning to tread new ground. He invites me over to his hostel and cooks me a chicken curry. We sit at a small table on an enclosed deck. The table is covered in a red and white chequered plastic cloth; wine and candles give it romance. Outside it's pouring with a tropical downfall and my senses are alive with the scent of rain and spices. Gusts of wind make it hard to keep the candles alive.

I choke down the last piece of chicken, my throat constricting with the sadness of what's coming.

Then he reaches for my hand and says, 'Come with me.'

'What?'

'You have two more weeks, no? Spend them with me. Let's travel together.'

I am completely unprepared for this. 'Are you sure? Do you really want me to go with you?' Excitement is rising in me.

'Jessy, please come, I don't want to say goodbye yet.'

'Me neither. Okay then, let's do it.'

A million thoughts jostle to be noticed. He wants to be with me, this amazing young man; but what if I fall for him even more? Our inevitable separation will be even worse. But I can't miss out on this time with him. Just enjoy it, I tell myself: don't think. Be happy—*live the moments; breathe, God damn you.* My heart is beating so fast I feel faint.

That same night I meet with the girls for an urgent huddle.

'Am I doing the right thing? Am I setting myself up for a more painful end?'

'Enjoy it for what it is, a holiday romance—with a very cute, much younger man,' says Amy, grinning.

'You'll regret it if you don't go,' adds Jen, a wry smile planted on her lips.

'Go, Jessy, you deserve some fun,' says Chrissie.

I hug them all, forcefully. I almost break the wafer-thin Chrissie. Then I fly off to my room to pack.

Four

THE NEXT MORNING I stand again above the waterfall and look once more over Cusco. The farewell to her tears at me. She has been a wise teacher and become a friend. But somehow I know it's not the last time I will walk her narrow cobbled streets. She has claimed a piece of my heart and etched herself in.

I look down at my tattoo.

This is the right thing to do, isn't it? Go with the flow.

Paco comes into view, rising up from the steep steps. He gets bigger and bigger, closer and closer. An over-stuffed backpack contains his whole life; his surfboard is tucked under one arm. I laugh. A surfboard in the mountains! He is smiling so broadly I think his face might break.

The journey to Lima will take twenty-two hours or so. Our bus is the cheapest one available; a bus for locals, not tourists. When it crawls into view at the busy, dusty station, I gasp. It rattles to a halt, shudders and sits there. *Sits.* It looks as if it never plans to move again. Big, cracked side mirrors give the impression of insect antennae; the windows are huge blank eyes. Rust and dust obscure its colours, as if it wants to disappear. It's a mournful, fat bug of a bus.

'That thing looks dead,' I say.

Paco laughs.

We squeeze in and clamber over piled up bags of produce and some live, flustered chickens. Of course there's no toilet, no heating or air conditioning, no TV. There are rusted broken windows and mangy seats that were not designed for us long-legged people. We have to turn our legs at a peculiar L-shape angle to our bodies and squish in sideways. Once in, with the seat reclined as far as it will go, I estimate seven centimetres from my nose to the back of the seat in front of me.

Twenty-two hours. You must be kidding.

Off we rattle, down the steep, muddy and dangerous road. We try to talk. We cuddle as best we can as by nightfall it is freezing cold. The bus stops often to pick up more people, and chickens, which sit and flap, shedding soft white feathers into the aisles. With the new recruits, food arrives. We happily purchase anything that looks edible. It's good. I stuff my face with the wonderful flavours of a particularly spicy *papa rellena* (mashed potato, filled with spicy mince and hard-boiled egg, remade into a potato shape and deep fried). After ten weeks in Peru my fondness for them has become an addiction.

Hours later I start to feel terribly uncomfortable; everything is aching but euphoria courses through me, too. It's a strangely pleasant combination.

When the bus grinds and sputters to a halt at each small *pueblo*, we un-pretzel ourselves and jump off. And, if needed, we use the local squat hole in the ground. It's decidedly unpleasant. Ghastly smells hover. Stiff legs, unaccustomed to making a balanced squat, threaten to tip me over and expose my bits to the world.

'That looked like fun,' says Paco when I return.

I cringe. *Did he see that?*

Halfway into the trip our sick bus gets a flat tire; later a billowing black, diesel-smelling smoke cloud fills the back of the bus. The pitiful thing decides it just can't go on. We sit patiently with the locals on the side of the road, waiting for someone to come and coax it back to life. Eventually a mechanic appears and we get under way again.

The road is now especially rough and pot-holed. Our newly revived bus rocks violently from one side to the other; creaking and scraping sounds echo around us. After a particularly brutal movement a heavy metal bar suddenly breaks free from the skylight window above us and hits Paco directly on his hairless head. Viscous red blood drips, and then runs down his face.

'God, are you okay?' I am panicking, even as he blinks back into consciousness, pale as paper.

I wipe the blood off his head with my sleeve. 'Paco, *¿estás bien?*' I ask again, vocal cords tight.

'*Sí*, I'm okay. Shit.'

From that point on, the gangly, forlorn bus-boy has to stand in the aisle of the bus, his reed-like arms stretched high in the air holding onto the skylight so it won't unhinge itself and blow right away.

Minutes tick into hours. We are nearly there.

'Look, the sea,' says Paco, grabbing my arm.

We peer out the window, our bodies crushed together by another jolt.

'Thank goodness. We're almost there,' I say, all the tension leaching out.

On our last stop before arriving in Lima, Paco jumps off the bus and disappears for a long time, camera in hand. Sitting outside with the other passengers, I start to worry. Keeping an eye on the bus, I go and search for him.

I see him, crouched down, camera to his eye, on a flat-topped building a block away. He turns when I call his name, half-smiles and then returns to his task, absorbed in the moment.

I stop and watch from a distance.

He's surrounded by hundreds of empty green glass bottles. Some are neatly stacked, others thrown in haphazard piles. They are reflecting the light of the early morning sun. They look as if they're alive, flickering with shards of green and white light. I trail my eyes over him, in love with the sight of him in a glowing moment, a little in love with him, too.

I wonder if the photos will do the sight justice. I doubt they will capture it—the *feeling* of seeing.

Twenty-eight hours after leaving Cusco, Lima slaps us into consciousness—it's big and grey and broken. Dust and fumes hang in the muggy air. We go exploring, and then, come the night, we sleep as if in comas.

'Jessy, wake up.'

I struggle out of an early morning dream, open my eyes briefly and then shut them again in an attempt to catch the end, but it's already gone. My eyelids are sticking.

'I want to go surfing, come with me,' Paco says.

'Okay, give me a minute.'

I watch him adjusting his singlet and green and white board shorts in the mirror on the back of the wardrobe door. He checks himself out from all angles, making micro turns. Concern screws up his eyes.

I think, really, *what do you have to worry about?* His tanned back curves down into a tight waist, his legs are long and muscled.

I wrap myself in a sheet and sprint to the bathroom, self-consciousness catching me, too.

As Paco rides the waves I watch from the beach. I am fully clothed with a hat and sun-block protecting my pale Irish-Scottish skin from the rays. Not exactly a beach babe waiting for her surfer-man in a cute pink bikini. I don't care and he doesn't seem to, either.

This isn't a sandy beach; it's made up of smooth, multi-coloured pebbles. My attention becomes focused on building towers in matching tones. I drift away, totally absorbed in the play of it. The sky above is a sludgy white-grey, there's no blue. It feels otherworldly.

He stays out on the waves for hours but time contracts as my little towers of pebbles grow, topple and grow again.

'Jessy,' he calls out as he approaches.

I jolt out of my world of miniature castles and look up.

His dripping wet form, glistening in the muted sunlight, holds my breath hostage. The huge smile spread across his face sends the butterflies in my stomach *loco*.

I'm in big trouble.

We stay for four days in Huanchaco, a wide grey sand beach and mid-sized fishing village popular with locals and tourists. It is the haunt of occasional pickpocketers and passionate surfers, and home of the most divine *ceviche* in the world.

As Paco's meagre budget of a few soles a day doesn't extend to restaurants every night, he sweet talks a local fisherman into telling us how to prepare it for ourselves. Fresh white-fleshed fish cut into cubes, with loads of chopped garlic, fresh cilantro, salt and pepper, a chopped chilli—*aji amarillo* or the hotter *aji rocoto*, similar to a *habañero* pepper. Mix and then top with thinly sliced red onion. Douse with fresh lime juice and then leave in the fridge to soak for a few hours. On the plate, slices of boiled sweet potato and regular potato absorb the juices, and large dried corn kernels or slices of corn on the cob give it crunch.

We devour platefuls every day, peeking silently at each other's faces, mirroring the enjoyment as the flavours assault our senses. Our eyes roll, close, and we breathe deeply through our noses as we pull in the aromas. The citrus tones, chilli heat and fresh fragrance of the cilantro infuse themselves into the soft, acid cooked fish, accumulating into a clean yet explosive *fiesta* of sensations.

'Food from the gods,' I say.

'Food for gods,' he says, laughing.

As Huanchaco is only half an hour from Trujillo, I'm compelled to return and visit the children I volunteered with, before we move on up the coast. I make the trip alone, in a *combi* —a passenger van made to seat about fifteen people. I count twenty-four. I hurt all over. My body is pressed into a back corner, my head pushed awkwardly into the roof, my legs squished between the back of a profusely sweating older man and the head of a neatly dressed girl. Despite the physical discomfort and pungent body smells, I'm excited about seeing the children again. But I feel a curious sensation, too, as if a different version of me is returning to visit, even though it's only been a month since I saw them.

I knock on the door of the compound. It opens and a bright-faced blonde American girl says, '*Hola.*'

'*Hola*, I'm Jessica. I used to volunteer here. Can I visit the kids?'

'Sure, come in. I'm Becky.'

I feel like a stranger.

I ask about the other volunteers; three of the people I was here with have moved on, replaced by ten more. My eyes scan the courtyard; I don't see anyone I know. A tidal wave of new faces has washed away any trace of me.

I ask Becky about the almond-eyed girl. She's tells me she's not here today. It's disheartening, but I wonder if it's not for the best.

Two faces jump out from the fast-moving knot of kids playing football on the cracked concrete field.

'Oh my God, they stayed,' I say, pointing out the two little brothers to Becky.

'Yes, cool, huh? The younger one is so keen on learning; he's already starting to read.'

'That's great,' I say, remembering the state they were in when they arrived.

The day I met them they were as bedraggled as two small boys could be. Their thin bodies were marked with scratches and covered with sores that leaked under layers of grime. It was obvious that these two brothers, aged about six and eight, lived hidden under boxes and scavenged for food from the streets. The eyes of the smallest boy were barely visible beneath swollen, red-raw infected skin. When he wasn't rubbing and rubbing at his eye sockets with his knuckles, he used his hands like a blind child to get around. The older one stared at us sharply, puffing up his body and spirit when we inched closer to his sibling. He demonstrated with teeth and nails that his main mission in life was to protect the little one from harm. With a great deal of patience and some bribing, we eventually managed to persuade them to come with us to the compound to see the doctor. I held them and calmed them while the doctor looked them over, rubbed antibiotic creams into their sores and put drops in their infected eyes. As soon as she was finished they wriggled free and ran off.

The following day they came back, eyes less swollen though still wary, but feet more willing. We gave them a towel and soap and watched as they disappeared into the shower block. The sound of the water running had made them curious.

A long while later, two very different boys exploded out into the courtyard, lit up by the most incredible smiles I had ever seen. It was the first time in their young lives they had ever had a warm shower.

I stare at these children, who seem to have been transformed. I am transfixed. Becky mutters something about needing to prepare classes and she bounces off. As the brothers run around, trailing a football with their feet, I see wide-open eyes and filled-out bodies free from sores. I smile.

Not wanting to interrupt their play, I move slowly to the door and leave.

The last days in Huanchaco go by in a blur of sand, sweaty skin, caressing hands, food and beer. I can't grasp time and slow it down, though I would if I could. I don't want it ever to end. I don't want to release his hand.

I attack the universe. *You owe me.* I know it's not true, but that doesn't stop me from bartering about fairness and balance.

With his sleeping body lying so still next to mine I ask, *is he the one, or am I mad?* I wonder if maybe we are just two lost and lonely people crossing paths.

Then my heart fights back. This is special it says, our connection is real. I argue with myself as I struggle to sleep. I seek out all the moments that string together to make meaning, that make it real. Look at the ease with which we work together to cook a meal. We share a passion for creating food that massages the soul and satisfies all the senses. And we talk intensely about everything, even if not all the words are understood.

On our last night in Huanchaco we sit side by side on a beach, watching the day melt away—a ritual of ours, a marking of time. Pressure has been building inside me; I need to know what he's thinking. 'Paco, what's going to happen, when this is over, when I go home?'

'I don't want this to end so soon. I want to see you again. I hear there's a beach in Melbourne that has *increíble* surf. Maybe I can come to see you in Australia,' he says.

My heart speeds up and sends blood rushing to my head. I feel dizzy. I try valiantly to contain my delight under my carefully constructed, whatever-will-be expression.

'You want to come to Australia? To see me again?' I've been dying to say these words.

'Yes, I do, but not yet. I want to know more here. Ecuador, Costa Rica, Colombia. I have a friend in Mexico I want to visit. After—'

'How long? How long from now?' I ask, breathing carefully through my nose.

'I think six months, *tel vez* a year.'

After a torturous pause, I say, trying to keep my voice from cracking, 'Okay, I understand. You need to finish your trip. I'll wait.'

Alone on the beach the next day, I chide myself. I'll wait? What am I thinking? He's a twenty-five-year-old who has just broken off an intense four-year relationship—and will be travelling through the continent, alone. Even six months, let alone a year, is long enough for all his plans to change. Am I kidding myself?

The emotional storm passes as one day turns into the next. I shake myself free from worrying about the future of us and force my feet into the sand—into the present— soothed by the rasping sounds of the sea, the salty taste on our skins, the sun rising millimetre by millimetre each day over the vast ocean.

On a wind-swept Peruvian beach called Chicama, I let go.

The long, curved beach stretches out in front of us, interrupted only by rocks and hungry seagulls picking at some remains. It's just us and the waves. Each footprint I leave in the sand draws me into my body a little more. It's a gustily grey day and Paco and I run around like kids, playfully taking silly and dramatic photos with his camera. As time wears on, the wind gains strength, howling like a mountain wolf. I hold a sarong high in the air, with my arms stretched wide and high above my head. The beast in the air blows it straight out in a billowing arch behind me. I'm almost blown off my feet. I can feel the wind buffeting my face hard as the late sun warms my skin. In that moment, I'm infused with buzzing power—I believe it's possible to fly; that I am flying. A memory flashes in my mind. As a small child, I thought that, if I just wished hard enough, if I was good enough, I would lift off and fly away to another land. Here on this wild beach, in Peru, looking at Paco, I want so completely to stay in this moment forever.

'That's it, right there,' he says, directing me as he snaps away.

I smile, a real smile, with all of me in it.

I glance up at my etched hummingbird, beak pointing proudly towards the sun.

We arrive that night at the commercial, tourist beach of Mancora. It's our final destination—well, my final destination. In the morning we wake from an exhausted and scratchy sleep. The mattress under us is made of a thin cloth filled with straw. I didn't know such things still existed. As we lie there quietly side by side, I listen to the throaty rhythmic hum and hiss of the sea. With my eyes still closed, in that state between dreams and waking, it sounds like the slow hypnotic breathing of a huge mythical creature sitting on its haunches, enclosed in a cavernous grotto, mindful, waiting.

We go outside and a sweeping, almost white sand beach meets our eyes. There are palm trees, girls with bikinis and boys with boards everywhere. I feel happy, but there's a twist. I miss Chicama and its solitude. It was just us, now we are back in the world.

Paco runs off to unite with the sea and I find the nearest cafe and drink a bitter coffee while inhaling a wonderful trashy women's magazine in English that I find hidden under a pile of tatty papers, books and tourist pamphlets. It's a heavenly, indulgent moment.

Later I sit in the sand, watching the surfers, unsure if it is Paco's shiny-headed dot on the waves that I can see. I wonder, what would people think if he turned up in Australia to be with me? What would mum and dad in New Zealand think of this young, Spanish-speaking guy? Would they even care? How would I know, either way?

Over the years I had brought a few boys home to meet my parents (mostly separately, as they divorced when I was still in high school), but it was never possible to know what they thought— neither of them said anything. I think they were both wary of Daniel, though. It was as if they sensed he was balanced on the edge of a very scary place, and if he fell, he might take me with him.

The only time I remember getting a clear sign from either of them was with my first boyfriend, nicknamed 'Gaps', as he had a big gap between his teeth. I was fifteen. He was eighteen and a rebel, bright and artistic but wildly off course in life and from the *wrong* part of town. He was popular in the alternative kids' scene and I was a nerd trying desperately to be cool. Anything he asked of me was given without question. Mum was at home less and less by then and I was often alone with dad. Well, the part of him that remained. He would drift, grey-faced, around the house as our dog's big watery brown eyes trailed his every move.

One day I invited Gaps over. We were skulking around inside the house as teenagers do, when two ear-drum shattering shots rang out from the garden. Confused and scared, Gaps and I crept out into the back yard. Two mouths dropped in unison as we spotted one of Gaps' T-shirts (black, Iron Maiden) hanging limp and peppered on the clothesline, curls of smoke rising from the crusted holes. Dad had blasted it with a double-barrelled shotgun—both barrels. He was laughing. The barrels of the gun were still smoking.

'What did you do that for?' I asked, with eyes wide.

'I wanted to see what would happen,' he said.

The oddest thing was that Dad happily wore that T-shirt around the house for years afterwards. I never really understood that or him, but I guess it was clear he didn't think much of Gaps. I wished that he had told me about what was going on in his mind, but he never did. And he said nothing when I stayed out all night. I remember almost hoping he would forbid me from seeing Gaps. Maybe I chose him to push my father into caring.

Christmas Eve is our last night together. Paco and I go on a mission late in the afternoon to procure some goodies for a miniature feast for two. Some amiable locals direct us to a market near the edge of town. We arrive to the scent of rotting vegetables and the acrid smell of fresh meat, the salty wafts of fish. It's bursting with life and colour. It draws us in and we wander around for hours, looking for supplies. Paco snaps shots of the wonderful array of people and exotic fruits and strange foods.

At the darkest edge of the market we come across odd, fluffy little animals, like balls of cotton wool. They are crammed into tiny cages, their eyes half closed, sweltering in the heat.

'Are they for sale?' I ask Paco.

'Guess so.'

'For what?'

'I don't know.'

'Food?'

'Maybe pets, food for pets.'

I feel sick as I watch them. Some are breathing so slowly they look as if they are dying. Some don't move at all. Paco drags me away when I threaten to spend a small fortune on buying their—most likely temporary—freedom.

With the mournful furry creatures in cages behind us, we head back to our hostel with a bag bursting with fresh fish, bread, wine and fruit. The evening air is crisp, faintly salty; hardly a breath of wind circulates. The town's lights are low, giving a perfect view of a billion stars.

Paco asks our humorous host, Marcos, a squat man with cheeky, shiny eyes, if he can borrow some pots and cooking equipment.

'*Sí, sí, por supuesto*. Of course,' Marcos answers, as he heads off on his short legs.

Hobbit, I think.

'*Que personaje*,' says Paco.

'Yep, he's a character all right.'

We laugh as we hear banging and clashing sounds coming from behind the hostel.

Marcos looks very pleased with himself when he reappears. He drops a pot, a bowl, a small warped and blackened skillet, a sharp fishing knife, two green plastic plates, one fork and one spoon, on a small table.

'*Perfecto*,' says Paco.

Paco builds a fire and then positions a metal grate on top, balanced between two stones. We work around each other like two seasoned chefs, absorbed in our tasks. While Paco invents a wonderful spicy batter for the fresh fish, I make a colourful salad and cut up potatoes for frying. I run my hand across his back any chance I get. His face is alive in the orange glow of the flames.

As the bright hearts of the coals battle on, fed by a faint current in the air, we eat quietly, sitting on two wooden blocks. The wine bottle is passed back and forth. Fresh fruit, eaten whole, serves as dessert.

Words bubble up in my mind, but I can't mouth any.

'Jessy, I want to ring my dad, wish him Happy Christmas. There's a phone place in town.'

'Okay, cool. I'll stay here.'

'You don't want to ring your parents? You can buy a card.'

'No, it's okay. They won't be expecting a call.'

'Why not?'

'I'm a long way away.'

Paco looks confused but seems to sense not to push. I see him shake his head as he strides off.

A familiar sadness starts to creep over me. I crave what Paco has. It's an insatiable need that lies in my stomach. My parents feel like strangers; stranger and more unknown as time and distance grow between us. When I turned eighteen I ran to the furthest university from them, at the bottom of New Zealand's South Island. When there were no more exams to sit and papers to write, I flew to Australia, putting the Tasman Sea between us. I wonder if I place oceans in the way because it feels consistent with the emotional void separating us. When I grab for them, I get a handful of air.

I poke at the flames with a stick, lost to this train of thought. I have few memories of my mum and dad, of a childhood with them in it. My mother and father spun in their own worlds, bumping against each other and then flinging apart. My sensitive, solitary father was a ghost to me when I was growing up, and when things got too hard he lost himself in a bottle. He fluttered in the corners of the house and in my mind. My beautiful and extremely talented mother was a rush of energy, a wind, always moving, always absorbed in a project that took nearly all of her. Each of us would have her for some precious minutes, then she would whirl away again. I know they both loved us, but sometimes that's not enough.

There were four kids in the house: I was the eldest, followed by my brother Jonny, who was born two years after me; then there was a gap of eight years before Edward and Henry were born, two years apart. I largely missed growing up with the youngest two, as I left when they were eight and six. Jonny was in and out of home for years before he finally flung himself away to London, only returning to New Zealand recently, still lost, but now lost in his own country.

I get frustrated trying to visualise my family's faces. Frustrated they aren't clearer. There is guilt there, too. I could do more, try harder to know them, to reach out. I wonder what's wrong with us that we can't step in; we all back away, run away. I see Jonny's face; those dark pools of eyes that seem to reflect a bottomless longing, the mouth that's more comfortable in a scowl than a smile. I see him on stage, sitting alone, guitar resting on his crossed knees. I shiver, remembering his voice, so soft, then harsh, throwing out sad words into the crowd. He tried to suffocate his angst by immersing himself in music; when that wasn't enough he used numbing substances to dull the pain.

Edi ran from project to project, while gathering around him a buffer of friends. The youngest, Henry, hid himself away within his own skin. I shake my head at my memory of him and his magician-like ability to disappear; it was as if the very walls around him engulfed him. We were often surprised when he moved, realising he was actually in the room.

Paco has been gone a long time. Loneliness settles in. The words, *this can't be almost over*, start looping in my head. Nausea creeps into me and sends my head spinning.

As I watch the coals die, the cold of the night presses on my back. I'm about to abandon the hearth when I hear footsteps in the darkness. Paco comes into view, his face radiant with relief, but his hands are jittery.

'Sorry, Jessy. I have much problems with the card and then the phone. But in the end we speak for a long time, till the money goes,' he says, emotion showing, his English crumbling.

'How is your dad?

Paco sits. 'He's good. I miss him so much. I love him so much. It's hard to be away,' he says. His tears flow softly.

I give him space. He looks like a little boy. His adoration for his father is so tangible in his words. Sadness grips me.

Out of sight, out of mind.

I can taste the heaviness of the approaching farewell; my jaw is tight with it.

Emotional and feeling sentimental, we begin to toast those who aren't with us, and those who can never be with us again.

An idea forms clear edges. 'Why don't we have a special ceremony down on the beach?' I say to him.

'To say goodbye to Daniel and my brother,' he says, instantly in tune. '*Sí, vamos*, let's do it. I'll get some candles.' He strides off, looking for Marcos.

When he comes back he's cradling a candle and a plastic bottle, borrowed from our now highly intoxicated host. He sets to work, a man on a mission. I watch, enthralled. He roughly hacks the bottle in half. I realise he's making a protective shield so the candle won't blow out.

We make our way down to the beach. Together we dig a hole in the sand, place the candle in its sheath, in the hollow, and then he lights it.

Each in our own way, we say our goodbyes.

Hi Daniel,

I'm here again. It's hard to know what to say because I feel this should be my last talk with you. It's time to say a proper goodbye. I'm sitting on a Peruvian beach; it's very early on Christmas Day. I wanted to tell you that I met someone in Cusco. He's next to me, right now. His name is Paco. I think you would have liked him. You have similar ways of seeing the world; and like you, he has a big heart. He's saying a sad goodbye as well, to his brother. In front of us, a small white candle is flickering away in a hollow in the sand. I'm trying hard to imagine you here, sitting cross-legged in the damp sand. I think I sense you when it flickers strongly—perhaps it's just the wind.

I don't really know how I am right now. My head is so full of thoughts, my body with emotions. Still, I feel better, as if I'm occupying my own skin again, despite the turmoil. I think I love this man beside me. Eighteen days together. I've been counting. I know, it's not long, but I don't want to lose him, or this feeling. I don't know how to say goodbye to him, either.

We've made plans to meet again in Australia. I'm not sure if it will happen. I'm not sure if it should happen. Perhaps it's best to leave things here, as a beautiful holiday fling.

Don't grab on so tight, you would say to me.

No, it is special. And it's too excruciating to think I might be alone again.

Enough—I wanted to tell you I'm okay, and I am, despite what I know is coming. I'm stronger. This trip, the kids I met when I was volunteering, Cusco, old friends and new friends have all conspired to shake me back into living. I'm so grateful I had this chance, that I took this chance. You don't have to worry about me.

You know, Daniel, you were a bonfire when you lived; we all basked and burnt next to you. I think it's taken me so long to say goodbye because it wasn't only sadness I had to let go of. It was anger, too. I've never been good at anger, but it's gone now.

I hope you are peaceful, wherever you are. You never had more than fleeting moments of peace when you were alive. I'm trying to remember you in those moments. They are the ones for keeping.

I think it's important to let you go now. I need the space in my head and heart.

So... God, this is hard. Okay, this is goodbye, my amazing, bright and sensitive friend. I'll never forget you. I hope that in some dimension, somewhere, I will see you again.

Sleep tight, Daniel. I will always love you.

We wake late on Christmas Day, entwined, unwilling to separate. When we finally disentangle, I persuade Paco to go surfing so I can arrange a surprise and buy a gift. I go out looking for the perfect present. It seems that all the hippies from around the world are selling their beads, silver jewellery and dream-catchers by the side of the road. I want him to be surprised by something unique. I'm disappointed when the same things peer up at me. Then a simple necklace of big red and brown beads with a large smooth seed pod in the middle, grabs my attention. Surfer on his spiritual journey, I think, and smile. Perfect. It's something to leave behind (my mark, my claim). I also arrange, with two gangly bronzed boys, in my glue-mouthed Spanish, to take two horses for a ride on the beach. I grew up around horses, my love for them is written firmly in my memories. I have marks and scars and healed bones from our adventures together. They were my freedom and my friends.

I go to find Paco. His skin is traced with faint white paths—long trails of dry salt outline his firm muscles.

'Do you like horses? Can you ride?' I ask.

'I love them, yes I can ride.'

'I have a treat, then.'

We ride together along the beach, fast and wild. My hair whips across my face, the thick salt-encrusted strands sting. I'm flying. He's flying beside me.

After the horses are gone, we sit on the sand and talk.

'What is this thing we have?' I ask, again.

'Jessy, we have a strong connection. I know we will see each other again. I will come to you in Australia. I promise.'

'Really?'

'Don't worry. It will all be okay. It's not over.'

It's not over, not over, what does that mean? Do I say—

'I think I love you.'

I feel his body tighten slightly, and then he looks at me.

I look down at my hands.

'Jessy, *te quiero mucho, también.* I'm just not sure if it's *te amo.* It's too soon. I'm not ready.'

'What's the difference?' I ask, trying to stay calm.

'Well, it's like *te quiero* is what you tell close friends. To say you care deeply for them. *Te amo* is more powerful, more romantic,' he explains. He looks down at the floor.

'So *te amo* is like, "I love you with all my heart."'

'Yes, it's something like that. Like boyfriend and girlfriend, with a big commitment.'

'I know it's too soon for that. I understand,' I say. Tear ducts tingle and my jaw stiffens to shutter them.

At the bus stop I give him his new necklace and he puts it on. I brush my hand across the seeds, wishing all sorts of things. We hug. It's crushing. I breathe him in. We kiss.

I get on the bus and when I reach my seat, the tears explode, running down my face, flooding into the corners of my mouth. I pull back the curtain, tugging roughly at it as it opens too slowly. I want one last look. I see him standing on the footpath, looking bewildered. I absorb the image, and then he turns quickly and I lose sight of him. I sink into the seat, wanting to disappear into the soft grey sponge.

Something makes me look up.

He's standing right in front of me, in the aisle of the bus. My insides shake.

'Jessy, please take this,' he says, handing me his own black, fine shell necklace. The one he never takes off. 'Look after it for me until we see each other again,' he says, his voice cracking.

We kiss again. I feel our tears mingling. He turns on his heel and is gone.

Five

I MAKE IT ONTO the plane in one piece—at least in the physical sense. Emotionally and mentally all the bits of me are splintering, and each fragment is competing to be heard above the din. Trains of thought spill out, some run to the end, others are intercepted. I grab at each one, trying to hold it before it flees. I need time to contemplate them in turn, but they continue to pour out, tumbling over each other.

Will I see him again? Should I see him again?

No. It was a holiday romance. I should let it go, enjoy the memory.

Hope swells and fights back. *It was special. We will see each other again. A chance, that's all I want... a chance.*

I'm losing it. The ping-pong match in my head has no winner. My mood fluctuates violently, from elated to depleted, optimistic to miserable. I keep shaking my head in the hope that the thoughts will settle.

'Shut up,' I cry out suddenly.

A few heads turn, people stare.

Then I get scared. Maybe this will tip me over into madness.

I try to breathe calmly. I close my eyes and attempt to be mindful. I count sheep. I go to an imaginary beach to listen to waves. It's a mistake; I see salt on his skin.

Be calm, Jess, breathe.

I wake feeling a little better and wondering what Buenos Aires will be like. I have a twelve-hour stopover there on the way back to Melbourne. Paco has arranged for two friends to pick me up from the airport and show me around the city. The plan is then for them to deliver me to Paco's home, where his father Pepe will feed me my first Argentine BBQ, or *asado* as they call it. Sadly, his mother won't be there. She's working on a cruise-ship off the coast of Miami; the economic crisis has pushed her into working far from home for the past three years.

I find it astonishing that his friends and father are going to do this for me. To them, I'm an unknown Kiwi girl who just happened to travel with Paco for a short time in Peru. Other travellers on the South American trail had told me that Argentine people were very hospitable, but still, the gesture is bewildering. I bite my lip to stop the tears rising. They disobey me.

What will they think of this dishevelled, puffy-eyed foreigner?

I can picture his parents: well, the essence of them. Paco told me that his mother is an artist and his father a graphic designer. Creative people— people who think in images and use their hands and minds to create a story. With his eyes misting over, he described his father as having a huge heart and a voracious appetite for learning and good food and good wine. His manner and words softened when he talked about his mother. I created a picture of a quiet centred woman who loved with gentle actions more than words. My chest would tighten ever so slightly when I listened to his tales of them.

'Your parents sound wise and very loving,' I said one day.

'*Yo sé*, I know, I'm very lucky to have them.'

'I can see you are very close.'

'Yes, it's common in Argentina: we say *un cordon corto*,' he said, smiling.

'A short cord,' I translate. He nods.

My cord is too long, so thin—frayed to a mere few strands.

I listen to the humming of the plane's motors and ruminate on my total lack of knowledge about this huge South American country. I remember—feeling a flush rising—that Evita Peron was an important figure, but I only know this because Madonna played her in the movie, *Evita*. 'Don't cry for me Argentina' rings annoyingly in my head. Okay, Evita/Madonna, oh and Diego Maradona, the football hero… something about the 'hand of god' 1986 World Cup goal that my English footy fan friend still rages about. Good meat. Tango. Polo. Is that it? I berate myself.

I try to recall scenes from the only Argentine movie I have ever seen, *Nueve Reinas* (Nine Queens), which is set in Buenos Aires at the time of the 2001 economic crisis. Ironically, it was my anti-Maradona friend who suggested we go and see it, in Melbourne. With eyes closed I picture the angry hordes, banging pots and scrabbling at the barricaded doors of banks, desperate to know what has happened to their money. There are flashes of miserable, furious, lost faces. Faces of people whose world had tipped so violently that many could only watch as all they had fought for and saved for slipped into an insatiable black hole. The movie allowed a glimpse into the chaos that followed the financial meltdown and the fall of the government but now the people are more real, they have faces I know. I can imagine Paco and his family living through the uncertainty, watching their beloved country rip apart at the seams while the world looked on, shaking its head. Now, I feel it.

I had asked Paco about the impact of the crisis when we were in Cusco. We were sitting on a disintegrating Incan stone wall when he slowly and carefully described the realities of life during that time: four presidents in a matter of weeks, hyperinflation and merciless devaluation of the peso, unemployment and deadly riots. He talked about how dismayed and enraged the people were.

'You could catch it in the air,' he said.

'You mean, "You could feel it in the air."'

'Yes, feel, but almost catch it, too. Like you could reach out and hold the anger.'

'I know what you mean.'

I could hear pain and, tucked between the words, a desperate love conflicting with bitter disappointment.

Now I pick, with a plastic fork, at the plastic tub of plasticky looking fruit salad. A movie is flickering on the screen, but I can't find the energy to watch it. I realise how lucky I am to have lived my whole life in two stable countries. Maybe it's sensible to be going back home. I wonder if part of my problem is that I have too much privilege. Not enough to fight for and too much free time to indulge in angst.

Paco's mother comes to mind again. As I picture her (my imaginings of her) working, alone, for months on end in other countries, a lump lodges in my throat. She must feel lonely, so far from home. I wish I could meet her.

That's Paco's fault. I remember his words. We were sitting on the beach watching the tide breathe and the sea foam form intricate patterns on the water, when he turned and said to me, 'You are so like my mother.'

His face was animated in an expression of surprised realisation.

'Really?'

'Not just how you look, your hair, pale skin. There's something so similar in how you are,' he added, before looking out to sea again.

Is that a good thing? My head buzzed as I searched for meaning in his words.

We are nearly there. I look down past the wing. There it is: a huge city, fanning out from the dark river. The glaring morning sun illuminates it through the shadows of clouds.

Paco's friends are waiting for me at the international arrivals gate, holding a roughly handwritten sign high in the air.

It's strange to see my name, to see people waiting for me.

'*Hola*. I like the sign,' I say, pointing.

'*Hola*, Jessy,' says the curly-haired one. He moves in for a hug and kisses me lightly, once on the right cheek (once, same as in Peru, not twice like the Italians and Spanish). 'I am Estefan, nice to meet you,' he says in schoolboy English.

I promptly receive another hug and kiss. 'I am Daniel.'

'*Gracias por buscarme*, thanks for picking me up,' I tell them both.

'*De nada*,' says Estefan.

Daniel takes my pack, Estefan my suitcase.

As we walk towards Estefan's car, I feel a strange urge to skip, relieved now of travel weight. I find it easy being with them, familiar somehow. I see instantly why they're loved by Paco. Both have cheeky wise grins and trendy jeans, though Daniel's apparel is more neatly put together. Estefan has a scrupulously arranged scruffy-art-student look.

On the way into the city we dodge a virus of yellow and black taxis, and buses that seem to think they're holy cows in India. I shove my white-knuckled hands between my knees. It's a long, lane-weaving sprint. I watch the city's cluttered outer neighbourhoods flow by, and then we are engulfed by stunning, enormously wide avenues and incredible turn-of-the-century architecture. Domes, columns and triangular neoclassical facades, ornate iron-worked balconies, opulent entrance ways. Wildly elaborate art nouveau buildings with steeples and sculptured flowers and animals peeping out from under arches, tall art deco buildings; they all rise up proudly around us in a cultural melting pot of Europe's most beautiful architecture. The view distracts me from my nerves.

Estefan suddenly pulls over and Daniel gestures that we should get out. I look at them both with a 'what now' expression.

'Sorry, I can't stay,' says Estefan. 'I must study. I have class in University,' he says in stale English.

'It's Saturday,' I say, confused.

'Yes, even Saturday we have class. I take your backpack to Pepe's place. See you later for *asado*.'

Daniel and I watch as he speeds off, nearly clipping an oncoming bus. I gasp and look over at Daniel, who is unmoved.

It isn't lost on me that I am spending my first morning in Argentina with a tall, sweet-faced man called Daniel. I don't know what to make of it and perhaps it's best not to think too much. I watch this Daniel intently as he carefully, in stuttered English or simple Spanish, tries to answer my questions and educate me on the sights we see.

We spend the crisp but sunny morning traipsing around leafy wealthy Recoleta. The more we wander, the more mesmerised I become. Parks and many plazas dilute the cityscape with green space. In the residential zones modern apartment blocks sit alongside colonial-style buildings, elegant concrete museums, churches and private houses. The older buildings nestle just under the canopies of hundred-year-old trees.

I suddenly understand the 'Paris of the South' reference. I don't feel as if I'm in South America anymore. Some architecture is similar to the older colonial zones of Lima, but it is still somehow different here. Perhaps it's the people who look different; the Spanish and Italian bloodlines are obvious in the streets. I feel as if I'm in a big weather-beaten European city that's found itself lost in South America.

In the well-maintained parks stand statues of *conquistadors* mounted on muscled steeds. Swords and proud noses point into the air. I feel momentarily transported back in time, and then the traffic tears me back to the present. The drivers are demented, manically weaving in and out, no one indicates and they sit on the horn. You cross with your hand on your heart, praying to make it to the other side. Daniel saves me twice from certain demise when I look the wrong way before crossing. Feet firmly on the rough, cracked footpath, I do a neat quickstep to avoid the dog excretions that smudge it.

When our feet get too tired we take the musty smelling subway to Pepe's home. Daniel buzzes the door to the laneway, steps back and we wait. I feel the flapping of tiny wings in my stomach.

The wooden door at the end of a long passageway swings opens and a large bearded man lumbers through it, blinking in the light. As he approaches us to unlock the tall, elaborate iron-gate, I see Paco's grin, and his kindness, glinting from two big brown eyes. He's attractive, even though well into his sixties. He edges through the gate

'Jessica.'

'*Hola.*'

Two big arms envelop me in a warm, smothering hug that threatens to burst the dam of my tears. It's a father's hug, or how I imagine one to be. In my mind I allow Paco to occupy my body for a second. A connective string forms, spanning a continent, and then it snaps back. My knees lose strength. When I look up at Pepe's face I see his eyes moisten with tears. I feel loved. There's no other way to explain it. I wonder what Paco has said about me.

Paco's home is small and simple and whitewashed, with long thin wooden patio doors opening into a wild green garden flooded with sunlight and bursting with overgrown plants in pots of all sizes. In one corner of the patio, twisted vines form a natural roof, and when the breeze weaves through them, the large rust-tipped green leaves shimmer into life. The fingers of the thick vines dig desperately into the peeling paint to cling on. The worn black and white tiles underfoot make me think of Paris, I'm not sure why.

Pepe gives me a tour of the house. Everywhere I look there are paintings, books and many beautiful wooden carvings. It's a house where many little treasures live cluttered together in dusty corners. Two dark grey Siamese cats greet me by twining figure of eights around my legs. One is long and thin, the other very fat.

Pepe looks surprised. 'The skinny cat, he don't like people, but he likes you.'

Estefan arrives later, as if driven by his nose. His timing is perfect. The thick slabs of beef are being served, along with white bread rolls and a fruity, sharp tasting wine. It's the best meat I have ever tasted. I knew Argentine beef was considered world class, but I wasn't expecting the joy I feel.

I watched the barbecuing process carefully. It's slower than back home. The meat is cooked in large pieces over barely glowing coals, and then cut into smaller pieces and shared. Pepe tended it so gently, as if it were the last piece of meat in the world. The end product is moist and tender with a divinely crunchy, salty crust.

When the sun disappears behind the house we move inside and collapse around a wooden table that wobbles when we move. Pepe reaches down to adjust the folded up paper jammed under one leg. Estefan opens a new bottle of wine, our third.

We talk for a long time about Paco and our trip together. Pepe seems to be living each detail as if he is travelling beside his son. I love listening to his rusted English. It lurches and then fades into silence as he searches for words. Words I feel he once spoke well but has lost over time.

I ask a lot of questions about the wooden carvings that sit on shelves and mantelpieces. I see the artist in him when he speaks about them, showing me their curves and markings. He tells me carving is a hobby. I visualise him sitting focused on a chunk of wood, turning it slowly in his big hands before whittling away in search of the lost form within.

The carvings are beautifully made copies of indigenous animal designs, tools and bowls from diverse countries. He opens a series of tired and dusty books, with broken spines, to show me where the carvings came from. I find myself especially attracted to a little pig. 'This is beautiful,' I say, running fingertips over the intricate white diamond patterns etched onto its back and sides.

'It's a design from Papua New Guinea.'

'I love pigs,' I say. The words hang in the air. Pepe's unruly eyebrows rise into two high arches.

'You love pigs?'

'Yes. A bit strange, I know. My dad does, too. My brothers and I grew up on a small farm and always had pet pigs.'

'Pet, is that like *¿mascota*? A pig *mascota*?'

'Yes, exactly. My father especially loved one pig. Her name was Gloria… well, her full name was Miss Gloria Bouser. She was his favourite: huge, black and prickly. She thought Dad was hers. She went everywhere with him; she wouldn't let Mum anywhere near him. She used her snout to force away any other person who tried to get close,' I explain, with some over-exaggerated miming.

A deep rolling laugh rises from his belly and echoes through the room. Daniel and Estefan look over, briefly. Then they rebound back into their own story. I have Pepe all to myself. 'A pig *mascota*,' he repeats, more to himself than me.

'It was the funniest sight, seeing them walking through the farm. My dad's very slim and Gloria had a large black bottom that swung from side to side. Mum would trail behind, looking furious.'

'*Furiosa*,' he translates. Then he laughs and shakes his head. 'So funny your dad, *pobre* your mother.'

'Yes, poor Mum,' I say. I feel animated, telling my tales, so I continue to pull out memories, giving them life and clarifying meaning with my gestures.

'I loved Gloria, too. She used to meet my brother and me at the gate, exactly on time, every day after school. We would find her there, sitting on her haunches, um, her back legs…' I say tapping my thigh. Pepe nods.

'…waiting patiently to *permit* us to scratch behind her ears. Then she would lead us right to the front door. She was the boss. You can't make a pig do anything it doesn't want to.'

'Stubborn, is that the word?'

'Yes, very stubborn,' I say. I wonder to myself whether to mention that Dad's nickname is 'Pig' (he chose it for himself), but I decide it's too hard to explain.

'What happened to Gloria?'

'She ran away with a cow from the neighbour's farm. My dad was very sad. He tried to get her back with cake soaked in cream.'

'It doesn't work?'

'No, she never came home. She fell in love… with a cow.'

'Good story,' he says, and then adds, 'you want more wine?' His eyes beam. His high round cheeks are rose coloured.

'*Sí, gracias*, just one more,' I say.

He gets up uneasily. I see a grimace, a pain too sharp and quick to be masked.

While he's gone, memories of Dad and that pig flip through my mind. I think perhaps it was easier to love her than us—way less complicated. Definitely way less complicated than loving Mum.

When I leave, after my incredible lunch, I say a very sad goodbye to Pepe. As we hug and he wishes me a good journey, he squeezes something solid into my hand. It's the little pig. I protest and say it's too much.

'I see how much you like it. I want him to have a good home, please take him,' he says.

'*Gracias*, Pepe, *gracias por todo*, thank you for everything.' I have more words, but they are mislaid in my attempt to translate them into Spanish. I feel sad and happy and overwhelmed. I hope to see him again someday.

I disappear into his farewell hug, completely soaked in its warmth.

'One more place to show you,' says Daniel, when we reach the car.

They drive me to San Telmo, an arty, eclectic neighbourhood near the commercial centre. Daniel tells me it's the oldest part of the city. I can see that some of the Spanish colonial-style buildings have been carefully renovated; others have been left to decay—once stunning carved wooden doors hang warped and worm-eaten, iron balconies are rusted red brown, walls crumble like week-old cake and sprout vines and weeds. I'm in love; it's edgy and full of antique shops, tango salons and makeshift artisan stores crammed together along the street.

We finish the day walking beside the wide slushy grey-brown Rio de la Plata (the Silver River) in Puerto Madero: a bright and shining, reclaimed river-front suburb. I buy the boys ice-creams. It doesn't seem enough to thank them for all they have done for me. On the way to the airport I recount the day in my head and I swear to myself that I'm going to return to this big, humming, city. In one beautiful day it has imprinted itself on my soul.

Six

I DON'T FEEL THRILLED when I look out the window of the plane and see Melbourne stretching out below me, and it had always made me happy before.

I don't ever quite land. Well, not all of me. All the fibres of my being rebel; I don't want to be here. In the first days back I feel like I'm floating above the ground, my toes only softly scraping the surface of the earth. My mind starts making the decision to go back just a week after arriving home.

Nausea sits constantly inside me and worsens every day on the trip to work. The thoughts and dreams that fill my head on the ride down the crammed motorway batter me like a slow, cruel torture. I search for signs that confirm that I'm not where I'm supposed to be. I check my email three times a day, and sometimes there's a treat of a quirky, warm email.

> Hi!! beautifull aussy chica!! I miss u so so so so much!!
> Okay, I have a few minutes, so... I hope that the asado was really good!!
> oh! It's so difficult to write in english!!
> I'm in Montañita jaja!!! I think I can get a job here!!
> It's amazing, really!!
> Again, I miss you very very much! I'm sure of go to your beatyfull place!!
> Kisses all over your body and a big huge hug!!!
> I MISS YOU!!!
> Te quiero mucho
> Paco

I receive an email from Pepe that leaves me awash in sweet tears.

Dear Jessy,
Happy New Year! Thank you for your mail. I was very happy to
meet you. I'm happy for the travelling Paco is doing, but I miss
him. You must come back to BsAs and we will go to my house
in Tigre and we'll make the greatest asado you see in your life.
I'm sorry that I can't express my feelings more correctly but is
very hard to me to write in english, I hope you understand and
I also hope you can see Paco in a very short time. I send you a
big abrazo y un big big beso.
Chau Jessy
Pepe

I hear him in the words. His face appears, clear in my recollection.
I smile at the memories of my one perfect day in Buenos Aires, of the
feeling of being connected, of the wine-soaked talk of pet pigs and the
delicious, still steaming meat. I wonder if South Americans really are so
different from us, or am I projecting my own feelings onto them? I can't
say, but they seem to me to wear love of family like a badge.

As the weeks crawl by, a massive gust of wind starts pushing at
my back. I make a decision to return. I can't wait for Paco to come to
Australia. I give three months' notice at work because I feel guilty about
leaving for good so soon after getting back from my trip. I don't want to
leave a mess behind. I book my flights. Relief fills me.

I tell everyone, a little manically, that I've made the decision
to go. I immerse myself in their advice, their warnings, concern and
encouragement. Everyone has something to say. I pick and choose,
ignoring some words and grabbing onto others.

'Go… don't stay. I see you dying here; don't end up a shrivelled husk
of a person. I know you; you will survive anything. But go for you, not for
him,' says Helen, the wise mother-hen of the clinic.

Another workmate advises, 'Be careful of the fantasy of a better
place somewhere else.'

Some say, 'That's a brave move.'

One person at the clinic says, 'You are so close to long-service leave,
why not wait a bit?'

Elle says, 'Jess, just go, believe that good things and good people will find you when you need them. You can always come back.'

'God, why not? Follow your dreams,' says Amy.

When I nervously ring my father with my news, he says, 'I thought you wanted to buy an apartment. You have a good job. Why?'

I find myself explaining my decision; I outline the value of learning Spanish, of making connections over there, for some kind of future business, maybe? When I hear silence on the line, I fall into justifying. 'I never got to travel and live overseas. I went from school to university to work with no break. I need this.'

'Okay. I guess you're going, then. Good luck,' he says, and the conversation is over.

I ring Mum.

'Is this about that Paco guy?' she asks.

'Yes and no.'

'He's very good looking.'

I smile. I can't help it. 'Yeah, I know…'

'You looked happy in that photo you sent.'

'I want to see what happens with us. I can't wait for him to come here. I need to know, so I'm going back.'

'I understand. Will you be okay if it doesn't work out?'

'Yes, Mum. I'll be fine. I have good friends over there.'

'Well, let me know how it goes.'

Sitting in silence after talking to her, I feel heard. It was a good conversation. I realise she knows something of the search for love, and the risks of the journey.

Just weeks before I leave, I seek out my friend and de facto shrink, Dave. I know he will see through my constructed layers. He's the one I mostly tell the truth to.

We struck up our strange and wonderful friendship some five years before while he was on rotation through our clinic as a psychiatry intern. Something about him charmed me instantly. He looked exactly like my imagined archetype of a super-shrink. Thin and crooked with a pointy straggly beard, no moustache. Slightly unkempt dark clothes, a face lined with a lifetime of thought, eyes deep with wisdom and melancholy. He's blessed with a gravelly but somehow liquid voice, which he uses well to calm lost souls. I remember thinking, he's a little odd but perfectly cool—a character.

One Thursday evening, we find ourselves in an English-style pub, one of our favourite haunts. It's our habit to meet on a Thursday, every few weeks, for this kind of talk. It's dark in the pub and smells of stale beer. Huddled in a corner booth, we order a bottle of wine.

'Is this crazy?' I ask.

'Maybe, maybe not. I do still worry about *why* you're doing it.'

'Because all my fibres are pushing me to go. I just can't stay. Too many memories. Too trapped. In some ways, I never really left South America.'

'Paco?'

'Yes, it is about him; but it's not all about him. You know I was thinking of going back even before I met him.'

'Yes, I do know. You were kind of high on Cusco.'

'It's like South America and I have unfinished business.'

'God, not the bloody psychic again…'

'No, well, maybe. It's a feeling, I can't explain it,' I say, a flush heating my skin.

'I can see there's going to be no changing your mind. So go, do what you have to do.'

'Does that mean I have your blessing?'

'My blessing. Very funny. Yes, but be very careful; you're still fragile. And what if it doesn't work out with Paco?'

'I'm trying to be prepared for that. He's been hard to contact lately. It scares me, but I have a backup plan if it all goes to pieces. I have some friends over there. I'll go to Cusco, maybe Buenos Aires again.'

'You can always come back; you do know that, don't you? You're not alone here, whatever you may feel sometimes.' He looks at me intently.

I stare into my glass before I answer. 'Yes, I do know, now more than ever. It's funny, sometimes it's only when you're about to leave a place that you realise you are loved and will be missed.'

Once I've sold or given away everything I own: my car, my bed, a set of drawers, a sofa, a coffee table, a tool kit with electric drill, kitchen appliances, clothes, shoes, colourful pillows, paintings… I have enough to live on for six months or so, if I stick to a super-tight budget.

Shoving my fears away, I pack my travel-weary backpack for another journey.

Backpackage. I laugh when I remember Paco's word for it.

As the plane to Panama takes off, I look over the tapered wing, out into seemingly endless space. I say a doleful goodbye to Melbourne. I sense I won't see the city for a long time.

My mind goes white, my body tingles and I'm suddenly overwhelmed. I feel as if I'm floating above the plane but I can see inside. I look down. I see myself as a strapped-in speck, contained inside a huge metal bird—so small, so insignificant. I take a few long calming breaths, fall back into my skin. I let hope in—maybe the plane will carry me to love, to a new life, a new home. I still can't decide whether I'm mad or brave, whether I'm running away from something or to something.

There's an empty seat next to me. An elderly man occupies the aisle seat. I'm curious about him. I heard him talk to the flight attendant in broken English with a strong Latin American accent. He has an open book resting under his twisted, wrinkled hands. He seems lost in thought. I have a special radar for sadness. He seems sad. His eyelids are heavy with it. I wonder why.

His sadness returns my mind to my own worries. I begin to fret, again, about how I will cope in Panama alone. No matter how much I try to be positive and determined, a persistent dread paces around my heart, and then a burning lava current of anger erupts in my head. Why does Paco keep changing his plans? What the hell's happening?

I dissect and ruminate over every word of his most recent, very infrequent emails. Our original plan, forged via email and awkward phone calls, is in tatters. He was supposed to be in Central America by the time I arrived. The idea had been to travel through Costa Rica together, and if things were going well, to continue to Mexico. But Paco has got stuck in Ecuador. He is still in Guayaquil, on the coast, sharing a flat with an 'amiga'.

Summoning the last dregs of female pride, I have informed him casually that I want to travel alone for a couple of weeks in Central America. I named beaches and ruins to make it real. If he was still in Ecuador after my explorations, I could, perhaps, travel through Colombia and catch up with him then. His reply was something along the lines of,

Okay, see you when I see you.

Maybe all of this is a terrible mistake.

I wonder if I'm conjuring up more than there is. I know I have a tendency to do that. My own nature confuses me: I'm both pessimistic, always thinking of the worst possible outcome, but then I can be so elated in my hope. It swells and consumes me.

Finally, after a long fight with myself, I fall into a deep sleep. When I wake, my dream lingers, entering the light of day. I can smell his skin, taste his lips. It's a dream of the magical reunion—feeling his arms holding me, the kissing and the tear-streaked, happy faces.

I am jolted back to reality when the attractive, mahogany-haired flight attendant hands me the landing documents for the United States. I have a twelve-hour stopover in Los Angeles. It will be my first time in the US and I'm curious to see even a little of it with my own eyes. She hands over the same documents to my row companion. He looks suddenly confused and tries to stop her leaving, but she swishes away too fast.

'Hi, are you okay, *¿estás bien?*' I say to him.

'*Hola, sí y no… tengo problems* with English, *no sé como…*' He fades off.

'Do you need help?'

'Yes, please, help,' he says. Relief washes over his face.

I smile at him. I'm happy to practice my Spanish. '*Hola, soy Jessica. ¿Y usted es?*' I attempt to be formal.

'*Soy Pedro. ¿Eres de Australia?*'

'*Sí, estoy de Melbourne. ¿Y usted de donde es?* I'm ecstatic I can do the basics.

'*Soy de El Salvador,*' he says, smiling shyly.

I find out he's been visiting his son and his son's family in Melbourne, and now he's travelling to see his daughter and her family in LA. He tells me he is very sad to say goodbye to his son and grandchildren as it will be years before he can see them again. But he's happy that he can see his daughter and her family.

I carefully go through each section of the documents and help him fill them in. He's very grateful and I'm proud to be able to help.

On arrival, Pedro and I bumble our way through Immigration together. Then, somehow, we get separated. I stand, looking for him, lost. I wanted to say goodbye. About twenty minutes later, as my eyes scan the room for a place to store my luggage, I spot him in the very centre of a family huddle of wet eyes and crushing hugs. It aches a little.

He looks over. His expression opens like a flower. I sense he has been searching for me, too. He calls to me, a wide smile on his face. Before I have time to slide off my heavy pack, the pack that contains my whole life, his daughter, her husband and their two teenage kids pull me into the huddle.

The granddaughter says, 'Come home with us… please spend the day with us. We'll show you around LA.'

What should I say? It is a wonderful generous offer, so I stammer, '*Sí, por favor, gracias.*'

Just as I was in Argentina, when I met Pepe, I'm surprised at how easily this family includes me in their lives. Back at their small apartment Pedro's daughter and her husband fuss over me, and then they feed me and send me off for a short nap under a colourful patchwork bedspread. Later in the day we all cram comically into an old blue Ford Falcon and drive down to Hollywood. It's an overcast grey day as we walk along Hollywood Boulevard, stepping over the stars of the famous.

I love the way they interact: the frequent touching, the light sparring and humorous jabs they launch at each other. We tell stories of life in our home countries over two greasy feasts: McDonald's for lunch and then later, back at the apartment, Tex Mex for dinner. I feel full in every sense. When the day draws to its end, I thank them all, in terrible mumbled Spanish, for giving me a very special and totally unexpected experience in LA.

At the airport, Pedro takes me aside and tells me, 'you can call me *Tío* (Uncle).' It feels as if he means I'm now a part of his family. A deep sob threatens to break from me when we hug goodbye.

As I stand in the queue for the check-in counter, tears start to leak uncontrollably down my face.

On the flight to Panama I'm seated next to a very different character. He looks as if he belongs in the movies. I see Mexican gangster: tough, squat, with pockmarked skin. Gold chains weave their way through mounds of chest hair, rings adorn stubby fingers. I discover he's actually a Guatemalan cigar salesman and quite sweet, despite his looks.

Something about his incongruous look reminds me of a story my friend and fellow child therapist Joe told me years before. She had just moved house with her family. The following day, someone rang the doorbell. Through the spy hole she saw a huge man with shaved head and a muscled body completely covered in badly etched tattoos. *Shit*, she thought, *what does he want? Should I open the door?*

She did. There he stood, casting a shadow and cradling in his big hands a batch of freshly baked bread. With a very shy smile he said, 'I see you guys have just moved in. I'm learning how to make bread so I thought I'd bring you some.' He held out the wondrous smelling and still steaming loaf. She welcomed him in, and amongst the boxes of household things, they drank tea and ate fresh bread with butter and jam. He became one of her favourite neighbours, always there to lift heavy things and fix broken things.

Joe told me her theory on his frightening appearance. Her thinking was that he had probably lived through a terrifying childhood and wore this shield of muscle and tattoos to make himself feel safe, but inside he was still a sweet, hurt little boy. Joe was such a strong person, but her eyes moistened when she finished her story about him.

I wonder if Sergio's gold jewellery is his armour.

I start to cry as I think of Joe. Just as she started to really enjoy her life, she lost it to cancer. The one thing her giant neighbour could not fix. Her office at the clinic was next to mine and when she wasn't with people, her door was always open. I visited her often, with a hot coffee cup in hand. She was Dutch and had a wonderful way of seeing to the core of a problem without sentiment clouding judgment. Her opinion on the wisdom of returning to Latin America would definitely have been worth listening to: she would have given it to me straight.

When she died, the door was closed and the room remained unoccupied, tomb-like, for many months. Her name, printed in clear black letters, still claimed the door. No one had wanted to be the one to take it down. I miss her.

Sergio's English is good, so we end up talking throughout the flight, enjoying each other's stories. He has a one-night stopover in Panama, so I ask him if he knows a good place to stay. I tell him I'm on my way to see 'my boyfriend' in Ecuador but will spend a few days in the city, seeing the sights before continuing my travels.

'Come with me. We can share a cab. I know a decent hotel close to the city centre.'

I'm still high on my experience with Pedro, so I think, *why not?* When we arrive at the ugly Seventies-era hotel I start to feel a little less enthusiastic. We are escorted to our rooms; his is just down the hall. Mine has a musty dank smell. The curtains are drawn and greying at their edges. All the furniture is painted black. The bedspread is black and the sheets are a rich blood red, which gives the bed a ghastly open mouth appearance. I feel as if I've walked into a brothel. When I manage to find the right button to switch on the TV, I see channel after channel of the worst kind of porn; grunting beast-like men pummelling vacant-eyed women.

God, what have I got myself into? I think, shivering involuntarily.

I go downstairs to the lobby to try to get a feel for the place. Sergio is there already. He acts as if it is a perfectly normal Panamanian hotel. Maybe it is. I don't know what to do, as it's getting late and I'm in a strange city, with little Spanish. My desire not to offend Sergio and the general sensation that he's not dangerous, outweigh my doubts, so I stay.

We eat at the hotel restaurant. I start to relax. Sergio is polite and thoughtful; he makes me laugh with his stories of a salesman's life. The rest of the hotel's clientele seem to be a mixture of perfectly normal people. At the end of the meal Sergio invites me to a dance club called 'Foxy' located nearby. Foxy, *really*? I fret. I weigh up all the pros and cons. The pros win. I'm too curious.

Foxy is shiny, tacky and jammed full with people slithering sexily on the dance floor to catchy Eighties songs. Some brave souls in the crowd are trying to mouth the words of 'I want to know what love is,' by Foreigner. I laugh: it couldn't be more apt.

'What would you like to drink?' Sergio asks, breathing into my ear.

'Gin and tonic, *gracias*.'

His hand slides down my back, not too far, as he manoeuvres me to the bar and buys two drinks.

My eyes watch like a hawk's as the barman pours it. I try to enjoy myself, but I feel distinctly like a small white lab-rat lost in a jungle full of sleek dark cats. Sergio does a stellar job at protecting me and he maintains his respectful manner; it's like having a bodyguard. But even so, the men's stares and roving hands wear me down and it's not long before I beg him to cut the night short. He obliges reluctantly and we return, safe and sound, to the hotel. I thank him for the *interesting* night and rapidly retire to my room. I detect, behind his politeness, that he's hoping for another kind of thank you.

No, thank you.

Just as I tuck into the red sheets, I hear a tentative rap rap on the door. *Oh god, here we go.*

'Yes, who is it?' I say through the closed door.

'It's Sergio. I was wondering if you want some company?'

'Oh, Sergio. Sorry, but I have a boyfriend so I'd rather not, thank you.'

There is a lengthy silence.

'Okay, see you tomorrow at breakfast. Sleep well,' he says, sounding seriously disappointed.

'Good night, thanks for everything,' I say, overly cheery.

I wait till his footsteps fade away and I hear a door close, and then I check again that my door is firmly locked.

Relief washes over me, but I feel rotten. Poor Sergio probably thought he was in with a good chance. I warn myself sternly to be less naive from now on. It could easily have ended badly.

I slip back into the red mouth and its silky sheets caress my skin. As I drift off to sleep I find Paco's soft lips in my dreams.

Seven

I LAST TWO DAYS IN PANAMA. The 'white lab-rat in the jungle' feeling continues unabated. I'm too scared to go anywhere or do anything, especially at night. Not even the famous canal lures me. The Panamanian men loiter, with backs pressed against walls, seemingly all day and all night. They stare and hiss, serpent-like. It's hot and humid. My clothes stick to my curves, making me feel more vulnerable.

Unable to stand it any longer, I sit myself down in a grubby-looking internet café and write to Paco. I tell him the truth about feeling unsafe and inform him simply that I need to see a familiar face. I give him the details of my flight out of Panama to Ecuador, which I've just booked for the next day.

Email sent, I feel a little better; at least now I have a plan. But it's been agonising to make the decision to leave so quickly; it feels like some kind of failure. I wanted so badly to look independent, to be independent, and to travel on my own through Colombia before going to join him. I slap my spirit but it refuses to come out of hiding. Finally, I admit to myself that I want to see him, and soon. Part of me worries about how Paco will interpret all this but most of me is just relieved to be getting out of Panama.

As my plane touches down in Guayaquil, my whole body tingles with anticipation. No more waiting and wondering. I barely look around me on the bus trip into town, but when I extract myself from my inner world, I see modern buildings outshining old stained ones that seem to be strapped together with snaking cables, streets heavy with traffic and alive with people. Guayaquil is Ecuador's biggest and most commercial city and I feel I could be anywhere in South America, looking at the same mix of decay and renovation.

I step down from the bus. Standing on the curb, backpack pressing into my shoulders, I try to get my bearings. The air smells faintly smoky, the light above is hazy. I unfold a map. Eyes find me. I feel on the edge of safety. Obviously foreign. Lost. I follow the marks I drew earlier and eventually locate the hostel. I'm its only guest. It looked better in the photos.

Settled in, I go in search of an internet café. I need to check if Paco knows I've arrived.

It seems to take forever for the each click to resister. I wait, picking at my fingers. Yahoo opens.

Nothing. I try to stay calm. Maybe he doesn't check his email every day; perhaps tomorrow, then. Tomorrow comes, again a blank in-box. Three more days go by, nothing.

My routine becomes my safety net. Every afternoon I wander to the Parque Seminario, or the 'Park of the Iguanas'; a green haven for hundreds of these giant, scaly lizards. Pigeons flap and peck at debris on the pathways; children stare, fascinated, and tourists take photos. The iguanas amble, carefully picking up and placing every limb, across concrete and grass, with their heads held high—the obvious owners of the zone.

On my fourth day in Ecuador I go to the park, find a park bench unoccupied. I claim it as mine.

'Hi, Willy,' I say quietly, when I spot him.

He's one of my favourite ancient, mossy green, stripy tailed friends. Over the past few days I have learned to pick out some of the iguanas, not only by their features, but by their personalities. Willy has a particularly high clump of spikes on his neck and an expression of gormless contentment. He is slower than the others, always last to the food scraps. I spot Grumpy, Sleek Yellow Skin and Old Pig (not hard to guess who he reminds me of).

I've been focussing on the iguanas to calm my mind and distract me from the hurt. I'm trying to really see them, understand them and their behaviour, to meditate mindfully while watching their daily antics. I feel like a biologist on a mission.

I'm glad that I can manage to laugh at my predicament: alone, waiting for my lover (ex-lover?) to appear, talking to iguanas. Willy turns his head slowly and looks at me. I laugh again.

But I am desperate to talk to someone, anyone. There's one person in particular.

Hi Daniel,

I know I said goodbye, but I'm feeling lonely. I'm wondering if my sanity is slipping. I'm in Ecuador. I came back to find Paco. Stupidly, I thought we had something; I think I was wrong. I think I generated a fantasy all on my own. There were signs he had moved on but I refused to see them. I didn't want my old life back, so I used him to get out. Look where that's got me. No job, no home, stuck on the other side of the world. I've been emailing him every day, nothing. I feel like an idiot. But it wasn't all me. He could have been clearer, told me not to come.

I don't know if I feel numb or full of a scream. Do I let my rage fly at someone, at Paco? Or do I just try to feel it, try to understand it and then allow it fade away? I've been attempting to do the latter. I'm trying to do a Buddhist mindfulness exercise, in the park, with my new iguana friends. I'm trying to find a state of being right in the moment, right in my own body; to allow my thoughts to just be what they are, to flow at will, without attaching myself to them or judging them. I'm letting them float away, like a leaf riding the current of a river.

I have no idea what to do next. Where to go? I can't go home, I'm too emburrassed. Cusco, maybe? Buenos Aires? BA is Paco's city, so going there might just be me refusing to face up to reality. What's wrong with me? I know. I get it. I have to be okay on my own. I just don't know how. I'm a bit tired of me.

It feels good to talk to you. Good that I talked to you in Peru. It did help. I think I put some of the painful stuff about you, and us, to bed. Talking to you now feels less sad, as if I'm just chatting to a friend.

Can you come along for the ride a while longer? I think I'm going to need you.

Five days is enough for me. I remove Paco's fine shell necklace. I'd worn it constantly for the last four months; it even appeared in my new passport photo. I hold it for a minute and then wrap it up, along with the Super8 camera I had been minding for him. I leave both at the hostel reception with a note. A minimal, formal email is sent telling him where they are so he can pick them up.

Okay, so I'm on my own.

I book a bus ticket to Quito and leave that night. When I get there I check in to a hostel and then find myself in an internet café again. One finger click of the mouse opens this email from him:

Jess!! I not even finish the mail to answer you. Okay. My number is 2 20___ house,
and 2 20___ job.
Sorry Jess but I have been in Montañita for the Easter weekend and now is the first time I check the mail! Why Quito? I'm so sorry, all this seems like I don't want to see you but be sure that is wrong! Don't worry. Please call me at the job. Jessy. No te enojes!! (don't get mad) Te quiero MUCHO y quiero verte loca!! (I love you a lot and I want to see you crazy girl.)
Ciao!
Paco

During those five long painful days I was so focussed on hearing from him, seeing him, that I hadn't realised it was Easter weekend. No wonder he hadn't responded to my emails.

God, now what do I do? What do I think?

I ring him.

'Paco, is that you?'

'Jessy, what happened? Please come back. I didn't know you were here.' He sounds upset.

'I thought you were ignoring my emails. I thought you didn't want to see me. It was horrible,' I say.

'No no, please don't think that. I was in Montañita, there was a big party. I didn't even check… I'm sorry. Please come back. I want to see you.'

It's tempting to free fall and go, but something has got through to me during those melancholic days watching iguanas. I feel more resolved, clearer that this is my life and I need to take control. I take a long, slow breath.

'It's okay, Paco. I understand now. It's my fault, too. I came here way sooner than I told you I would. I want to see you, too… but I think I need to stay here for a few days first.'

'But will you be alright?'

'I'll be fine. Quito is more tourist-friendly than Guayaquil. I want to take some Spanish classes and go into the jungle for a few days. Anyway, you're busy, right?'

'Actually I am. We need finish up an advertising campaign, then another one. I will be crazy for the next week, or more,' he says, his English awkward. I hear relief.

'It sounds like meeting in a week or ten days will be better.'

'*Está bien*. But I need to see you, *te quiero mucho*, Jessy,' he says.

'I'll let you know how it goes here. Then we will work out how and where to meet. *Quiero verte también. Te quiero mucho*, Paco,' I say. Somehow I don't feel it. My heart is wound tightly in a heavy blanket.

I hang up. I hear my pulse thumping in my ears. I feel twitchy. My mind is clearer than it has been for weeks, though. I know I need to do this.

Quito's home is beautiful, high, like Cusco's, huddled in a valley between two mountain ranges. On the day I arrive the clouds are hiding. I stand looking upwards and see snow-dusted volcanoes threatening to pierce the perfect blue sky. I have the sensation I'm enclosed in a balloon; one sharp prick and the world would disintegrate into long jagged slivers and fall away.

People surround me, busy with their days; but I'm alone, walking to my own tune. I am comfortable in my aloneness. I even seek it. I make regular escapes into the green hills that encircle the capital. Oddly, for me, I become drawn to the ubiquitous white colonial-style churches that sit high on round hillocks, surveying the people below. I feel almost compelled inside them by the ornate gold altars, stained-glass windows and the rows of pure white candles whose wicks dance softly to strange winds. I finally understand them as places to sit and think, and be still.

Venturing further out of town, I find myself immersed in tropical lush vegetation. Massive leaves and surreally huge bright flowers dwarf me. I imagine names for those that jump out of the green: yellow parrots' beaks, red love hearts with long yellow noses, pink fingerless gloves and fat yellow spotted ballet dancers. Florescent butterflies dance around the blooms while larger than life insects hum as they pollinate. Under the leaves, shiny black beetles forage in the moist soil. It's a worthy playground for a girl who grew up exploring the dense bush on our little farm.

I don't wander too far off the track as I've always been fearful of the dark unknown things that hide in cool places under the canopy of trees.

Time to be brave. With the storm inside quieter, I book a three-day trip into the jungle with a local guide and two other girls, plus their dog. I arrive the following day at the bus station with my pack hoisted on my back, ready and excited.

The guide, Stefan, a jolly, round-faced man in his late forties, waves me over. I had met him the day before. As I approach, my nerves start to play a sharp tune. I can see flushed cheeks and sparking eyes. When he kisses my cheek, my nose is assaulted by the heavy scent of alcohol.

Do I want to go into the jungle with a drunk man? I ask myself.

With only ten minutes to go before our bus leaves, my apprehension multiplies.

'Where are the other girls, and the dog?' I ask him.

'Oh, they are not coming. *Problemas*. Not sure what. It's just you now,' he says, smiling wanly. Then he continues, 'We can still go… I will be your guide, all for you.'

What? I feel torn when I look at the expression on his face, but I know that I do not want to be in the jungle alone with him for three days.

'Sorry, but I don't want to go on my own. I have to cancel,' I tell him.

'No, please, we can still do the trip. It will be fun.' His face drops; I see panic in his eyes.

'I'm sorry, but I'm not going. I thought there were other girls coming.'

His shoulders slump in resignation.

I feel guilty. I don't know whether to kiss him goodbye or just leave. I kiss him; I repeat my apology.

Walking away I feel deflated, angry at myself for saying sorry so many times, and angry with him for being drunk.

When I tell the reception staff at the hostel what happened they say cancelling was absolutely the right thing to do. Stefan's drinking had previously been a problem for other tourists. They look as if they wanted to say more, but don't.

All the built up excitement about exploring the wild jungles of

Ecuador fizzes out of me. Behind the disappointment lurks a profound relief—a sensation of having just escaped something.

Over the next few days I go to Stefan's office several times, with the idea of trying to get my money back. It's always closed. Getting angrier as each day passes, I wonder if I have fallen for some kind of scam.

Just as I'm about to give up, I'm surprised to find it open. Ready to fight for my rights, I barrel in but I'm stopped in mid stride by the looks on the faces of the two guys inside. Momentum slowed, I slide up the desk and quietly ask them if it's possible to get my money back.

'He's dead you know,' says one, ice in his voice.

'Who's dead?'

'Stefan. Your guide.'

'What? What happened?'

'After *you* cancelled, he went drinking. They found him dead, outside on the street, the following morning.'

Hang on a minute. If he drank himself to death, or had a heart problem or something, that's not my fault. I don't say that, I say, 'I'm really sorry, he was a nice man, but I had to cancel. I wanted to go in a group, not alone. He was already very drunk at the bus station. I didn't feel safe.'

They deflate and concede. Begrudgingly, my money is returned, minus a substantial 'administration' fee. I feel eyes boring into my back as I leave.

Feeling overwhelmed, I go straight to a tiny, flower-lined garden close to the hostel. It has become my special spot for sitting and thinking.

I remember the face of Stefan's wife, worried into lines, with staring eyes. I had met her and their young daughter the day before the scheduled trip. The little girl, aged around eight, smiled shyly at me from behind her mother. Stefan had taken me to meet them on the way to the bank to pay for the trip. His home was very humble, crumbling and dark. I could see they were struggling. He wanted me to see that.

I had heard from other locals that the dollarization of Ecuador's economy had affected its people terribly; the gap between those who lived well and those surviving on the edge was widening daily. Losing the money from the trip would have been devastating for Stefan, and now his family had lost him. I remember his excited face, a needy smile... *Come on, it will be fun.*

'Sorry, Stefan,' I say into the air.

When the guilt subsides, relief replaces it. I'm thankful I didn't end up in the middle of the jungle, on a riverboat with Stefan's ice-cold body beside me.

Before I can recover completely from the shock, the day I will see Paco again arrives. I feel as if I'm standing in a tiny dinghy, floating in the middle of the sea. The hairs on my neck are tingling, like they sense a tsunami could whip up at any minute and smash me out into the cool dark water.

I take a bus back to Guayaquil, fretting all the way. Am I ready for this? What's going to happen? What if…? The bus grinds and slides down the steep and perilous roads. My body feels bruised all over when I arrive. I am unable to think straight and my legs lead me back to the hostel I stayed in before. It was such a place of misery for me, I'm unsure why I return. It's familiar.

I ring Paco. He says he'll be over in an hour or so. I get ready, in all the ways I can think of—mind and body. Thoughts fly, my mouth is dry.

There's a call from reception. 'There is a man called Paco at the door,' the guy says. He asks me to come down, for security reasons.

My legs take me down the stairs. A breath catches in my throat. He looks stunning, unreal somehow. His tan is deeper, he seems taller. A shiver runs along my spine.

He smiles warmly and gives me a huge hug and a kiss on the cheek.

'Jessy, I'm so happy to see you again.'

He kissed me on the cheek. Oh no. What happened to that moment? The one I dreamed about; the movie moment I played over and over in my mind. Where is the passion, the tears of joy? That kiss was friendly.

'Let's go for a coffee. I know a cute place.'

'Okay, great,' I say, with a fake smile. Here it comes: the talk, the truth. I feel sick. I thought I'd prepared myself for this scenario, but it doesn't feel real.

We arrive at the small café, with outside tables cluttering a small cobbled patio. I find myself distracted by the sight of some stunning vermillion red bougainvillea flowers. They are weaving their way up the brick wall and over the roof of the café. How beautiful, I think.

I listen as he speaks. His words sound strange, as if they're coming from far away. He tells me he cares about me deeply and is happy to see me, but he has realised recently that he doesn't love me in the way I deserve. It's not *'te amo'* and never will be. He says he doesn't want a girlfriend right now, or for me to be his girlfriend.

'What do you want?' I ask, feeling numb.

'I want you in my life. I can't lose you. I want you to be my friend,' he says, reaching for my hand. It's a cool lump in his.

I feel thin trickles of spirit leak out of me.

'I'm sorry, Jessy. I've been really confused. A lot of things have happened. I wasn't clear about how I felt, but I am now.'

I wish you could have told me this before I travelled half way round the world to see you again.

I don't say anything. I swallow it. My eyes focus on the clustered red flowers. I am trying desperately not to splinter. *Can it get any worse?*

'Remember I told you that you remind me a lot of my mother? I love that about you, but I think that's why I can't do this with you. Well, part of it. It feels wrong, strange.'

Apparently, it can.

'I don't want to say goodbye,' he continues. 'Can we hang out, not sleep together? Just friends. I missed you. I think I need you.'

Of course you can't sleep with your mother... but you need one.

'Okay,' I find myself saying.

We hug for a long time. I breathe in the familiar earthy-boy smell of him. I realise that I want to keep him close, even if the story continues differently from the dream. I can't let go. My brain clicks and calculates. I morph into the actress, playing the part of a cool, centred girl.

'I was thinking of hiring a car and driving along the coast,' I tell him, improvising my lines. 'Up to Baños and Quito, then back again. Do you want to join me? We can stop for the full-moon party in Montañita on the way. No strings.'

'What do you mean—no strings?' His confusion is showing.

'No commitment, just as friends.'

I can see he's mulling over the offer. *Please, just a little more time. I'm not ready to be alone here.*

'Okay, *vamos*, let's do it' he says, suddenly excited.

Two days later we pick up our bright red car—blinded by very black tinted windows—from the airport at rush hour. Paco doesn't have a licence so the driving is my job. I hope I'm up for it. I went for my licence just days after my fifteenth birthday. It was a way to escape from the strains of being at home. Driving was second nature to me after seventeen years behind the wheel, or so I thought.

It's harder than I imagine. The whole 'driving on the other side of the road' thing isn't the main issue. If you just breathe and follow the flow, everything seems to work. The problem is that the car is on the wrong side of me. I nearly kill two pedestrians and three cyclists in a matter of minutes. I can't force my head around the fact that the whole car is now protruding out from the right of me, not the left. My brain's wires cross over and it smarts.

'Jessy, watch out on the right.'

'Sorry, I can't get used to the car being the wrong way round.'

I look over, Paco's face is white and his hand is gripping the armrest of the door.

'Shit, a cyclist!'

I swerve in.

'Who are you trying to kill, me or them?' he says, with a swallowed laugh.

I wonder, for a second, if subconsciously I do want to swipe him.

Eventually the strange rhythm of the road gets instilled in my body. No one follows any rules except one: do what you want, just don't crash into anything. Remarkably, the chaos seems to work. I become fascinated by how it makes me feel. I'm so alert and awake, but calm. It's a pure mindful state. And it seems everyone else around me is in the same state. It feels as if we're all connected somehow and can sense what someone else is going to do. There's this natural ebb and flow; a collective spiritual experience while driving the crazy roads of Ecuador.

There are no signposts in the small villages. We get lost every time we enter one; it's like they want to keep us from leaving. After circling a few times and coming back to the same spot, I shoot a frustrated look at Paco.

'Okay, okay,' he says, and begrudgingly seeks out someone to ask for directions.

I see hand movements and confused faces, more indicating, some chin rubbing.

'He thinks it's up there, straight, then first left, then 100 metres, then right, oh, or left, shit,' says Paco.

When we finally escape the villages, we find other perils in our pathway. Bright green snakes make rapid zigzagging crossings, and every few minutes I have to swerve violently to avoid enormous ragged pot-holes. Paco seems to be able to sleep through anything.

'What the hell is that?' I say loudly, jarring him from his dreams.

He rubs his eyes, blinks and says, 'Crabs, I think.'

I slow the car but there is no avoiding the onslaught of orange bodies with skittering legs trying to cross the road in front of us. In seconds, horrible, popping, crunching sounds surge up from under the car.

'Poor things,' I say.

'That's life; some make it, and some get crushed.'

We look at each other, appalled, and laugh.

When we arrive in Baños I'm dead tired after driving for more than eight hours. We had underestimated how long it would take to get here on roads as changeable as the climate on mountains. The sight of the picturesque mountain village wakes us both from a driving doze-state. It's hidden in fresh, overgrown brush and its neat little houses nestle snugly in the palm of the enclosed valley, circled by rivers.

We drive into the tiny central strip, stop outside a lean-to roadside store and then order homemade hamburgers. The scent of fresh warm yeast, melted cheese and grilled meat sets off a Pavlovian response. I'm starving. I shove it into my mouth as soon as the greasy paper is torn off.

'Jessy, wait. Let's have a picnic, up there.' Paco points into the hills above the village. 'I'll go get something to drink.'

I stop, mortified, my stomach throwing a loud fit of rumbling noises at being denied. 'Okay, but hurry, I'm dying here.'

He runs off. Turns out of sight. I wait. Two minutes later he comes running back, like the boy that just scored the winning goal; a bottle of wine raised in the air. 'Now we are ready. Up there, by that road,' he says.

The motor struggles as I accelerate round the tight bends. He indicates a dirt road off to the left. 'In there. We can see the mountains and watch the sun set,' he says, grinning.

The back wheels of the car slip on the muddy path, and then we lurch forward along the rough track.

I leave the car door open so we can hear the music while we eat.

Sitting on top of a large flat stone, we look down on the comings and goings of the village below us and eat our burgers. The bottle of wine is the only thing passed between us. We are close, I can feel his warmth, but nothing is touching. There is a gap that can't be wriggled into.

Then the sublimely ethereal song 'Angel Gabriel' by Lamb starts paying on the battered, barely functioning CD player. The lead singer's penetrating, raw voice vibrates its way right through to my soul. Every single word tingles its way down my spine and echoes softly from my mouth. She sings of needing Gabriel's wings, perhaps it's his encouragement to fly or a breath, *aliento*, to lift her.

The words are so perfect in the moment it's as if she's singing the song to me alone. She sweeps me up in her words about being strong, but still having a deep craving for unconditional love, for some light, and for someone. The song is so beautiful it hurts.

I turn slightly and watch Paco. He's illuminated by the car lights, calm in his own thoughts. He looks so lovely, but I'm not *allowed* to reach out. As I murmur the lyrics, I feel like a tiny girl alone on an iced-over lake in a violent snow storm. Sadness leaks out of me and is whipped up in the wind. I'm not sad because I believe somehow that Paco is 'Gabriel' but because, in that moment, my angel Gabriel is everyone and everything important that is missing for me. He's Daniel, my grandparents, lost friends, broken ties and missed chances. Something tugs at my heart. I want desperately to be connected to someone, anything. I feel as if I'm freefalling, watching my life slide past my eyes, faster and faster.

Feeling nauseous, I move quietly away from Paco and closer to the edge of the rock. I watch the villagers in the valley below, as the light fades. A memory surges into my head; a memory of the day I truly realised I was on my own.

It was a Saturday. I was about eleven years old. I woke up and went downstairs to get something to eat. No one was around, so I grabbed what I could find and consumed it in the kitchen. As I was sitting there, I wondered if my parents would miss me if I was gone. I suspected they wouldn't. My mind devised a way to test the thought.

I went outside and climbed a big leafy tree in the paddock behind the house; from there I could look down on the house and yard and see if they missed me. I sat there for hours and hours, watching my mother go in and out of the house, my father drive away and come back an hour or so later, life going on. I waited, hoping and fantasising that at any moment they would discover that their daughter was gone. Once they realised I was missing, they would call out my name; when there was no reply, they would get frantic and scream it out, and then, finally, taken over by desperation, they would run around trying to find me. I would let them suffer a bit, then I'd climb down and there would be a long session of huge hugs and happy tears. I would be missed and then found.

Nothing happened. When it started to get dark and cold and hunger got the better of me, I climbed down and went inside. They hadn't noticed. No one said anything. There was no family dinner, so, after rummaging around for some food and something to drink, I took myself off to my room. I had been up that tree, hoping to be missed, for about eight hours (unseen since dinner the night before).

I think I have spent a good part of my life hoping for the imaginary reunion that was missed that day.

I'm surprised by how vivid the memory is. I can almost feel the branches digging into my legs, and the hunger, a hunger for more than food.

I get up and walk away from the edge. Some distance away I stop and stare at the lightly frosted mountains, and then I realise I've been dancing with a dream; a dream of a boy, a boy folding me into his arms, and everything being right. The fanciful music in my mind disappears and I'm left standing, arms outstretched. No one is there. My body doubles over, as if I've been kicked in the stomach. Tears and ragged breathing choke me.

Then the storm stops, one second to the next. I come back into myself, depleted but calm. On a patch of rough grass, I sit down and then rest my forehead in my hands. I can hear the music playing faintly behind me. Paco hasn't moved from his warm rock seat. When I peer up through my splayed fingers at the mountains again, they are aglow with the last soft rays of the day. Then I focus on the grass, hoping to see life; a bug, some ants carrying their irregular loads along winding trails made with a million ant steps.

I can sense a smile twitching in the corners of my mouth. There she is, my little hummingbird, positioned in the perfect place to fulfil her promise. With my head resting in my hands I can see her fuzzy form gazing up at me from my forearm.

She seems to be saying, *I'm here, and remember, you can…*

Two blurry days later, we find ourselves standing right in the middle of the crowded and grubby Guayaquil central bus station.

'So this is it?' I say, looking at his face, seeing sadness reflected there.

'It's just goodbye. I know we will see each other again,' he says.

'Maybe I'll see you in BA. I would like to go back there for a proper visit.'

'You should.'

'Maybe I'll get to eat a Pepe *asado* before you do!'

'I hope you make it there. Pepe will look after you.'

'I know.'

We hug. There's nothing else to say. I board the bus and don't look back.

As the bus grumbles off, I focus on my destination: cobbled streets, mountains, bright colours and finger puppets.

Cusco. I knew I would see you again.

Eight

Cusco welcomes me with a day so clear and crisp I feel wide awake, as if I've emerged from a cool dark lake into the light of morning.

My nest room at the hostel where I stayed before is available. The same bright bedspread, the little lopsided wooden table—they cause a sublimely sweet ache. I switch on the lamp and its dull orange glow makes me smile. They fixed it. I curl up on the bed; it's scratchy. I try to create an image of how I'm feeling. I've always done this. I also did it with the kids I worked with in the clinic, as a way to give emotions a shape. I never felt entirely comfortable using psychological language, or talking in diagnoses. I tried to help the children and their families tell their story—to be explorers of the past, protagonists of the now and narrators of tomorrow—while I walked beside them.

Now an image comes to mind. I have woken up in a life raft, unharmed physically but lost at sea. There is a rope hanging over the side of the little boat, I pull it up and my heart constricts as the frayed end rises from the water. I look around for the big boat, for other rafts; there is nothing. I have survived something.

My mind focuses as I concentrate on this image. I begin to feel better able to work out what I'm going to do next. I'm still not sure, but I'm grateful to Cusco, for its strange light, for this little room, for friends I will see later. As hurt as I am, hope sits with me. I make a conscious decision to use the time to think, to piece myself back together.

I unpack. Then I sit and let the thoughts flow.

This is grief, a feeling I know well. I went to see a psychiatrist after Daniel died, because I was so sad I couldn't move and it hurt to keep breathing. He told me I was suffering from complicated grief. I think my life has always been complicated with grief, not only for those who have gone, but for those who live. It's a grief for something that's not there, a frightening grief for some unknown thing.

I go into the attic of my mind, scrabble through the boxes of memories. If I can just make sense of them and try to piece the story together, perhaps I will be free.

I go back as far as I can. I don't have any memories of my very young life. I know we spent a year or more in London. Dad was studying his medical speciality, Mum was interning at a law firm. I know my grandparents came over to visit and then brought my baby brother and me back to New Zealand with them. I was nearly three. Mum came home some months later, and then Dad. I remember Nana telling me, in a rare moment of openness about emotional things, about her first sight of me at Heathrow airport. She told me she was expecting her heart to explode with joy on seeing her first grandchild again; instead she froze, mortified by the sight of the tiny waif, with a pale face and gangly legs. When she took me up in her arms, I was stiff—a little rod already in my spine.

I realise that I want to know why they sent us away, back home. I know I need to ask, but how do I ask without hurting?

Sitting on my bed in my Cusco sanctuary, I try to see my parents, to conjure up a picture of their young selves. They must have felt all alone and ill equipped in London. I know they felt lost there. Mum was only twenty-three when she had me, and both of them were just starting their careers. I know—from said and unsaid things—that they were trapped on an unpredictable ride of powerful feelings and unheard thoughts. I imagine them trying to survive in a wild and angry sea. Mum rode her sailboat up the steep glistening surface of the large waves, but then plunged into the unforgiving surf. Dad sat, in his row boat without oars, as it was whipped in circles by the rough undercurrent. They needed to rope their boats together and guide each other to shore, but neither knew how. Perhaps they tried to save us from those waves by handing us over to Nana.

My childhood memories feel like flickering light filtered through leaves. The strength of the wind, the direction of the sunlight: they cause different patterns to be revealed. I try to see from all the angles, but there are so many gaps; it's like reading a badly printed book full of blank pages and illegible text. I want to know the story. I recreate what I can.

I know there was love between my parents, but they were terribly mismatched. Over the years, their jagged edges ground against each other, and their love and individual spirits were whittled away in the process. Bright painful sparks would fly but were never referred to. A massive avalanche of rocks fell some years before they divorced and was bulldozed off without a word. I think my brothers and I got lost under the rubble. I made a cave and stayed there; Jonny fought his way out, hurting himself in the process; Eddie picked his way through, refusing to acknowledge the debris and Henry lay completely still so as to not cause any more slippage.

My family never talked about emotional things, about what was really going on. I know some other families were different, but in part it is a cultural thing. We are stoic, us Kiwis, we are tough; we are taught not to cry over spilt milk, to buck up and move forward. It doesn't matter if there are burning secrets, fears, desires and hurts around us or behind us. I think that culture is changing, but there is a tendency not to seek help or look into the past and understand where the flames originated: that's for weak people. Some of us drink too much, too often. We are not the worst drinkers by far, but even so, it's almost a national tradition to drown problems in alcohol.

I tried to drink the aching away; I started too young, following the family tradition of washing away hurt. Every weekend from when I was fourteen years old was spent getting 'trashed', 'wasted', 'plastered' and 'wrecked'. The aim was to obliterate everything I felt. I started to grab onto boys then, too; one after the other—buoys in the sea. It became a habit. After Daniel's death there were times where I held onto anyone who seemed remotely interested; it didn't even matter if I liked them. Then I would stop: stop going out and stop actively looking, for many months, perhaps a year. I would fill the space with activity: art classes, photography courses and acting lessons.

I went to acting lessons hoping that if I could just learn to act out different emotions, I would be able to feel them—distinguish them one from the other. I remember that the teacher once said to me, 'That performance was so intensely sad, well done.' I felt like shouting, I can do *sad*, what I want is to know joyful, excited, angry!

Of course, not quite subconsciously, there was always a hope that maybe a nice handsome man would be taking the course or the class. It was comical, the first day of each one, everyone looking around, faces open, hopeful. Then a collective sigh as we realised we were all women in our thirties and forties.

It's dark now, in my nest above Cusco. I gather up the colourful bedspread and wrap it tight around my shoulders. The years in Melbourne feel both close and like another life: a blur of work and men and sadness, going out and being busy and hoping. I know I'm not the same girl now, but I could be her again, if I'm not careful.

Going through the messy dusty boxes in the attic of my mind extends long into the night. I pull up the good memories, too. I smile at Mum's amazing original bedtime stories about Baggety the witch and her enormously long fingernails and crazy adventures. My heart warms when I picture Dad's strange habitual gift of a crayfish and a bottle of Bailey's Irish Cream, sitting on the kitchen bench. This gift was always waiting for me when I came home for university holidays, and I know it was his way of saying I care. I try to stretch the lovely memories over the blank pages.

It is hard, going through the boxes, but it feels important to sit with the memories and snapshots for a while, and then quietly arrange some things in slightly better order, before putting them back neatly, less laden with old dust. The new 'Paco dream' files still have pain hanging onto them, but even they are less heavy now.

No more boys. I seek out girls. The following morning I return to 'my' café in San Blas plaza to look for Bree, the tall redhead who had so kindly poured large glasses of wine the night Amy and I spilled out our troubles. I was just starting to get to know her when Paco exploded into my world and whipped me away.

Her face lights up with surprise when she sees me. 'Jessy,' she says, coming round from behind the counter for a hug. She bends down. I'm tall, she's taller, but she has this way of presenting herself that reduces her stature. She stands with shoulders slightly rolled, head bowed and one knee bent. I wonder if it's a new trait born of Cusco's low ceilings and petite people, or whether it's a lifetime's habit. An urge comes over me to pull her up to full height, like a puppet master.

'I knew you would come back,' she says, in her lilting Irish accent.

I don't quite know what to make of this, but I smile, nod. 'You're still here!'

'Yes, getting close to a year now.'

'And Brian?'

'Yep, crazy as always. He's playing here tonight; you have to come. Hey, what happened with Paco?'

'I saw him in Ecuador; I came back for him… sort of. He had moved on by the time I got there.'

'Oh, no way, Juicy,' she says, using the nickname she gave me before I left, which I'm not convinced by. 'That's tough. You okay, though?'

'Better now.'

That night I walk into the café above the waterfall and I feel, at home. Its bright colours and the smiling faces jolt me awake. Brian is playing guitar in the corner and singing the insanely infectious song, 'I'm Gonna Be,' by the Proclaimers. His eyes are closed, head swinging back, orange curls bouncing around his face.

Bree is behind the bar, a pisco sour in her outstretched hand. 'Thanks, love,' I say as I reach for it.

'*De nada*, Juicy.'

It's impossible not to be merry.

I spend my nights trailing behind Bree and Brian, soaking up the fun that follows them around. In the day I take Spanish classes and wander the city alone. I don't think of tomorrow; it's still scary. I do fantasise about staying in Cusco, making a life, but as the days go by the shine starts to rub off. An American friend gets mugged on her way home from a bar late at night. She's alright physically, but it makes us all tense. Bree has been trying to obtain work papers for months. She breezily updates me on her struggles with hand-rubbing, smirking officials. She doesn't complain; any troubles get buried in laughter. I don't know whether I could be so resilient.

One Saturday I watch a scene in a café that jars me and strengthens my resolve to maintain a contemplative space between me and men. I see an English guy sitting beside an extremely pretty, petite Peruvian girl with silky black hair and big eyes. His long, painfully thin legs are bent up in an awkward position; he appears almost folded in on himself. His face is sharp, hawk-like, with deep inset eyes.

'This is Maria,' he says, introducing the beautiful girl to the group of people they're sitting with. Someone asks him how they met. He launches straight into the story, full of a jittery energy. People lean in, curious, captivated by his intensity. I listen, too.

'We met in Mama Africa, on the dance floor,' he says. 'I saw her there, dancing and I just fell, instantly. It's been a month and we are so in love.'

He looks down at her, briefly, before continuing with his tale. I have to struggle to concentrate as my stomach lurches: Mama Africa is where I met Paco, and something about this scenario is making me feel uncomfortable.

'We're living together,' he goes on. 'I rented a place here. I want to learn Spanish. She's learning English. I think the plan will be to go back to London in a few months.' It all comes pouring out.

As he's telling their love story, she has one limp hand—with perfect manicured nails—resting on his knee, while the rest of her is staring into space. Every few minutes he looks adoringly at her and she smiles a weak smile up at him. His eyes drift to the hand on his leg, as if it's a huge comfort—he is hers, she is his.

As I sit there watching them, I find myself questioning the love story. The body language on display undermines it too noticeably. I can't help speculating about what might be going on, even though I know I'm probably reading things into the scenario that are about me not them. I wonder what they want, and especially, what she wants. I imagine that she aspires to a better life, that perhaps she is under pressure from her family to land a foreign man and get away (maybe even to finance them, too).

My throat constricts. I sense that both of them need something so desperately that the fantasy in their minds cannot be dismissed by the truth.

I know that place well.

When his story comes to an abrupt end, he laughs oddly, his face grim. She looks up at him, her face passive. I hope I'm wrong, but I feel an acid taste in my mouth; a nervous sadness.

I go home to my nest room, climb the rickety stairs.

What do I want? What?

I sit on my bed, frustrated. I want what my grandparents had. The warm and loving threads that joined them were almost visible. After forty years together you could feel they loved each other genuinely and firmly.

It was subtle, there were no big gestures. It was shown in the way they looked at each other and the things they did for each other.

When we were kids and stayed with them at the weekend we were allowed to hop in bed with them in the morning. We would snuggle up warmly between ample Nana on the right and stick thin Granddad on the left. Being in the middle of that loving energy gave me some of my most cherished memories. All doubts and fears were just washed away in it.

I start to cry. I miss them. It was with them, in their humble weatherboard house, that I felt more connected. Their house was a home, but that sense of home was ripped away when they left us, just one week apart. More than ten years have passed, but my sense of loss hasn't.

The last time I saw them was when I came home for Dad's wedding. I was twenty-one and confused by my feelings about him marrying again. It made me happy that he had someone; for a man who likes solitude and mistrusts people, he didn't cope well alone. But my house felt even less like my home. It had been splashed in pink. I've never liked pink. My mother had been totally erased. His wife, Cheryl, is so different from my mother, but they both have the same propensity for forward motion. Neither of them ever walks. Cheryl trots, leaning slightly forward; my mother strides, back stiff.

When I left after the wedding, to go back to university, I turned to look at my grandparents standing in the driveway. Granddad had his hand up in a still salute; Nana waved and put on a smile. They suddenly seemed so old. I found myself taking a mental snapshot of them.

Later that year Nana tore a ligament in her shoulder when she fell over a large pumpkin in her wild and abundant garden. During surgery, a pulmonary embolism burst and her breath was sucked permanently from her. Unable to live without Nana, Granddad took his own life, exactly a week later.

I have relived that day a hundred times. Now I relive it again. I feel almost that, if only I could remember every small detail, then somehow I could change the ending. It's mad-making, but I can't help it.

Mum asked me to pick him up and bring him to her house. We had given him some time alone as he was relentless in asking for it, but we all felt that he needed company. I vividly remember parking outside his garage, already sensing that something was wrong. When I entered the house and couldn't find him the panic began to pulse through me, rising further when I saw—laid out neatly on the bed—his and Nana's documents, other envelopes and one of Nana's nightgowns.

My mind shouted out as my seemingly detached body raced around outside in search of him. Every turn of the garden was dreaded, every tree feared as I looked up at its branches. When I arrived at the side door of the garage I spotted the handwritten notice pinned there.

DON'T COME IN

CALL THE POLICE

The side door was locked and the garage door pulled down. I'll never forget the intense fear of that moment, and the sense of helplessness.

Should I try to break in? What would I see?

Was he dead? Could I save him?

I called his name but no one answered so I ran inside and rang my mother. The police came ten minutes later and broke down the door. The young officer's face said it all when he emerged from the dark. Granddad was gone. He had somehow put in working order an old World War II rifle. Then, after covering the floor with plastic sheeting, he had shattered his heart.

I felt so powerless and defeated, knowing that I couldn't save him. It was a feeling that lingered and then gained strength when Daniel died seven years later.

I'm exhausted by the memories so I get into bed and pull the covers up, so high I'm almost burrowed under them; nothing is exposed to the cool Cusco air. My last thoughts as I drift off into an exhausted sleep are: *I couldn't save them. Maybe I need to save me.*

Nine

I HAVE ONE MONTH left on my tourist visa. It's time to decide what to do next. Do I stay in Cusco, go back to Melbourne, or continue on this journey? Do I try my luck in Argentina?

Perched, one afternoon, on the edge of the mermen fountain in the main plaza, I start my analysis of the last option. When the ideas keep looping back on themselves, I just stop thinking and start running my fingers through the waters instead. As I watch the ripples arch out and fade away, a warm feeling of calm fills me. Then I see something in the water. Sitting separately from the other smooth stones and some coins, an irregular grey stone catches my attention. I pull back my sleeve, reach in and pluck it out. It's shaped like a heart.

Okay then, Argentina it is.

It feels right, indescribably right, as if a concrete-soaked scarf has just been lifted from my neck.

I wonder if it's me or Cusco or something else that gave me this crumb to follow. This small city in the sky inspires a belief in mystical things. Or is it just magical thinking? Are these signs real? Perhaps they're merely random coincidences—not fate but serendipity? I struggle with the questions. I don't know whether there really are cosmic forces that place pointers and people in our pathway for us to find, or whether we *know* deep down what we want to do and we search for and find a sign that confirms it. Maybe sometimes we search for a sign to confirm something we *want* to do but know we *shouldn't*. In the end I think that the world can appear so arbitrary and uncontrollable that humans need to discover form in the waves of events, to detect patterns in the stars and follow signposts on the rough, beautiful and frightening road of life. Maybe it doesn't matter where these things come from; they're kind of magical, either way. They keep hope flowing and feet moving.

Two days later I receive two emails in response to the one I sent everybody saying I was Argentina-bound. The first one, from my shrink-friend Dave, says

Jess
I need to escape for awhile so I booked a ticket to Cusco. I was going to surprise you with a visit. So, stay a bit longer as I arrive next week. Then maybe I can change my flight and return from Buenos Aires? You can savour my wonderful company on the journey there.
D

I write back: what a wonderful surprise and yes, absolutely book from BA. Dave is currently separated from his wife, Anne. He is having a difficult time, so I understand his need to run away. He could probably benefit from a bit of South America-inspired perspective, too. I can't wait to see him. The earth under my feet moves again, propelling me forward.

Everything seems to be pointing south, to Buenos Aires. Of course there is a tiny grain of hope still sitting there, itching away; the tiny pea under a hundred mattresses. Eventually the wandering Paco will return home. I try hard not to allow it to rule any of my plans, but…

The itching is not helped by his father, who sent the other email.

Hi Jessy
How're you doing?
Like mi slang? I read your mail. It seems that South America get into your self, no? It's necessary to us (Latins) to be recognised by beautiful people like you, who enjoy our people, our landscapes and our language and our asado!!
Of course, if you pass by Buenos Aires, you are absolutely obligated to call me, so I can go to buy the best asado I can get!!! And we'll do it, slowly, to eat it faster with many bottles of good red Argentine wine.
My two sleeping cats also will be waiting for you, so you can't fail. By that time I hope your *castellano sea mejor qué mi ingles*

(I hope your Spanish will be better than my English).
I send you a great *abrazo y un gran beso*! (A hug and a big kiss.)
Pepe

Dave, my grumpy angel-friend, is knocked about by the altitude for the first few days after he arrives. He moves slowly and I buzz around, waiting for him to come back to life. My happiness is almost manic.

'Jessy, slow down,' he says.

'But there's so much to tell you and show you.'

'I know, but chill a bit.'

'Okay, okay. I'm just happy you came.'

'I'm happy to be here. Just this damn headache…'

'Sorry, I'm not helping.'

'Give me a day.'

I can't believe my luck. Once again a wise friend is accompanying me on the walks through Cusco's stony streets.

After a week in Cusco and the surrounding valleys we start the journey south. Our first stop is the picturesque town of Copacabana, on the shores of Lake Titicaca. It's a strange little place; I can't help feeling we are in a cove beside the seaside. The lake is so immense that it gives the impression it's a sea. There are sandy beaches at its edges and real lapping waves—albeit tiny ones.

We take a trip out to the famous floating reed islands, home for the Uros people, who not only pre-date the Incas but also survived them.

'I hope that thing is safe,' says Dave, when he sees our reed canoe come into view.

It looks like bundles of tightly bound straw, shaped into a canoe. On its prow an animal head has been sculptured: large ears point up, alert, and its open mouth, with painted teeth, grins at us. It looks both proud and comical.

'I'm sure it's fine,' I say as we get in.

'Looks like the Loch Ness monster to me.'

'It won't bite you.'

Dave is less than amused when the canoe rocks from side to side as it cuts through the water. I'm not sure whether the rocking, or the fact that he's stuck beside a very large man with a big belly and a bigger belly laugh, bothers him most.

As we approach one of the floating islands, our guide starts telling us a story about the Uros people who live on them.

'There are lots of islands on the lake, and each has a family, or some families living on them. When there are problems between these family and those on other islands, they just grab a big stick and float their island away. When the anger goes, they get happy again, and they float it back.'

We all laugh. Dave's seat companion crushes him when he roars.

'That's handy,' I say, trying not to giggle at Dave's pained expression.

'Bet a lot of people would love to float themselves away from their neighbours,' he says, while elbowing himself some space.

'Or away from their families,' I add.

Walking on the island is like trying to get your balance on a water bed topped with loose green straw. The surface is uneven and patchy. With every step I feel I might lose a leg into the cool dark water underneath. Four small, simple houses have been constructed on this island, all out of reeds. They look like the huts my brother and I used to make out of hay bales, but with woven reed walls. Tiny sliver-grey fish lie, split open, drying in the sun, in rows. Sleek gull-like birds hover nearby, spying on us, waiting for the right moment to dive and steal. Lying on colourful mats are artisanal products, woven hats and gloves and some silver jewellery. Three women sit by their wares, weather-worn faces expectant.

'What a strange way to live,' says Dave.

'I kind of like the simplicity.'

'You would be bored out of your mind in two minutes.'

'I know. I just like the idea.'

Not long after dusk the following day our bus drives over the crest of a hill—still on the road, thankfully. We had heard horror stories of busloads of people being driven over the edge, hanging for a minute fragment of time in the air, before plunging into the valley's throat.

'Wow, now that's a sight,' says Dave.

'That's La Paz, right?'

'Must be.'

I look down into the lit up city's valley home. The world flips upside down. It's like gazing at the night sky, or a reflection of it. Instead of stars there are a million tiny individual lights spattered, seemingly randomly, across the valley floor and up the bases of the high hills around the city. It's disorientating. Breath catches behind my teeth. The sucking sounds of gasps can be heard around us.

We spend two days in a daze wandering around La Paz, breathing in barely enough oxygen to make coherent thoughts. It's on the second day that we stumble into the Witches' Market.

'Oh, that's a little gross,' I say, pointing to a row of llama foetuses hanging by their necks, limbs curled. They are bone dry like petrified wood, their eyes frozen half open.

'Not a pretty sight. Curious, though,' says Dave.

I see baskets of dried toads, insects, bright berries, herbs and strange pods.

'I imagine these are for rituals.'

'Begging favour with the spirits, probably.'

'I guess. A bit yucky, though. I heard they perform live sacrifices.'

I find out later that the Aymara or Aimara people do use these strange things for asking favours of the earth goddess Pachamama, for luck, for love and fortune. The Aymara are an indigenous culture that populated the region before the Incas and then the Spanish colonised it.

I'm a little scared of the ancient ladies, with sharp eyes and nails, who sit patiently and serenely by their wares. Their eyes bore into us as if they are reading something there.

I smile and think of Henry's face. My youngest brother would love the Witches' Market. I imagine him here—poring over every foul, dead thing, and every unusual plant or artefact. Wanting to keep it, and study it on rainy days.

When Henry was little he had a collection of the skeletons of small animals, neatly arranged in his room, which didn't smell exactly but looked as if they should. His favourite set, however, was a human skull, spine and hand—courtesy of Dad's days as a medical student. At age three he could put all its pieces together—harder than you might think when all the cranium bones and segments of spine were separated, like the pieces of a puzzle. It's not a 'normal' toy for a little boy. I think Dad liked to shock people when they came to our house, by setting Henry in the middle of the room to piece together all the human bones.

It wasn't just bones Henry liked to collect; it was rocks, and strangely-shaped sticks, and seeds and pods. He didn't speak a word until he was well over two years old—but when he did he made it sound like a declaration. 'Rock,' he said proudly, before diving head first down a large hole in search of one he had spotted. I remember someone grabbing a leg before he totally disappeared.

People, including me, often thought of him as an odd little boy. But when I think about the man he is today, his peculiar hobbies don't seem so out of place. Like all of us, he's just searching for his own way to make sense of what he found in the world.

A day later Dave and I find ourselves standing, mesmerised, on the famous Salar de Uyuni salt flat, which spreads over 10,500 square kilometres, making it the largest of its kind in the world. It's so otherworldly that it's disorientating. Its planes are so flat and white that space and distance become both contracted and expanded. Hills in the distance appear to float above the earth and are much further away than they look. If you crouch low to the ground and focus on an object close to you, people barely metres away appear tiny, suddenly miniaturised. An American and his Chilean girlfriend spend hours, wild-eyed, cameras grasped in hands, playing games with the weird perspectives. They show us some photos, grinning wide. There is one of her standing tippy-toed on a Coke bottle; some others of toy figurines become man-eating monsters, hungrily chasing her across the stark whiteness. Nothing is normal here. Small pointed pyramids of salt cut the smoothness of the plains in neat rows. The salt crunches like icy snow underfoot, but you don't feel cold there, pressed between the white earth and the clean hot sun. Dry and cracked into pentagon patterns, the surface gives the impression of a vast pure white snakeskin stretched out across the earth. Giant, ancient cacti growing on a hill look bizarre silhouetted against the backdrop of 'snow'.

I watch Dave. He's looking into the white, standing very still. 'You there?' I ask.

'Oh. Yes.'

'It's so strange here.'

'Kind of beautiful.'

I look out over the patches of water on the salt. The clouds are reflected so perfectly that I suddenly feel squashed even thinner between the earth and sky. 'Humbling, too. A little magical, even.'

'It's a sight I won't forget.'

Is this childlike joy I'm experiencing? Do children really become wide-eyed at sights like these? Maybe we have to be grown-up, knocked down a bit, to appreciate how majestic it is, to be truly awed.

Later, in a small low-roofed café, we come back to earth.

'What lovely people,' I say. 'And the guide was so good; not too intrusive. He let us explore the place, and…' I stop. I know I have started gushing. I glance over at Dave.

'Jess, you think everyone is nice and means well. I worry about that.'

'What do you mean?'

'You always see the best version of people and explain away things that don't fit. That's great in some ways, but it makes you vulnerable to disappointment.'

'Okay, fair enough. I promise to put clear lenses in my glasses.'

'I think you do need this experience, but you could easily lose yourself if you're not careful.'

On the walk back to the hostel I look down at my shoes. They are dusty and worn. I feel like an adventurer, moving towards something new. It's exciting and terrifying. I have a chance to expand, to learn, to see and breathe new things, to express myself in a new language. It's on the edge you find out who you are. I want to know the girl in the grubby shoes.

Maybe everyone needs to be lost at least once, so they can go find themselves again.

From the pure white of the salt flats we cross the border into Argentina. White turns into red. On the bus trip to Salta our seats are on the upper deck, directly above the driver. We have windows all around us with an unobstructed view of the landscapes around Jujuy, on the extreme north-west edge of Argentina. It's like suddenly being placed in the glass bubble of a vehicle traversing Mars. High undulating hills tower over us. They look as if they have been forced out from deep within the earth. Hundreds of distinct red, yellow, purple, grey and brown tones lie next to each other, in layers, giving the hills a zigzagging, stripy appearance. It's like weaving through the squeezed out peaks of icing on a gigantic, colourful, sculptured cake.

'I'm hungry,' I say.

'You're always hungry,' says Dave.

'I hope they have good cheese in this country.'

'I hear the wine is great.'

As the kilometres tick down to Buenos Aires, a wind of excitement starts welling up inside me. Through the soft vibrating hum of the bus I feel a deeper thumping inside, as if my heart is bigger and stronger than normal.

Part Two

Landing

Ten

DAVE AMBLES, I PACE, but we find a rhythm that suits. After the quiet otherworldliness of Bolivia, Buenos Aires assaults us. As we walk down Avenida de Mayo we become engulfed in the heavy smoky fumy aroma of tar-sweating streets overrun with traffic. A disharmonious opera of raised voices, screeching brakes and violent accelerations raises heart rates and leaves us off balance. The incessant tapping and banging of building sites echoes around us and gnaws at our temples. We come to the massively wide Avenida 9 de Julio, stop, and stand there, contemplating for a few seconds. 'What do you think?' I say. We watch as people start running to make it to the median strip before the lights change.

'Looks like it takes two goes to get across.'

'We can rest in the middle.'

'Not so keen.'

'Tomorrow, then?'

'Yep.'

We are buffeted by a tide of workers in rush mode, with stressed faces. There are long queues of people waiting for the chaotic stream of buses. I can't understand a word of the conversations going on around me. It's a blur of passionate syllables and talking hands. I wonder to myself how long it will take before I can eavesdrop on a conversation. *Will I ever fit in here?*

'Which way?' I ask Dave.

'That way,' he says, pointing back towards where we started from. It seems that Dave is all out of the desire to explore.

As we weave around people, senses alert, I'm suddenly reminded of driving in Ecuador and the sensation of mindfully finding a space that's yours, in amongst the ever twisting river of cars.

'Too early for a wine?' Dave looks at me with a glint in his narrowed eyes.

'Come on, really, we've only walked a couple of blocks.'

'I'm tired. Shall we try that place?' he says, pointing to a large café, wrapping itself around the corner.

I'm tired, too. 'Okay, guess it's never too early.'

We fall heavily into our chairs and rest our elbows on a table near the large sash windows. It's quieter in here, but alive still with the hum of voices, interspersed with the clinking of glasses and plates.

An elderly waiter swans over, dressed in white with a perfectly pressed blue apron. His hands are crossed in front of him. He leans in slightly, an attentive expression in place.

'*Un vino, por favor,*' I say.

With a nod, he swiftly gets us a menu.

'Malbec, right?' says Dave, running his finger down the list.

'That's from here?'

'They're known for it. I have some at home. Pretty nice drop.'

Dave indicates to our *mozo.* 'This, *por favor.*'

It arrives less than a minute later. 'Oh, that's good,' I say, taking a long sip. The travel tension starts to wear off me. It's like I'm shedding a too tight skin.

Dave savours the wine in his mouth before swallowing. 'So… A few days of looking around?'

'May as well take advantage of your company before you go.' I grin at him.

Suddenly drumming, chanting and shouts break into our world. We peer out the window as a group of around fifty protesters stampedes down the street outside. Angry faces and fixed eyes flash past us. Banners inked in spray paint flutter in the light wind. I can't catch a single word of the impassioned cries. I turn and look back into the café to see brief flicks of heads in the direction of the noise, before conversations are resumed.

'Wonder what that's all about?' I say.

'God knows, but they're not short on passion,' replies Dave.

'Nope. From the lack of reaction in here, seems like this is pretty normal.'

We stare out the window. 'What have I let myself in for?'

Dave raises one grey-specked, slightly out of control eyebrow.

That night my dreams are vivid and bursting with the faces of friends and people we met on our travels. I can't understand what they're saying to me; the mouths form words but nothing is said. Their expressions are urgent but I don't know what they want. Then the image whips away. I wonder what it means.

Am I making a mistake? Was I supposed to get off here?

On the street in the morning the intoxicating scent of caramelising sugar drifts around the corner. I see a slim man with leathery oversized hands standing over a metal contraption heated with a blue-yellow gas flame. In a disk-like pan he's patiently turning over peanuts soaked in a bubbling sugary liquid. There is an intriguing stillness about the set of his face. Then I see a large stand, overflowing with colourful blooms and foliage, green and orange and blue and pink forms beautifully break the monotonous greys and stiff lines of the street—a tiny oasis. It makes me smile.

'What are you so chuffed about?' asks Dave.

'I'm not sure. Flowers? The smell of syrup?'

Later, on the docks of Puerto Madero, the recently renovated New Rich waterfront area of the city, our legs start burning from effort and our minds wake up.

'The women are a sleek-looking lot,' says Dave.

'Yep, I can see that. I feel decidedly underdressed. Grubby, too.'

I scan each woman furtively as she walks by. Dresses, dress pants, pressed skirts, neat shirts or feminine tops, long hair neatly tied back or free flowing, manicured nails, elegant shoes or sandals with matching bags. Earrings and necklaces, unobtrusive bangles and watches on wrists. Made up, but not overdone faces. I do a double take when I spot all the small tattoos peeping out from under clothes: on arms, backs, necks and ankles.

'Lots of tattoos,' I say with relief.

'Kind of weird, because otherwise they look quite conservative.'

'It's like the opposite of London, with the crazy hair-dos and clothes, the variety, girls with short hair, boys with long hair.' I remember how much I loved people watching on the streets of London, when I went to visit Jonny there, one summer. 'But I guess we are in an upmarket, office-worker part of town.'

Dave has picked up on my unease. 'Jess, you'll be fine,' he tells me.

'I need new clothes,' I say, pointing out the worn patches on my pants and the small holes opening under my arms.

'Who cares?'

I check out my reflection in a shop window. You can take the girl away from New Zealand, but not the hippy-Kiwi out of the girl. Layered loose clothes in black or earthy tones with colourful headscarves and big pendants, comfortable shoes, wild hair, little makeup and no earrings have always been my staples. I have never had a manicure and my feet look as if they have never worn shoes. I feel scruffy, out of place.

The day before Dave leaves, we spend a whole afternoon in the botanical gardens in Palermo. It's a charming haven in the middle of bustling chaos. Trees and plants of all shapes and sizes share space with fountains and a lovely old building with a glasshouse full of flowers attached. I notice a cat—large, fluffy and orange, with very green eyes—dart across our path, then another two lying stretched out in the sun, then two more, another one… ten. I can only see grown up cats sauntering around their inner city habitat, so I wonder about the fate of the kittens. The gardens are unusually quiet. There is a distinct lack of twittering from small, winged species.

When we tire of wandering we find a spot under a tree, its branches filtering the sun so it splatters us with tiny irregular prisms of light. It's a good place to talk. I lie on my jacket, my head resting on my daypack. Dave props his slender body up against the trunk. Perhaps we have subconsciously assumed Doctor-Patient positions. They have become almost too comfortable, these roles we play.

Dave seems gloomy. Worry digs three lines across his forehead. 'What's next, Jess?'

'Not sure exactly. Find a place to live. Get some work.'

He sighs. I feel slightly exasperated with him.

'Please don't worry. You're not abandoning me here. I can do this.'

'I know, but I worry anyway.'

'Don't. I'm a bit scared but I feel good about what's coming.'

'What happens when the novelty wears off? You might be left with a big hole to fill, disconnected in a strange culture. It's a risk.'

'True. But I'm already acquainted with that kind of hole. As you know.' My hand goes to my chest, automatically. 'I know I've gone over and over this, but I think if only I could find the key, some memories, then maybe I would finally understand this horrible sensation of having something vital missing. I feel empty. Sometimes I look at myself in a mirror and I don't know who I am. I hate it…'

Silence. A long silence. 'Sorry,' I say.

'No, don't be sorry.' He pauses. 'You have to ask your parents about those missing years.'

'I know… I know. But—'

'It doesn't have to be an attack, if that's what you're worried about. Take your emotions out of it a little and just ask for some things to be filled in. Maybe it will be a relief for them, too, to talk about it. Those early years sound as if they were tough for everyone.'

I nod. 'Lots of stuff buried there.'

'There must be something behind you kids being whipped back to New Zealand by your grandmother. You were two?'

'Near three, I think.'

'That's something to explore.'

'I know some things. Jonny's birth was hard for many reasons.'

'You're the type of person who needs to know more. So ask.'

'When? I never see them.'

'You will find the right time. Be patient.'

I look over at Dave. His hooded eyes are following the sashaying gait of a black and white cat as it drifts past us.

'I'll be alright, right?

'Yes. Just don't fill the hole with boys.'

I feel like a fourteen-year-old girl having a very uncomfortable talk with her dad. 'I won't.' I don't like the whine in my tone.

When he sees my face he adds, 'Look, you don't have to be perfectly bloody together to look for love. If we all waited for that, the species would die out. But you have to be okay.'

'A more okay version of myself than this, you mean.'

I see the corner of his mouth curl up in a smile and detect a tiny shake of his head, like he's heard all this so many times before.

'God, enough of me. Your marriage? How are you feeling now about seeing Anne when you get back?'

'I don't know. Not confident.'

'Sorry, my stuff's been drowning you out lately.'

He huffs. 'No words left.'

'You can—'

He cuts me off. 'Truth is, I'm happy to be distracted by your shit for a little longer.'

'I'm going to miss this. I feel so close to you after this trip. I don't know... it's like you are the big brother I never had, a kind of dad, maybe. I will miss you.'

He closes his eyes and seems to go inward.

My hand automatically reaches out and squeezes his bony knee. Hugging isn't really our thing. Our intimacy always comes from words.

'Yes, me too,' he says, eyes still closed.

The following day I lose my tired, thoughtful, gruff counsellor. Our hug goodbye is awkward. I watch him get into a taxi, folding in his thin legs. He makes a tiny wave and pulls the door closed. The exhaust fumes momentarily suffocate me. I cough, wipe my eyes. His taxi is swallowed in a tumultuous sea of weaving taxis, buses, cars and motorbikes. I feel a pull and an ache and then a snap. Then I turn and walk towards the hotel. A chill runs along my spine as I absorb the idea that I am alone.

Three days later I turn thirty-three. I remind myself I'm a Leo and I should be brave, but I feel small and frightened in this huge, busy, intense city that I'm sure has swallowed its fair share of people. I email a friendly Finnish couple that Dave and I met on the bus in Salta. They email back and invite me out for dinner. This warm gesture, from two almost strangers, washes away some of the aloneness that's already starting to grip me.

I ring Pepe a couple of days later. I hadn't felt sure about contacting him, because of how things were with Paco. The Kiwi in me didn't want to be a bother to him.

'*Hola. ¿Pepe esta?*' I say nervously into the phone.

'*Sí, soy Pepe.*'

'*Soy Jessy, amiga de Paco…*'

'*Jessy, Jessy, hola, ¿cómo estás?*' he says, bubbling with enthusiasm.

Relief fills me. '*Bien, bien.* Sorry, can we speak in English? My Spanish is *pésima*, especially on the phone.'

He laughs and says, 'It's hard to speak another language. Don't worry you will be good soon.'

'I hope so.'

'You come for an *asado* with me?'

'Yes, please.'

He invites me to his little weekend cottage in Tigre—a town on the banks of the Río de la Plata and bordering a nature reserve—the following weekend.

'That would be amazing,' I say.

'*Listo*, done.'

'Bye—'

He cuts in. 'Wait, Jessy, do you want to meet Monica? She's back in town.'

My stomach lurches a little. Even now, when I am determined that the 'Paco dream' file has been closed, this mention of his mother makes me anxious.

'Of course. I'd love to,' I say, already busy with imagining what she will be like. 'In Tigre?'

'No, no Tigre is my special place. At her art studio. You will get on very well, I think. I know how much you like art.'

Will we? I hope so. I'm nervous, but I'm also intrigued. I want to understand what it was that Paco saw of his mother in me.

I'm sweating by the time I arrive at Monica's studio out in the suburbs, two days after my call with Pepe, having negotiated the subway and then a long bus trip through the sprawling streets. The studio is in a large building with a corrugated-iron roof. I hear the doorbell echoing a long way off. Pepe warned me that even though she had spent a lot of time in the US, Monica was very shy about her English. I run some Spanish through my head, which only makes the nerves worse. I hear her quiet footsteps as they approach the door. When she opens it, it rattles and threatens to fall off its hinges.

She smiles at me, her eyes slightly averted. My shoulders drop two inches. She gives me a shy hug and a kiss on the cheek.

'Welcome, Jessica. I am Monica,' she says in her highly accented and very sweet English.

'*Hola, Monica, gracias. Estoy feliz, me gusta visitar a vos,*' I say in return, in ghastly Spanish.

She looks at me with gratitude and recognition, and I sense that both of us feel less ashamed of our faulty language skills. She leads me into her cavernous studio—a big, airy shed that she shares with other artists. That day we are alone there, swimming around in the huge space.

Initially, communicating is a struggle. We both use our hands and a lot of facial expressions. In time we find a rhythm and relax into each other's company. As I watch her explain the techniques she used to paint her amazing murals, I realise Paco is right. We are similar. She's smaller and slimmer than me, has curly dark hair, pale skin and fine features, but it's more than physical; it's as if our energies vibrate at the same frequency. I sense that, like me, she is also shy, slightly uncomfortable around people but warm and still—still despite all the thoughts and feelings that are churning quietly and constantly inside. She too has loss marked in her eyes—the excruciating loss of a child, Paco's older brother. I recognise myself in her. A light of comprehension switches on. I now understand some of Paco's confusion. It's comforting in a way. Looking back, there were many times I acted more like a mother than a girlfriend.

I'm excited about seeing Pepe again. With him and now Monica, I feel as if I have a semblance of family in Buenos Aires. If I ever needed help, they would be there. On the one hand it's anchoring, but warning thoughts race around my head. *Am I trying to get them to love me so Paco will too? Am I really over him?* I push them away. What does it matter? Right now I need a Pepe hug.

I know I'm privileged to be invited to his retreat. I try to imagine the house, full of his things. His man shed. I smile at the thought: a space to potter and ponder and eat uncensored…

Saturday arrives quickly. Pepe and I meet at a train station to travel together out to Tigre. The long awaited and imagined hug is given with gusto and is so warm my tensions melt away like winter snow on a warm spring day.

'Jessy, too long time. I'm so happy to see you,' he says, still hugging me tight.

'*Yo también*, me too.'

God, I love Argentines. There's going to be no shortage of hugging here.

We buy tickets, hop on the train and sit side by side. Luckily I have a slim behind, as his takes up more than its fair share of the tattered seats.

The train stops in the centre of a pretty little town with lots of trees and low buildings. When the slushy wide brown river comes fully into view my mind dives into a memory. I think of *Charlie and the Chocolate Factory* and its river's chocolate currents. I don't see a dirty brown, thick as soup, river. I must be happy; the adjustment of perspective makes it magical.

Then some lyrics from the 'Wondrous Boat Ride' make an appearance in my head. It's a strange song about uncertainty and dangers at every turn. No one knows where they're rowing, nor where the river is taking them, but they keep rowing anyway. I played the role of Willy Wonka in our local drama society production when I was about thirteen, but it still surprises me how well I remember the words. I was a good actor, or perhaps just good at acting.

Everything seems vivid as we make our way towards the river. I feel my toes in my shoes, my feet firm on the path. The actress in me takes a break from the stage.

Pepe and I squash into a lovely old wooden passenger boat, called a *lancha*, for the forty-minute ride to his home on the river's bank. We pass by broken-down red-rusted barges and boats leaning on their sides in the water. Rowing clubs line the river; beautiful old colonial-style buildings in various states of repair rise up from wide river-front lawns. I can see about seven battered, rotted and web-adorned life-jackets jammed into the rafters of the *lancha*. I don't imagine they would be much help, but I figure we must be safe enough as we grind through the water, fine spray peppering faces.

When we arrive at Pepe's hideaway, I see the cottage is perched precariously on fragile looking wooden foundation blocks. It looks tipsy, like an old drunk that may fall over any minute. It's a simple square-shaped, weathered and extremely weary looking house, but its shabby front door beckons us warmly. I know good things reside inside.

When Pepe opens the door, a faint smell of dank wood and musty mats makes its escape. I watch him lurch around on his one bung hip (an old injury, made worse by the weight of a life lived well—too many *asados*). I imagine him suddenly disappearing through the floor, in a crunching dusty explosion of fragments of wood. He seems to trust it can bear his weight, but I'm not so sure.

Everywhere little treasures lurk—old books, paintings, carving gear and half-carved things come into view around every corner. I imagine him sitting, whittling away into the night, thinking quietly, mindfully. On the train on the way here, Pepe told me that for more than twenty years this has been his place of solitude, and on other occasions of warm meetings with family and friends. I feel lucky to be here.

After the brief tour Pepe gets stuck into the task of preparing huge slabs of beef. As we wait hungrily, we drink a cheap but tasty Malbec and we talk. It's easy. I love the sound of his deep honey voice, halting and then finding its way to the English words it speaks so infrequently. He attempts to get me to speak in Spanish. My temples pulse with the effort. We find our way back to English and our favourite subject.

'What do you think of our food?' Pepe asks me.

'It's great, but I'm used to more variety and more flavour. It seems as if people only use salt to favour things!' I worry that I sound too fussy.

'Yes, that can be true. We have simple flavours but good ingredients. Our meat is the best in the world.'

'The meat is wonderful,' I agree. 'It's just, when I lived in Melbourne, in one street you could find Arabian food, Italian food, Polish food, Indian food, oh and Thai food. I miss Thai food. I miss the flavour, the aromas and the heat. I miss chilli in food. They have *ají* in Peru, but here?' I'm ranting, so I stop.

Pepe laughs. 'You can get *ají* here, and chilli. I love chilli, too,' he says. Then he gets up suddenly, climbs the teetering staircase and disappears into the tiny kitchen. I hear him rummaging around in the fridge. I think, for a moment, I've offended him with my negative ramblings. He comes back out with a tall glass container filled with a sauce of some kind. He's smiling.

'*Chimichurri*, I make it myself,' he says, poking it under my nose.

I smell garlic, parsley, olive oil and a whiff of chilli (the mild dry flaky version—but still, chilli).

His timing couldn't be better as the meat is finally ready to eat. We place large pieces on fresh white bread and smother it all in the sauce. The flavours of the meat and garlic and olive oil run over my tongue. I become lost in the moment. When I finally look up, Pepe is shining a long, wise smile at me. I wipe dripping grease from my chin and smile back.

When we finish the first course of many, he tells me his favourite version of the story of how *chimichurri* got its name. Back in the nineteenth century, some British prisoners of war were so desperate for food with some flavour that they begged their guards to 'give me curry,' or 'che-mi-curry' (mixing English and the local Spanish expression *'che mi salsa'*: meaning 'please condiment my food'). The phrase later morphed into *chimichurri*. There are other versions of its possible origins, revolving around some corruption of names: that of Jimmy McCurry, an Irishman, who was said to have invented the mix, or was it the Englishman Jimmy Curry?

I like the 'give me curry' version best as I can vividly imagine the desperation in the men's voices and the aching in their bellies, as they shook the prison bars. I feel similar every day as I restlessly search for flavour on the streets of Buenos Aires. I remind myself that unimaginative food is a small price to pay, given that for as long as I am here I will not go without either fantastic red meat or hugs; that I'm sure of.

On the boat trip back to Buenos Aires I find my thoughts absorbed in the trails of white froth, frosted on brown water, as they arrow out behind us. Perhaps life is like a boat trip. We can sit passively and go where it takes us, or we can jump into our own small boat and row where we want to go. We might crash violently into big rocks, get pulled by an undertow down a fork we didn't plan on taking, but then we still have oars and can fight the current when we need to, or ride it when it takes us where we want to go. Mostly, we can choose which fork to try.

My battered boat has been too full of heavy packages bulging with sadness and anger and fear. It's time to toss more of those packages overboard, while row, row, rowing in a new direction.

Eleven

I can't find a place to live. It quickly becomes clear that Buenos Aires is not particularity friendly to long-term temporary hopefuls in this respect. When I bumble in the door, wide-eyed and scrambling my Spanish, the real-estate agents try to charge me three times the normal rent. Or they ask for six months' cash in advance.

Monica, Paco's mother, comes to my rescue and gives me the contact details of a friend of hers who rents out a small apartment in Palermo, near the parks. We speak on the phone and arrange to meet. Her English is perfect.

Later that day an impeccably dressed middle-aged woman approaches me, hair and bag swinging. 'Jessica?'

'Yes, you must be Valeria. *Un gusto.*'

'Spanish, then?'

'No, no, please; English for now.'

She ushers me through the doors of the ground-floor apartment we are standing outside.

'Living room,' she says, throwing one hand out in a wide arc.

'Oh.' Dark, tight and forlorn, it's begging for light and colour. The small rectangular room contains nothing but a set of built-in bookshelves and a beaten up white plastic table, with two matching plastic chairs. I try to paint the space with life. I imagine books and small things—Pepe's pig—in the shelves and something colourful hanging on the wall, perhaps a bright tablecloth to hide the table.

Three long strides and we are in the bedroom.

'You have to keep the window closed, and blinds. You can see it's on the street,' says Valeria.

'Is it safe here?'

'Yes, safe enough, but be careful walking around alone at night.'

A metal bed with a paper thin, stained mattress lies under the window. Valeria briskly opens the wooden doors of the built-in wardrobe. It's cavernous. Enough room for ten times my current belongings. 'Should be enough space for you,' she states, and then turns on her heel and is out the door.

When we enter the minute kitchen, I think *not enough room to swing a cat*, echoing my grandmother's words. It has an old stove, some shelves, but no fridge.

'It doesn't have a fridge,' slips out, a little too loud.

'No apartment here comes with a fridge,' Valeria says, tossing her hair as she leads me out.

A voice in my head tells me, this is just a start.

'*Gracias*, Valeria, I'll take it,' I say.

I start to feel queasy as she outlines the rent and expenses and bills. It's more than I can afford; steep, but less than the usual foreigner rates. I will need *flitmates*. I can practically see Elle, laughing at me.

Two ex-Cusco Irish lasses bunk down on mattresses in the living room for a few weeks, and then a trio of naughty but very charming twenty-something Aussie lads take over the space left by the girls. The noise of them rocks the little cave into life, but they also have a tendency to leave trails of stiff, smelly socks everywhere. I name them 'the three musketeers'. They stay a couple of weeks and then move into a sunny, tenth-floor, furnished apartment, which they nickname, 'the mansion'.

With the boys in greener pastures, I find myself alone in a now somewhat musty and lifeless space. I email everyone I can think of, looking for replacements. Meanwhile I start to explore, in little circles and then larger circles from my home, as if I'm pacing out my territory. I get braver and go further every day. I start intensive Spanish classes across town. I make friends with the greengrocer, Marcelo, who claims a wide corner near the apartment. He's a big man with a bulging belly and slightly protruding eyes. He smokes constantly but cradles the fruit and vegetables, in his yellow-stained fingers, as if they were precious things.

'*¿Comó se llama eso?*' I ask.

'*Apio.*'

'*Apio*, celery.'

'*Albahaca*,' says Marcelo, shoving a fresh bunch of basil under my nose. It's divine, rich and intoxicating. I smile at him and he smiles back.

'Pesto?' I say.

'*Sí, sí, pesto.*'

I run through the produce I know. '*Manzana, naranja, acelga, lechuga, zapato…*'

His laugh is so deep it reverberates through me and the two women who have just arrived. '*No, no. Zapallo, no zapato,*' he says, pointing helpfully first to a pumpkin and then to his shoe.

'Oh,' I say, biting my lip.

He's patient. I get better each day.

Loneliness seeps in. After nearly two weeks of lone circling and exploring, I decide to talk to someone who can only listen. I don't want to hear advice, see frowns form on foreheads.

Hi Daniel,

I'm a bit confused. I've done this big thing, moved to Buenos Aires, and now I dream sometimes of going home, of having a comfy bed, a job, a goddamn fridge, and my old friends close by. I feel stupid for doing this but I can't admit that to anyone. I have very little contact with my parents or my brothers. I may as well have fallen off the map. It's my fault, too. I don't contact them either, anymore. I've given up.

I feel alone in this big crazy city. But there is something very special about this place. It gets under your skin so fast. It's alive, it breathes. I feel alert here. There's so much warmth in the people I meet. I have a kind of unromantic crush on the greengrocer. He thinks I'm hilarious. I go visit him nearly every day, you know, due to having no fridge. He's a funny guy. There's a kindness, a willingness to connect, I don't know how else to describe it. People get kissed at least ten times a day. But the city can be cruel and confusing, too. I know some people have taken advantage of me, and I can see faces on the streets that are tired and sad. I feel vulnerable now, alone in the flat. I feel so many different things here—free and fearful, independent and needy, special and totally out of place.

Spanish is getting the better of me. It makes me so mad that I don't get it. I feel dumb and you know I hate that. And then there's Paco. If I really dig deep, I think I came here hoping that he would come home, see me, and change his mind. He's been writing me emails. He says he misses me, and that I meant a lot to him. Am I waiting for him? I tell myself I'm not. I want to let go but I worry I'm drifting round and round in the same circles. Darkness is nipping at my heels again.

Sorry. I'll be okay.

Goodnight.

Two days later the buzzer from the front door of the building rings. I cross the flat, open the door and look towards the entrance.

My heart jumps when I see her standing there, with the glass panel between us. Her head is cocked quizzically, her red hair glowing around her pale face. I can't open the door fast enough.

'Bree,' I gasp loudly. We collapse into each other.

'Yep, it's me,' she says, squeezing me tight.

'You're here, you came.'

Bree had promised that she and Brian would come to visit me in Buenos Aires when I got settled, but I hadn't expected them for a few weeks yet.

'I know it's a little earlier than planned. Things changed.' She suddenly looks vulnerable. It's a new look for her.

'Are you okay? Where's Brian?' I ask, while already sensing what she's going to say.

'Gone, we broke up.'

I direct her inside the now cosier living room and pour two glasses of wine. She tells me the story.

I was aware before I left Cusco that its darker charms and nightlife had got hold of them both. What I didn't know was how deep its fingernails were embedded. Bree, now folded tight into her chair, quietly tells me she became tired of the night and wanted to reach back into the day, but Brian wasn't ready or able to join her. Having been sewn together for years by a deep love, it was Cusco's temptations that tore them apart.

As I watch her pretty face twist in sadness, a memory comes clear into my mind. I don't know how we found ourselves talking about it, but she once told me that she and Brian slept together all night, legs and arms totally entwined, faces pressed together, sharing the same breath. I had imagined them, then, like twins in a womb. I wonder how night feels for her now. Three years enwrapped and then, nothing.

Bree's story slows and then she stops talking, abruptly, as if she's run out of words. I see her eyes are shining, but then she looks away. I can feel so strongly the rawness of the space next to her, where he once was.

I wrap both arms tight around her. I want my hug to fill the space, even briefly. In seconds she lightly pushes me away and wipes her face with a hand. A new expression appears.

'I'm here now,' she says simply.

'I'm very happy to have you to play with. Bummer it's in this way,' I say.

Her unexpected arrival at my door is taken as another sign; I can't help myself. I called out for something, for someone, and she came. She makes a new nest in my living room.

With Bree close by, I feel reenergised.

One cool but bright spring day we are wandering down Avenida Santa Fe, one of the main roads that cuts through the city, looking for black pants and top. Bree has recently found work in an Irish bar and needs the standard uniform.

I imagine we are a sight. Both of us are tall, one with bright red hair, the other wild curls. We are obviously foreign: our casual look, pale faces, the way we are openly curious about everything. There is something extra, too, in Bree's energy. It radiates out from her; pulls looks to her. It fills me up just being near her.

A grey-haired man in a suit walks past us. Turning his head slightly, he whispers in Spanish, 'God, two angels just fell from the sky.'

We laugh, turn to catch him, but he's well up the street. I feel both flattered and irritated. 'I'm not sure I'm used to that yet.'

'Oh, it's just a bit of fun, Juicy.'

Over the course of the next two blocks we get two more rapid-fire serenades: '*Hermosas*, beautiful girls.' Then, '*Mmm, para comer.*'

'What did he just say?' I ask Bree.

'For eating!'

'Really?'

'Bountiful day we're having.'

'We are the queens of *piojos*,' I say.

Bree buckles over with laughter.

'What?' I demand.

'Jessy, no, no, no. It's *piropos*, not *piojos*,' she says, eyes tearing up.

'Oh god, what does *piojo* mean, then?'

'Nits. We are the queens of nits is not what you were aiming for, I hope,' she says, as she throws her arms out wide, and adds a curtsey.

'Seriously, Bree, I'm never going to get this bloody language,' I say, feeling a little raw.

'You will. It just takes a while. Don't stress. In the mean time, you make me laugh.'

'Please don't tell anyone, it's really embarrassing.'

'Can't promise anything, but I'll try,' she says, glancing at the ground.

She tells everyone.

I start to wonder if I will ever understand and produce a reasonable form of Spanish, or *Castellano*, which is the word they use here. Argentine *Castellano* has some minor differences from the Spanish I learned in Peru that I find tricky to get used to. There's the pronoun *vos* instead of *tu*, and the *y* and *ll* sounds are pronounced as *sh*. Argentines speak fast with a strong Italian flavour and a sexy tone that wins me over despite my continued confusion. I had thought I would be speaking well by now, with all the intensive classes and the months in Peru, but the words always seem to get tangled in my head; they go in and out distorted, and being wrong most of the time eats away at my precarious self-esteem.

My perception of my skills and worth is not helped when I start teaching English for a small language institute that sends its teachers into office buildings. I don't have any relevant qualifications, but it seems that being a native speaker is enough. It's the only job I think I can manage as a visa-less and new long-term temporary. I can't imagine wanting to go back to psychology, even if I could somehow swing it. Working in a call centre would drive me crazy and waitressing terrifies me more than teaching. I'm used to one-on-one and talking. It can't be that hard.

My first class is in an office in the middle of the busiest part of town. I'm already frazzled by the time I arrive, late.

The secretary looks up at me through her long eyelashes. She glances over my clothes and face furtively, and her eyes open a little wider.

I pull at my top and try to stand a little taller.

'Oh, you must be the new English teacher,' she says, in Spanish. 'Welcome, please wait here.' She points to a sofa.

Ten minutes later a serious faced young man comes into the reception.

The secretary waves a manicured finger in my direction.

'Hi, you must be Jessica, no?' he says in English, leaning in to kiss me on the cheek.

'Yes, I'm your new teacher.'

'My name is Pablo.'

I follow Pablo into a small office. I have a lump in my throat like I'm going into a job interview.

All goes well until he asks me about the present perfect tense.

I tell him firmly, 'We don't really use present perfect that much, so don't worry about it for now.'

He looks at me and says, 'But you use it all the time, as in how long *have you been* teaching?'

I realise as the weeks go by that my knowledge of the finer workings of the English language is troublingly scarce. I quietly curse my tiny, country primary school. While I was there they decided to trial a system that concentrated on story and creativity rather than spelling or grammar. It's a lovely idea in principle, but I came out not knowing anything at all about grammar. Over the years I have managed to piece together a semblance of how it works, but gaping holes remain. It's embarrassing when they get exposed in front of people.

Now I live every day constantly alert, consumed by an old fear that someone will ask me to spell something on the board or out loud. It's a fear that has been there since my earliest schooldays. Like my father before me, I have struggled with dyslexia my whole life. My brain has its own system for remembering and reproducing words, but it's not quite right. It's as if some vital wires are tangled around each other and the messages don't get through in the intended fashion. I endure each class I teach, slightly leaning forward, not quite comfortable, ready to run if I need to.

I have a group class early on Mondays. The students are a lovely collection of personalities. There are six of them, all smiling and friendly and curious. One day we are working through a workshop on medical conditions and illnesses when one woman asks me, 'What is the little sore cut that comes in the mouth sometimes. When you are stress-ed?'

'Stressed,' I correct.

'Yes, stressed. Here.' She points to her gum.

'Oh, yes, ulcer,' I say.

'How do you spell that?'

My chest tightens. 'Um, give me a minute,' I say, while frantically scribbling down, *alcer, aulser, ulser* and then ulcer! Six pairs of eyes watch me as I shrink before them.

I slowly recover over the rest of the day as I remind myself that most of my students are tired of grammar classes and formality; instead they just want to talk and listen, and improve their fluency and confidence. These are things I can help with. It doesn't take long before I relax into it and start to enjoy my new role. The job is, after all, primarily a means to a very modest income, and more than that, the possibility to stay, if I decide to.

A month later, on the sweaty, crowded bus ride home after a long working day, I tot up the day's tally of kisses: twelve—six hellos and six goodbyes. I don't really feel like a teacher any more. My students are beginning to become friends. Perhaps it's all the kissing. The intimacy and human touch of everyday life is still surprising to me, still wonderful—a once dry lake is overflowing and I can jump joyously into it every day. It feels as if I'm happily caught up in the warm fibres of an interconnected web. It's comforting.

My students are curious about New Zealand and Australia, about why I came here. I tell them various versions of the truth, depending on who I'm talking to. Most of my tales include a need to experience something new, to learn another language, to test myself and to escape a job that was whittling away at my spirit. I tell some of them about Paco and the return trip to see him again. The women shake their heads in sad recognition and say, 'typical of Argentine men'. The men shake their heads differently, in an 'I could have warned you,' way. I don't talk about Daniel. It's not the place and I don't need to anymore.

I start out of my thoughts when the bus bumps and grinds to a halt. The doors flip nosily open, and then I watch as an elderly lady starts slowly negotiating the stairs. She barely makes it to the top when the driver accelerates with a violent jolt. She stumbles back, fear glints in her eyes. A hand grabs her and she's escorted to a seat, recently vacated by a teenage boy, just for her. I think of craziness and kindness. This is a country of contradictions. Nothing is predictable.

I watch the city race by and think about conversations with my students on the subject of Argentina. Their eyes are bright, almost too bright, when we chat about the incredible landscapes, beautiful people, prime meat, and all the other abundant resources. They rave about their culture, the tango, and their writers, such as the much loved Jorge Luis Borges (the only one I've heard of), and are proud of their football players and sporting stars. Then a moment always comes when a cloud crosses over—darkening the mood. Embarrassment, sometimes shame, tinge their voices when we find ourselves discussing politics, the troubled economy, corruption, poverty and inept bureaucracy. They try to make jokes to hide it, but it lingers in the tone of their voices.

I make a mental note to ask my favourite student, André, more about the economy when we meet later. He has class at his office at 9.00p.m., so I have to make another trip into the chaos of downtown in a few hours. I'm happy to do it for him.

Every time I see Andrés, I feel like laughing. He looks like a little boy trapped in a man's body. The word 'scallywag' comes to mind. I guess he's in his early forties, but he refuses to tell me. He has a floppy, pushed over fringe, its tips dyed blond. His hair is long at the back, cut in a slightly disturbing mullet style. He has some small badly drawn tattoos on his arms and chest. I saw them during our last class, when he whipped off his shirt to show me. The shirt was impeccably ironed and looked very expensive and he always wears gold cufflinks. It all adds up to an intriguing combination.

He orders me tea and biscuits from Mario, the old, bent over, pleasant-faced caretaker of the office building, who attends us in a quiet unassuming manner every week.

So, Miss Jessy, how's your day been?'

'Good, busy. You are my lucky last, as usual.'

'I know, it's late…'

'No, it's no problem,' I cut in.

'Too much work, no time; you know how it is.'

'You love working,' I say, baiting him.

I'm following up from our last discussion, when I surmised that he works so hard and so many hours because he's avoiding thinking about some important psychological issues. I already know his whole history: a dominant mother; a father who died suddenly, very young; a series of steady 'nice' girlfriends, and then the 'fun' girls on the side. He let me in little by little, seeming to enjoy the light sparring about his womanising.

I was surprised at first that he was so welcoming of my attempts to psychoanalyse him. He, without fail, laughed me off, but only after hearing me out. These half-English classes, half-therapy sessions (both ways) were strange for me at first. I've always tried very hard not to play psychologist with friends (at least consciously), but here, people actively seek it. They want you to know them; they are not so scared of the dark places, of being exposed as human. Argentines, especially *Porteños* tell you quite happily that they have a therapist and have been seeing them for five years, or ten years, twice a week or more. Andrés, mind you, swears to me that he has never been.

'Ha, not that psychobabble again.'

'You love my head-shrinking attempts. I should charge you more.'

'You should.'

'I've learned some things from you, too. You are my source on all things economic. Although I still can't get my head around why Argentina is where it is. I wish there was a simple way to tell me what went wrong.'

'There isn't. It can't be done in a few phrases.'

'Something, I don't know. A graph? Give me a scenario or something to picture in my head. I understand pictures more than words.'

He thinks for a few seconds, smiles to himself and says, 'This might help. Simon Kuznets, a Nobel-prize winning economist, said: "There are four kinds of countries in the world: developed countries, undeveloped countries, Japan and Argentina."'

'Ah...'

'It's sad and funny because it's true. Japan is so small, it doesn't really have many natural assets, but it forced its way up. The people there make it work. Here, we have everything in our fingertips—' he says.

'At our fingertips,' I correct.

'Oh, okay, at our fingertips, but we mess it up.'

'I understand what you're saying. It just seems baffling.'

'Baffling?'

'Very confusing.'

'Yes, very confusing. We have everything we need, but we stuff it up by fighting each other,' he says. His brow creases and then he continues, 'Maybe if we had less, we'd work together. Fight harder for our country. I don't know.'

'Is corruption as bad as I've heard?' I ask.

'I'll show you something,' he says, typing into the search bar of his desktop computer. 'Look. The Corruption Perception Index.'

He explains that the index is a ranking of levels of corruption in 176 countries around the world, released each year by an NGO called Transparency International and based on opinion surveys and expert assessments.

'Ha,' he says. 'Look at your country: New Zealand is number two.'

'What?'

'No, no, it means least corrupt country. You are just beaten by Finland.'

'Ah, of course.' For a moment there, I was worried. 'Where's Argentina?'

'I'm still looking,' he says as he scrolls down through the countries, looking more peeved by the minute. 'Oh, here it is, we come in at 108.'

'108. Oh. But hey, it's not the worst.' Feeling scampish, I add, 'Perhaps if you had been colonised by the English rather than the Spanish, things would be different.'

'Ha, Jessy, very funny. Don't say that to everyone; I don't think they would like it. But yes, probably it would be very different here.'

'A lot more boring, and not as friendly either,' I say.

'*¿Qué sé yo*? What do I know? It's complicated. We are complicated,' he says.

We sit in silence for a minute.

'Do you think things will get better?' I ask.

'I don't know. I hope so. We need to change many things but I'm not sure it's possible.'

'I hope it comes right. I'm starting to love it here, despite *el quilombo*.'

He laughs. '*Quilombo*, eh? You're really getting the slang now.'

I grin. I'll take all the compliments on my Spanish I can get.

'It sounds like its meaning: total chaos.'

'Great. But you know it's borrowed from Brazilian Portuguese, right?'

'Oh.' Typical: my favourite new word isn't even Spanish.

Twelve

I'M NOT ALWAYS a teacher of English or a student of Argentine history and economics. On the weekends, I'm someone else. With Bree at my side, I go a little wild. The pull of the night catches us and throws us tumbling through the bars and *boliches* (nightclubs) that open late and close when the sun rises. Buenos Aires dances at night, alive with lights and swarming with people. I can't resist. I make excuses, tell myself that I'm living the years I missed: the years I didn't spend partying in London, travelling in Asia, backpacking around the globe. I feel young again, as if I've shed something—the serious coat of a serious life, with the heavy job of helping the hurting.

Everything is new to Bree and me: the places, the faces, the rules and codes.

One Saturday, in a side booth in a large two-storied club in Palermo, we find ourselves watching 'The Game' as it's being played out in front of us.

'That's a very strange way to try and pick someone up.' I say, subtly pointing to a guy and a petite dark-haired girl. He's grabbing her arm and leaning in hard, as if he's trying to kiss her.

'It's a bit Neanderthal,' says Bree.

'I hate that kind of thing,' I reply, thinking about a couple of recent less than delicate moments of my own. 'She doesn't look very happy, either. Do you think some girls like it?'

'I just think they're used to it. Maybe it's a love-hate thing. It must work sometimes. Okay, look over there.' Bree gestures with her nose at a scene two metres from us. Another slim gorgeous girl in high boots and a very short skirt is holding her hand an inch from her pursuer's nose. Her face is turned slightly away, a look of absolute disdain on her pretty features. He keeps pleading his case. She walks off. He shrugs, and within seconds is on the trail of another girl.

'Unbelievable. They have no shame,' I say.

'A guy I talked to in the bar the other night told me this: "*El 'no'ya tenés*,"' Bree says. 'You already have "no", so just keep on going until you get a "yes". He also told me, "*We work the numbers, maybe we get lucky!*"'

'Sweet-talking liars,' I say.

'Exactly. *Chamuyeros.*'

'*Chamuyeros*? Ha, I knew there'd be a word for it.'

'I pick up all the good vocab at work,' says Bree. 'The lines I've heard, it's almost funny.'

I know what she means, it is sort of funny, if you can treat it all as a light-hearted entertainment. But that's easier said than done. And there is a dynamic that bothers me. 'There seems to be this horrible competition of *us* against *them*. The girls think all the guys are charming losers with only *one thing* on their minds. And the guys think all the women are complicated and needy and obviously only have *long-term* on their minds.'

'Ha, so true,' says Bree.

'*Hystericas*, that's what they say.' I am warming to my theme.

'Yeah, that word gets thrown around a lot.'

'I was chatting about how dating works here with a guy the other night. He told me, "All the girls flirt and kiss you and act like they want it, but then they don't go home with you." So I asked him. "If they did go home with you the first night, what would you think of them?" Do you know what he said?'

'That they were *putas*,' says Bree.

'Exactly, so I asked, "So could a woman like that ever be a girlfriend?" And he answered, "No way, if she gave it up the first night, no way."'

'Yay, so two options, *hystericas* or *putas*; it's a no win,' says Bree, slightly distracted by a handsome man who's just walked by.

'Poor women.'

'Well, yes,' I agree. 'On the other hand, there are compensations: at least the men look like him.'

We have a couple more drinks and decide to call it a night.

When I get home, I can't sleep. I'm turning over my various

encounters with unsuitable men which started not long after I arrived. There was the big, kind-faced psychologist who tried to seduce me, but the spark wasn't there; the very young, overly pretty boy who the Irish girls called Zoolander; the lawyer who tried to hide his live-in girlfriend and the barman at Bree's bar whose last girlfriend was also called Jessica… It feels surreal looking back at the chase, the catch, the rush and the disappointment. These are old games I thought I had put behind me. Why am I still playing them?

A week later I am sitting in Bree's Irish bar, waiting for her to finish her shift and having a drink. I watch an obviously foreign girl fluttering from one person to the next. Her animated voice, speaking in both English and Spanish, penetrates the room. Her tight clothes draw eyes. Bree brings her over to introduce us. 'Jess, this is Jennifer.'

'Hi,' she says. Her bright eyes look up at me through heavily painted lashes.

I give her a kiss, hoping she didn't see me watching her.

Bree disappears back behind the bar. Jen and I look at each other. 'So, how long have you been here?' I ask.

'Almost a year. You?'

'A little under four months. How did you get to be here, in this crazy city?'

'I work for a big international computer business, they posted me here.' She flicks her long blonde fringe out of her eyes. I feel her getting bored.

'Met any cute men?' I ask, to keep her interest for some minutes more.

She unravels a stream of names and experiences and troubles and hopes. I see fear in her eyes. She doesn't filter anything and I feel like putting my hand on her arm and saying stop. I don't.

I try to think of something soothing to say. 'They're complicated. Handsome, but complicated.'

'I'm actually waiting for Lucas to get here. He's my latest. So gorgeous. I really like him,' she says, looking over my shoulder towards the entrance to the bar.

'Nice name, where did you—'

'Oh, oh, there he is. Sorry, gotta go.'

'Okay,' I say, to her retreating back.

I watch. Lucas is tall. Dark waves of perfectly placed hair fall over his face. I see Jen leap at him, embracing him hard. Then she dives onto his lips. He closes his eyes for a second, opens them and starts looking around the room over her shoulder.

I see me in her and the impact knocks me so hard I'm stunned into place.

'What's up with you?' says Bree, concern showing in her eyes.

'Oh, just watching Jen and Lucas. He doesn't look that interested.'

'Probably isn't. She has a new one every few weeks. Such a super smart girl, it's…' Bree's voice trails off.

'Sad.'

'Yeah, she's lovely, but needy, too.'

'I can see that. I wonder why?'

'Not sure exactly, someone told me she used to be very overweight. She got a hard time about it.'

'Guess she still feels ugly.'

'I guess.'

Our scars are different, but the outcome is similar. I wonder if Bree introduced us on purpose.

I fight with myself that night. I think I know what's behind her behaviour, and mine. I've always felt that I didn't warrant being loved, but I couldn't bear the empty space around me. I hoped so desperately that I would feel better if it was filled, but I never truly thought I deserved for that to happen. I can't shake the belief that people either don't see me, or that they will inevitably leave me. I know these patterns started young (before there were words to make sense of things) and like rivers scouring ravines from the earth, they carved themselves into me. The deeper and older they are, the harder it is to shift their course. I know I must slowly and carefully redirect them, and find a way to calm the impulse to grab hold of anything or anyone that floats past. But sometimes knowing this is not enough; the need is so great it's like fighting off a tidal wave with a tennis racket. My biggest fear is that I will never belong anywhere, that I will miss out on being loved.

I wonder if I'm more like my mother and brother than I thought. I too suffer from peaks of activity, the fast thinking, the over-ripe hoping and rash choices; and then there are the dark, paralysing troughs and the life-sucking doubts, and the impulse to curl into a ball and not uncurl again.

Over the past few weeks I've gradually been losing strength. I don't sleep enough and a layer of fat has started to accumulate around my waist from the bread and empanada and meat and wine diet. I wonder if it's a floatation device produced unconsciously to keep me from drowning, to make me feel bigger. I need to pull energy from somewhere so that I can get strong again.

The following Sunday I find myself wandering through the bustling Plaza Francia, in the upmarket area of Recoleta. The square is lined with stalls selling handmade products and is situated alongside the gothic central cemetery, Eva Peron's resting place. The plaza is alive with couples hand in hand, families with kids and foreign strays in groups. I walk past the very simple but beautiful Spanish colonial-style church. It is pure white and firm, its wooden doors open. I walk on. I need to be outside.

I hear the rhythmic sound of drumming and singing as it pulses in waves up the hill. Curious, I wander towards it. I stop when I find the source of the deep rolling beats. There, standing in a big circle, is a group of people in wide-legged white pants. Varying coloured ropes hang swinging from their toned waists. A guy and a girl are sparring in the middle of the circle. It looks like a martial art, but it also resembles a dance. The high and low swirling kicks don't make contact; instead they swing past bodies or under feet, in wide arching circles. I stand transfixed, watching the teasing, sexy and smooth movements of the encircled couple. They are like two elegant birds performing some kind of exotic mating ritual.

'What is that,' I say to a blonde girl who is standing next to me, equally engaged in the performance.

'I think it's called capoeira; it's from Brazil,' she says in an American accent, without taking her eyes off them.

I approach the group shyly, to get a flier from a stunning young man with no shirt. He looks like a walking anatomy drawing. As I reach out my hand, a flush rises. He smiles at me. '*Gracias*,' I say, as I run away.

I'm enthralled by the strength and peaceful faces and flowing movements. I want to know more.

The very next week I start my first class. As I enter the long room, with smooth wooden floors, I see there is a good mix of girls and boys all standing ready to move. A blonde woman with the body of a Greek goddess approaches me, face serene and sure. She welcomes me warmly but swiftly, and then ushers me towards a tall, very thin Scandinavianlooking guy, who seems almost as nervous as I feel.

'Hi, I'm Piet,' he says, hand held out stiffly in front of him.

'I'm Jess,' I say, leaning past the hand to kiss him on the cheek. It's become an unstoppable impulse. He steps back slightly, his cheek blushing pink in exactly the spot where I kissed him.

I find out he's Dutch, and my instinct was right: this is his first class, too. His Spanish is years ahead of mine, and he says he's been here for two weeks, with no prior classes. I swallow the unfairness of that.

We make a comic pair. Two, long-legged, wildly out of time klutzes clash and duck and fight back frustration, while our extremely patient classmates and teacher try to help us. The class is an endless cringe-worthy stream of, 'No, you go first, no, no the other way. Right, let's start again. That arm goes there, the other leg goes back. Now. Stop. No. Again.'

Our companions' barely stifled giggles don't escape our notice, but we battle on, determined to better each other in our primal battle of the highly uncoordinated. Neither of us finishes well, but I return the following week and he is never seen again.

I find out later that capoeira was developed by the descendants of African slaves and native Brazilians. It was born out of a dream of freedom. The slaves would practice fighting under the guise of a dance so they could avoid detection from their owners. They developed skills to enhance survival, should they ever escape; hence the stunning mixing of fighting and dancing. Having good rhythm is necessary to do it well.

I ache and struggle during the two-hour training sessions, three times a week, but it's so powerful that I want to claim it. I become fixated in my desire to have those rhythms and kicks come naturally, despite the fact that my flying limbs betray me. It's mortifying and hilarious at the same time, but I refuse to give up. Slowly, my body finds the beat and my spirit gets regenerated along the way. I fall deeply in love with capoeira, not just because I'm learning to twist and move my body into new shapes, but because I'm reviving some long forgotten ones as well. I was a small child when I last cartwheeled or did a headstand. It fills me with joy, even though it's sometimes painful going back to those lost movements. I feel in my skin and strong again. Week by week my flotation device melts away; I can feel the outlines of muscles form under my skin. I have a core, and from it a novel feeling of strength radiates through me.

One Friday, when Valeria visits to pick up the rent, she causally says to me, 'Have you seen Paco yet?'

'What do you mean?'

'Oh, you didn't know? Monica told me he's been back for a couple of weeks now.'

My heart plummets, and something drains from my face.

'So he made it back for Creamfields after all. I thought he got work in Mexico and couldn't make it. He invited me to go with him to the concert.' I know I'm babbling.

'Sorry, Jessica. I think he has a new girlfriend.'

'Oh, really?'

I don't understand why she tells me about the girlfriend. Something about her tone makes me think she enjoyed the moment.

Once I've seen her out the door, I sit on one of the plastic chairs. I feel numb. Why didn't he contact me? I thought we were, at least, friends. I can't help imagining him walking around Buenos Aires for days and days. I wasn't in his head at all.

I email him; it's brief.

Hi Paco,
So you are here already. I didn't know. I've been looking forward
to catching up with you.
Tu amiga,
Jess.

He writes back.

Sorry Jess, I've been so busy catching up with people and
looking for work, time just went. Of course I want to see you.
You going to Creamfields tomorrow, right? You have to go. I'll
see you there.
Te quiero mucho,
Paco!

A group of us bought tickets for the big night out, weeks ago. I go to the huge outdoor concert with 'the three musketeers', Bree, two English sisters we met in Cusco and the Irish girls, who are back in Buenos Aires.

Their merriment keeps me distracted, but I can't help searching the crowd for a hairless head. There are thousands of people, moving like giant shoals of fish, following the music. Then I spot him. He looks up and sees me. Expressions of recognition, then surprise, and then confusion flick across his face. As he approaches I see his hand trailing behind him, holding onto a very pretty girl.

'Jessy,' he shouts over the music.

'Paco.'

We hug, hard, and then pull apart fast.

'I'm so happy to see you. We have to catch up later, dance together,' he says.

'Sure,' I say.

'Well, gotta go. See you.'

'*Chau.*'

He disappears back into the masses, girlfriend in tow. He never told me her name.

Bree appears in front of me. 'You okay?'

'No, but yes.'

She nods. 'Let's go and have some fun. You need dancing, and a stiff drink.'

Bree's right, I do. But a strange thing has already happened, a thing I wouldn't have predicted. I feel ridiculous, sure, but then I feel relieved. More than six months of waiting and denying I was waiting, and trying to fill the gap with other boys, and in two seconds I finally get it. He doesn't want me. And I don't want him anymore. And it's okay.

Strong male arms are grabbing me. It's the three musketeers. They pull me into the middle of a group photo and a crushing group hug.

The encounter with Paco seals something. I am pleased with myself for not wanting him; the thoughts of our past seem more peaceful now. I feel stronger, more able to confront the challenges this city throws at its inhabitants, and its inhabitants throw at me. I find myself looking around me and seeing what's really there. I become more and more affected by what I glimpse of a world of serious poverty just beyond my comfortable Palermo life.

A couple of weeks before Christmas I accompany Zoe, one of the English sisters, to the *Ciudad Oculta*, the Hidden City, one of the poorest *villas miserias* (shanty towns) that ekes out an existence in the vast sprawling suburbs of the capital. We go with a non-profit organisation that arranges group birthday parties for the children in these disadvantaged neighbourhoods.

After a train trip we flag a taxi. Our taxi driver wants to drop us ten blocks from the address we gave him. 'It's dangerous in there,' he says wiping sweaty pearls from his forehead. With a little extra cash waved in his face, he reluctantly continues driving. On arrival he abruptly halts the taxi, grabs the money and waves us roughly out its doors. '*Gringas tontas*, stupid foreigners,' hangs in the air as we walk away.

We are met at the entrance to the villa by some volunteers who have safe passage into the zone. The police don't enter here and neither do ambulances. The further we walk along the uneven, dirt alleys, the more miserable the sights become. Makeshift homes are made of large orange bricks stuck together unevenly by leaching cement, bits of wood and corrugated-iron are crunched together and on top of each other. Their bare brick or smoky concrete walls appear to tip into the earth as if they might just disappear. The roofs are weighted down by rocks and insulated with plastic sheets that lift and flutter in the wind. Electricity cables criss-cross haphazardly and dangerously above us. There are few people in the streets. I see some men in groups, on corners, drinking beer and smoking, and a few women walking with heads down, feet dragging, bags in hands and children tagging behind.

A huge multi-story white skeleton of a building looms ominously over the villa.

'It's called the white elephant,' says Zoe when she sees me staring.

'What was it?'

'It was supposed to be a hospital.'

It shocks me to see this level of poverty close up, again. Not since I was volunteering at the centre for street kids in Peru have I been aware of such a sense of hopelessness hovering. It's a stark confirmation that Buenos Aires contains two cities—that of the haves and the have-nots. They are intertwined, but as different as day and night.

After a jaw-tightening walk through the dirt alleys, we arrive at the community centre/food kitchen. It sticks out because it is one of the few solid looking structures. It had been painted white many years ago, now its walls are a mush of colours; the orange underlying brick shows through deep scratches, dirt and mould smudge its base, paint peels like ragged fish scales. Inside, its low ceiling and the pressing in of people suck the air out of the room.

Seated at a row of tables, a posse is busy making decorations for the room and the tree. Smiles shine through the rushing and chattering. Some local women are preparing small hamburgers and a bright orange drink. The rest of the volunteers are diligently wrapping small Christmas presents for the kids. Colourful silky ribbons flap in the air and get tamed into bows and flowers. I see plastic trucks, dolls, teddy bears, plastic animals and farm fences, books, marker pens and coloured paper.

I help make decorations. Many pairs of eyes watch Zoe and me, quietly and patiently. To distract myself from them I join another girl and paint fingernails. It's soul-warming to see each tiny face light up as they stretch out their hands and proudly show off their new coloured nails. A small gift, but it's something. Thirty small hands later, we run out of nail polish. I look up and see a pretty face drop. She looks no more than fourteen, already some six months pregnant. The child in her eyes is disappointed, again.

On the trip back home, I wonder if I will go back again. I tell myself I will but in my heart I'm not sure. I'm not sure I have the energy, not sure I can see the faces again and not take their pain home with me, as I did working at the clinic all those years, or at the centre in Peru. I'm not sure if I'm strong enough, maybe *good* enough, to go back.

I know that the Argentines around me see this stark difference in realities. I know my students are pained when they see the faces of children who have fallen through the net of society, but they are tired, worn down by holding up the people closest to them. There is little energy left over to open eyes fully to the sadness. As the villas get bigger and bigger and rifer with troubles, their people spill out more frequently into the city, often as humble decent workers, but increasingly as weapon-holding delinquents who fuel the constant fear of insecurity. Over the years the outer suburbs of Buenos Aires have filled up with security-guarded, gated communities next to the villas. High walls and barbed-wire fences separate them. All trust has long gone.

Tired and weary from my feet to my soul, I step into our apartment and the smell of pasta and garlic-infused tomato sauce wafts towards me. Bree pops her head round the kitchen door.

'Just in time, Juicy.'

I can't help smiling.

A week later I write an insanely upbeat and very long email (with lots of exclamation marks) to my family and friends for Christmas. I rave about capoeira and my lovely students. I tell them I'm in love with this crazy-wonderful city. I want them to know I'm good, that I did the right thing in coming here. I tell them I'm thinking of giving BA a year and then I'll see how I go.

Dave writes back.

So, Jess, it looks like you did land on your feet there. Capoeira sounds interesting. Very exuberant email? Is it really that good? I'm happy Bree is with you. She seemed like a bright spark, although she looks like she could lead you astray!!!
No mention of Paco. Is that a good thing?
I forgot to send you the Salta photos, some are quite beautiful. Will do that soon.
Keep in touch.
Dave

Elle writes.

Jessy,
Sounds like you're having a ball. I'm very happy for you. Maybe I will get by that way sometime soon. We have been touring a lot. We played a gig on top of a mountain in Japan! All's good on the home front. If you do eventually come home, you always have a place to stay.
Love you,
Elle

I receive an email from Dad, too. I know his wife wrote it by the tone and lack of spelling errors. After 'it sounds like you are having fun,' and 'great you have a job,' it falls into an impersonal, standard Christmas letter about dinner preparations and holiday plans and best wishes for the New Year.

I ring Mum from a phone booth as she's not quite computer literate yet.

'Darling, great to hear from you.'

'How are you, Mum?'

'Good, busy. It's a crazy time of year.'

'So…'

She cuts in. 'Wait, someone on the other line.'

'Mum—' She's gone.

I wait, and wait and watch the counter in the *locutorio*, call shop, tick over. When it gets to 100 pesos I hang up.

On the way home I wonder who was on the other line. And then I fume, thinking 100 pesos is eight English classes for me.

I don't want to go back to New Zealand.

On the last day of 2004 I go to the café next to our apartment, alone. I order a *cortado* and grab a dog-eared newspaper from one of the tables. When I unfold the paper, I gasp out loud at the headline. I read that during a band recital the night before a terrible fire had broken out in a nightclub called *República Cromañón*, killing 194 and injuring 714 more. Around 3,000, mostly young people, had gone to see the rock group *Callejeros* play, so the club was over full and bursting with ecstatic fans. The blaze was started by a flare let off in fun; a popular sport in nightclubs and other venues, even though it is banned. Its burning comet's tail had set alight the foam in the ceiling. Then the flammable decorations and materials fuelled the unstoppable flames as they roared through the building, consuming the air and replacing it with poisonous gases. Four of the six exit doors, some of which were fire exits, had been chained shut so as to prevent patrons sneaking in without paying.

Over the following days a profound mourning stalks me. I can't stop poring over the faces in the photos; all those young lives, gone. On the television news channels the parents of these lost children rage, faces set with inconsolable and gut-wrenching grief. It pierces through everything. Their eyes are so haunted I wonder if they will ever lose that stare.

How the hell could something like that happen? I roll it over and over, unable to grasp onto anything, some meaning, to stop the ruminating. It surprises me just how much I feel the sadness of it. It's as if I'm sucking it in with great grasping breaths.

It seems this tragedy was waiting to happen. In the weeks that follow, everyone looks for someone to blame: the lighter of the flare, the band, their manager, the owner of the club, the inspectors from the government and men in power. As I follow the news, I see a glimpse of the underbelly of Argentinean society; its fabric is so full of holes that many people slip right through. I see the passion and rage of regular people fighting against injustice and blatant corruption at all levels, right to the very top. Ignoring rules in order to save money and time appears to be a national pastime. Bribing and paying people to turn a blind eye is normal and in fact expected behaviour.

I ask my students, hoping they can help me understand. 'Yes, it is terrible, but what can you do?' they say, seemingly exhausted. 'It's just how it is here. Nothing will ever change.'

It takes the President, Nestor Kirchner, many days to respond to the screaming, and then he reacts by getting aggressive towards the newspapers, which he says are using the tragedy to attack him personally.

The Buenos Aires night is shut down in mourning. There's ample talk of new regulations, more responsibility and stronger enforcement but when the night cogs of the city do start turning again, over the following weeks and months, nothing seems to have changed. There's a flip of a page and a new drama surges into the public vista.

Life here is a test I can't study for.

Keep row row rowing, but where to?

Thirteen

January is a quiet forlorn month. With no night, paradoxically the faces of the day seem wearier. Even Bree's inner light dims. I start to wonder why I'm staying. I have friends and a job and a roof. But is it enough? I can see the city more clearly now. The contradictions are eating into my love for it. I have a terrible attack of ambivalence, stuck between believing something good awaits me just out of reach and a hungry nostalgia for my 'easier' life in Australia. Maybe I should I go back? Would returning feel like failure? Do I have the energy to cross oceans, start again?

Stay or go back? Go back or stay?

On a muggy grey day the cry of a tiny baby girl gives me my answer. I'm sitting in a crammed café in the centre of town, my spirit depleted from giving classes all morning. The weight of a day only half finished hammers down on me. My arms are leaden. Eating alone in a corner by the door, a gloom coat wrapped around me, I feel detached from the world. I find it hard to swallow the stodgy raviolis in front of me.

I stop, take a breath and look around the café. A few tables away from me, a young mum is seated, her tiny baby snug in a bassinet beside her. I catch a glimpse of the baby's face, all screwed up and red. A pink woolly blanket is wriggling with little protruding toes, elbows and knees. For something so small, the noise emanating from her mouth is brain rattling. No amount of soothing seems to be helping.

I look around the room full of men in suits having lunch meetings, waiting for them to frown in the woman's direction. I imagine them saying to each other, *I wish she would take that thing home, it's so disruptive.*

Nothing happens. The baby's loud wailing eventually evaporates and is replaced by soft strange animal-like snuffles. A big group of men get up, put their suit jackets on and start making their way towards the door.

I watch as they stop one by one at the table with mum and baby. They bend over and coo at the wrapped up bundle as they say kind words to the flustered woman. Some of them even reach in and gently stroke the baby's soft whiffs of hair. I can't believe it. The baby, despite its crying and disturbing the peace, is totally accepted; she belongs there. I had seen in the corners of my vision this intense love of children and the integration of them into all aspects of life. I had been surprised at hordes of little ones roaming around tables in restaurants at midnight, attracting attention at all kinds of gatherings and winding up under waiters' feet in fancy cafés. All they get are smiles and pats on the head.

Is it different in my two home countries? Children are equally loved, but I don't remember them being so much a part of everything. Perhaps I wasn't paying attention, though, or I'm not remembering it right? Then I recall a sign, scrawled on a chalkboard outside a café in Melbourne, which warned: *if your children are noisy, you will be asked to leave.* Or the one in another café that a friend told me about, that was only lightly flavoured with humour: *unattended or disruptive children will be given an espresso and a kitten.* Those signs would not exist here.

A strange warm feeling of knowing surfaces, and a clear thought flashes in my mind: *I want my children to grow up here.* Despite everything this country throws at its people, I know they would be accepted, hugged and loved in a way that enriches life and mediates the struggle of it. An odd click happens inside me, as if something has lined up and a valve that was closed, opens. It almost alarms me that I'm so certain. I feel patient. I'm alone, there is no man, children seem so far away, yet something tells me to wait. So I will wait.

The spring in my step and the smile in my eyes on the way back to work attracts more than an entire week's worth of *piropos*. The lightness of a decision made.

The Irish girls are back, again. They seem to pop in and out on a regular basis. I wonder when they will have to stop and go home. One has a weak-coffee-coloured tan and the other looks out from beneath a thousand new freckles after a long trek along Brazil's coast. I suddenly remember telling Pepe about them and promising him to bring them to Tigre.

I ring him.

'Jessy, is that you? Too long time. I miss you.'

'Miss you, too. Hey, the Irish lasses are back. I wanted to know if we can still come to Tigre for a visit?'

'*Por supuesto. Dale*. This weekend?'

'*Sí, sí, por favor*.'

'You bring wine, bread and salad. I'll get the *asado*, okay?'

'*Perfecto*.'

The following Saturday, the sun is a bright fire in the sky. Sitting on wooden blocks in a circle around burning coals, with steaming meat cooking on it, fills me with happiness. Bree is babbling away in Spanish to Pepe. Sarah, with her wild reddish curls, and Mary with her straight blonde hair and green eyes, are rehashing some stories of Brazilian bad boys for my benefit. They are a funny pair: Sarah is tall and loud, Mary smaller and watchful. Sarah's words tumble out over each other in an unnerving stream; Mary stops her periodically to make timely clarifications.

'It's so hot,' says Sarah, fanning her face.

'Nearly done, just ten minutes,' says Pepe.

'I'll get the *chimicurri* then,' I say.

'Please.'

I teeter up the precarious wooden steps and turn into the small kitchen. As I'm reaching down to get the large jar of sauce out of the fridge, I hear a screaming whoop. I look out the small window just in time to see Sarah strip down to her very tiny Brazilian bikini and run towards the brown water of the river.

'You're mad as a chook,' yells Bree after her.

I can see the back of Pepe's head bouncing up and down as loud chortles emanate from his belly.

'Is it safe to swim in?' I yell to him through the window.

He makes a so-so movement with his hand and shrugs his shoulders.

Sarah eventually climbs out of the sludgy water, shakes her head like a dog and comes over to eat with us.

It's a tiny moment of pure joy in being human, surrounded by other humans.

'So are we staying, then?' I say to Bree in late February.

'Yep, I think so.'

'This flat is way overpriced. Should we try to find somewhere else?'

'Yep. A fridge would be nice. A bedroom each would be nice, too.'

'I know. You're tired of living-room living.'

'A little.'

After some weeks of increasingly desperate searching, Bree spots an advert in one of the many free newssheets for foreigners. *American girl, looking for two flatmates to share a sunny, furnished three-bedroom apartment in Palermo.* Reasonable rent. She circles the ad with a flourish, in red felt-tip, as if it's already a done deal. I love that about her. I'm reminded of Elle and her words, 'I believe if you really need something, it will come to you.'

The following day, over two stale-tasting espressos each, we manage to charm Laura, the American girl, despite the fact that Bree still smells like a winery from the night before. In the end it's her Irish luminescence that wins us a chance to see the apartment.

Laura is tall, brunette, with a stunning movie-star face. She holds herself in that confident way Americans have. I find myself a little mesmerised, watching her talk. The painter in me is caught by the sight of her amazingly perfect top lip. It looks as if someone has pressed and moulded it out and up into a beautiful bowed shape.

The apartment is perfectly located, close to the subway, near the big green Plaza Armenia and close to a selection of great restaurants and bars. The living room has a comfortable blue sofa and an art-deco table with four chairs. There's a TV and some paintings on the walls. A small, slightly dangerous looking balcony protrudes out of the living room into the open air. We edge out onto it and gasp in unison. At sixteen floors up, we can see a huge slice of the city stretching out below us. The cars below look like wind-up toys; above us, towering apartment buildings reach up from the older lower buildings like giant fingers trying to touch the sky.

Laura shows us the bedrooms. They are small, but big enough for a double bed and a bedside table. The light-green tiled bathroom is small and functional. It has a built-in, slightly grey-rimmed bath.

'Jessy, come quick,' Bree squeals.

I cross the short hall and squish into the thin kitchen next to her. 'What?

'This,' she says, clinging to the fridge, her face pressed up against it—an expression of love radiating from her eyes.

'Oh, thank god,' I say, shoving her out of the way, in play.

'Big, white, cold, food inside,' she says.

I open and close the door three times. Bree sighs. Laura stares at us like we truly are *dos locas*.

'It's been more than six months without a fridge,' I explain.

'Oh,' she says, still looking concerned.

We sit down around the table and talk numbers. It's a good deal, but we have to pay six months in advance. I glance at Bree. She nods. 'Can we have a minute?' I say to Laura.

'Yeah, sure.'

Bree and I go to the balcony.

'I can scrape it together, just. You?'

'I might need to borrow a little. I'll pay you back with my tips,' she says.

We stand there, side by side, looking at the incredible view.

'Let's do it,' I say.

We step back into the living room. 'If you'll have us, we would love to stay,' says Bree.

'*Listo*,' says Laura, still looking slightly perplexed by the pair of us.

'We have a home,' I gush.

It feels like the start of a *proper* life in this city that has worked its way into our hearts. Even though I'm sixteen floors up, I feel my feet on solid ground.

With a warm wool jacket draped over my shoulders, I sit on the balcony that night, alone. Bree is working. Laura is out with her Argentine boyfriend. I find myself staring at all the little squares of lit up windows, across the void. I wonder about the lives going on inside all those homes. The line '*Little boxes... little boxes made of ticky-tacky*' fills my head. My speck of a life, with its woe and wow moments, is just one of thousands within my line of sight.

I try to imagine my way inside those holes of light. How many people in them are happy? How many are sad? What things are they worrying about? What does life hold for them? It's calming, pondering the ebb and flow of all the lives around me.

I feel a chill in my hands, which now grasp a cold drink from *our* fridge—another reason to thank the universe. Our pantry (a little high shelf, plus the top of the fridge) is lovingly stocked with basmati rice, tins of Thai curry, various sauces (oyster and sweet chilli), fresh lemongrass and many other things to condiment our lives and satiate our need for flavour. A settled feeling washes over me as my mind happily integrates this new life change into its complex networks.

This is what content feels like.

The following night, Laura cooks us a Thai green curry and I fall a little in love with her. But then, she's taken. When I meet him, I understand why she's staying. Julio is a year older than me; Laura is twenty-six but has a warm maturity that defies her years. When Julio speaks, in near perfect English, I can see he's smart and considerate. A musician, he plays guitar in a band of old friends, and makes a living from running his own small business.

I want one like that. Same make, different model. I love watching them together, the soft non-verbal connection and care they show each other. They radiate warmth, and it seeps into the room.

Of course, I know I'm idealising them, and him.

One sunset, when we're sitting on our balcony, I ask Laura how they met.

'Well, now that's a story,' she starts, a sweet smile on her lips.

'I love these kinds of stories,' I prompt her.

'Okay. I was stressed that day. I woke up feeling rushed, like there wasn't enough time. As I was hurrying down the street, just down there,' she points, 'I was preoccupied, my head was buzzing. He was walking towards me, I nearly bumped into him. I looked up and *bam*, I met his eyes. We held each other's stare for longer than normal, you know…'

'Yes, and…?'

'Then we walked past each other and kept going. I was thinking *wow, what was that?*' She drifts away for some seconds.

'Don't leave me hanging.'

'A block later we both turned, it was as if we were being dragged by some physical force, and retraced our steps. We met in the middle of the pavement, face to face, and everything sort of stopped in time. Someone said "*Hola*", I don't remember who.' Laura stops, looks a little sheepish. 'I know it all sounds a bit Hollywood…'

'A clashing of souls in the street. I love it.'

'And here we are, six months later.' She smiles. 'It hasn't all been easy. There's some cultural stuff to deal with.'

'What do you mean?'

'He can be quite jealous.'

'I've noticed that's an issue here. I have a male student who hasn't told his wife he takes classes with a woman, because he's worried about her reaction!'

'I know. It's too much. I'm used to being really independent. I have male friends here, and he's not used to that.'

'You guys look really good together. He's lovely.'

'He is. I love him. It's good, really good,' she says, her gaze dropping to the floor.

'I'm just delighted to see that they're not all *chamuyeros*. I was starting to wonder.'

'There are some good ones. Be patient. Don't try to find them in bars.'

'Ha, good tip. Thanks for the story.'

'*De nada*,' she says in her perfect *porteño* accent.

One afternoon I try to meditate mindfully in the botanical 'cat' garden, which is now conveniently at the end of my street. I watch two lithe white-bellied grey cats saunter past me, pacing so lightly they look as if they're floating above the grass. They appear peaceful, easily happy. As I continue to watch their parade, I start to laugh when a thought appears in my mind. *Maybe they're so serene because they've been neutered!*

I am calmed by the whispering leaves and that strange orange glow of a day near its end. I no longer feel invaded by the sensation of searching. Being alone, as I am now in the garden, is a choice. I have people to go home to: two strong women to cushion me from the hard edges of life. I picture Laura, so calm and soulful, so sure of herself. She never questions whether she is good enough, she just is, and she's happy with that. And then there's Bree, who lives so fully in the moments of fun, who lives with a certain lightness. Even when things are hard, she seems to trust that everything will be alright.

There is lots more to be grateful for. Capoeira is reforming me in more ways than just physically. Sometimes I can actually sense energy seeping up through my bare feet. It helps to connect me, to ground me. My students inspire me every day and I have enough of them now that I can stretch a little—buy a few things, some new clothes to replace the travel worn ones. Once again I decide that the decision to stay was the right one. I make it at least once a week, like a mantra. When I get up to walk home I'm content, not unlike the cats in the little green haven.

By the time I receive a long email from Paco, about four months later, I have had plenty of practice at being content in my new home. I haven't thought about him in a long time. Good thing, too, otherwise it might have really knocked me, seeing his name pop up in my inbox. The email fills me in on what's happened since our last encounter. He's single again. He tells me he feels stuck right back where he started; the year away from Buenos Aires is a distant memory. He confides that he's dead broke and fighting to find a job, to find some meaning again. He writes at the end, 'Can we talk? I need you.'

I close the laptop and sit for a long time on the balcony, staring across at a new building that is racing up into the sky. Men are swarming all over it. It seems to grow a level every day.

I'm too curious to say no, despite the flash of irritation I feel. I write back to suggest he comes round at a time when I know we will be alone. I don't tell Bree. She will give me that look of quiet concern and say, 'Jessy, be careful.'

It's a shock to see him. He looks smaller, thinner, but more real, too. The brightness that hung on him before has faded. The sexy confidence, maybe even cockiness, that I used to see, or imagine, is diminished. He is just a guy. My heart doesn't jump, not even a little. Instead it aches and is warmed to see him so human. When we hug it has a different quality. I feel love, but it's the kind I feel for my brothers and my friends. I'm slightly surprised; relieved, too.

I show him around; his eyes flick open when he sees the view. I make coffee as he stands leaning against the fridge, with the light playing across the lovely angles of his cheekbones. Nothing. I smile to myself. We sit cross-legged on the balcony and talk, coffee cups warming our hands, eyes squinting slightly in the bright sunlight. Many roaming thoughts make it into the air between us, others stay quiet.

He asks a question that I sense has been on his mind. 'Jessy, are you okay here? Are you going to stay longer?'

'Yes, and yes,' I answer.

'Could this be your new home? I mean, a permanent home.'

I feel myself stalling. 'I think so. I do see a future here, but sometimes it's hard. There are things I love and things I just don't understand.'

'But are you happy about the huge change you made in your life?' he pushes.

I detect guilt.

'Yes. I needed shaking up. Sure, it was a big risk but it doesn't feel like a mistake. Buenos Aires has caught me.'

He looks relieved. 'She does that,' he says, smiling.

'Are you okay? Your email made you sound so sad. Stuck,' I say.

'You know, I feel better today but it's been hard coming back. I thought I would feel different, ready to move forward here, but I feel restless again already,' he says.

'Like you want to travel more?'

'Yes, but I know I have to stay a while. I can't keep running.'

'You take yourself with you wherever you go,' I say. 'I should know.'

'Yes, true. *Mierda,* shit.' He laughs with his eyes closed. '*Sabès que sos mi amiga del alma,* Jessy,' he says breaking into Spanish.

'Your soul friend. I like that. I feel the same way.' It doesn't cost me anything to say this. I realise it's true.

After a warm hug as he's leaving, I think he looks a little taller, a touch more filled out. I'm about to shut the door when he turns suddenly, brightening up. 'Hey, Jessy, I nearly forgot. Pepe, Mum and the cats would love to see you again.'

I almost succumb to tears, but I check them by being jolly. 'I would really like that. It's been a while. You know, the last time I saw Pepe was the day I took the Irish terrors to Tigre for an *asado.*'

'Yes, he told me about that. He had a fabulous day with them.'

'The wildest one stripped down to a very small bikini and jumped in the river for a swim. Pepe was totally thrilled!'

'*Thrilled,* what does that mean?' Paco asks, frowning.

'*Chocho,*' I return with the appropriate Argentine slang translation.

Recognition flashes in his face. 'Oh, *chocho,* yes I'm sure he was!'

Later, after he's gone, I go back onto the balcony. Standing there, looking out over the vast city that never rests, a thought strikes me. Meeting Paco, loving and losing him, broke me open. It forced me to move, to look honestly at where I was and what I was chasing. I needed to have layers ripped off so that I could clearly see my inner workings, the cogs out of place. I needed to see inside in order to rebuild me. It was meeting him that led me to this place, this point in time.

Maybe I am supposed to be here.

The following weekend I find myself sitting at the dinner table with Paco's small clan. It feels as if I was there only yesterday, as I eat Monica's divine stuffed squid, still steaming in front of me. We have full wine glasses, crunchy bread and a simple tossed salad to accompany it. Pepe looks like a child without hope of dessert. I can see in his face that he is dreaming of sizzling slabs of meat. I suspect that for him, entertaining is not quite entertaining without an *asado*.

At the end of the evening, as I'm about to leave for home, I notice a framed photo sitting proud on a small shelf in the living room. It's me. I see the sarong flying out behind the girl with the quizzical smile on her face. I remember that day, on the beach: the wild wind stroking my face, the silly posing, the laughter and the sensation of flying.

Pepe smiles when he spots that I have seen it. 'I did that,' he says.

I catch Paco looking pink.

'Thank you, it means a lot that it's in your home,' I say, my throat tight.

'You always have a place here,' he says simply.

Later, back at the apartment, I am overwhelmed by the power of this gesture of Pepe's and the contrast with a particular memory. The last time I was at my old family home I noticed Dad's wife Cheryl had put up a big corkboard on the wall near the kitchen. Tacked on it were family photos, mostly candid shots—people having fun. I remember standing in front of it scanning every photo, once, and then again. I can see some of Henry and Edward. None of Jonny or me. In fact we weren't anywhere in the house, except in an official family shot taken on the day Dad and Cheryl married. There wasn't even a proud shot of me on graduation day, all dressed up in my robes, my Master's degree in hand; and I knew Dad had taken some photos that day. I felt erased.

This memory plunges me into an old familiar anguish. *Am I so forgettable?* I want to ask the crisp night, as I curl up on my bed. But something has changed. *You are not, at least not for everyone*, I answer. I realise that I do exist in the minds of others, even when I'm not there. Pepe's small, framed photo has given me that precious gift.

I sit up and decide it's a good moment to bring Daniel into the room.

Hi Daniel,

I haven't forgotten you; I've just been busy, making a new life. I decided to stay in Buenos Aires. It's complicated, but I love it here. I saw Paco the other day. We're friends now, which is great, but that's not what I want to talk about. He asked me a question: 'Could this be your new home?' It made me think hard about what home really means. Is it a house, a city, a country, a place with certain people or family connected to it? Is it somewhere you feel loved and understood? I had never really actively thought about it. Then I came across a new Spanish word the other day, hogar, it's close to what we mean when we say 'home', as opposed to 'house', casa. It also means fireplace, hearth—the heart of a home.

Something about fire and a hearth made me think back to anthropology lectures about the first humans. They were mostly nomadic. The fireplace, the hearth, was the centre of their lives. When they packed up and moved from one place to another, the first task in the new location was to make a fresh flame. Sometimes they even carried a burning coal with them, coaxing it back to life. This hearth and their kin sitting around it was home, wherever they were. It struck me that perhaps 'home' really isn't a place, but a feeling.

For me it's a magical sensation of being calm, fully alive and connected, all in the same moment. Present in my skin. I don't think it's a coincidence that I feel that same sensation when I stare into flickering flames and burning embers—their hot light warms me through and inspires dreaming. I think it is the 'something' I have been searching for; a primal awareness residing in my core. Here I feel it more often than ever before and I'm over a thousand kilometres from my birthplace.

My mind just keeps going and going—you know the way it does. It wakes me at night, thinking about this stuff. Why here? What is it about this place and these people? I feel as if I'm working it out, fitting the puzzle pieces together in my batty mind. Argentines really cherish the things that fuel that sensation. Family and friends are core elements to them; fire and food, too—steaming meat over hot coals. See where my brain is going?

The way we live is changing so fast; we are drifting apart. Families eat together less often; people spend so much time working to earn more in order to spend more that they hardly see the people closest to them and even less of their extended family; we allow, without realising, our connections to stretch until the fibres are pulled cotton thin or break completely. Maybe I feel it more, because of my own stuff, my own family. But I can't help thinking that back home we are taught to become independent too young and then we stay alone, or pair up, thinking that will be enough. I have seen so many people struggle with this, and too many desperately shove things into the void hoping to fill it up, while their hearts scream out.

I don't know, though. You were strongly connected to your family and you still chose to leave because you couldn't bear staying, even for them, even for me. Did you feel like a burden on us? Did you not know how incredible you were?

Too many young people at home and in Australia take their own lives. We nearly lost Jonny a couple of times over the years, his struggles so similar to yours. I never stop worrying about him. I don't understand it. These two amazing countries with good people and stability, and yet... There must be a reason—a lack of something to hold them, a sense of not belonging or being good enough, a fear that talking about sadness will make them seem weak.

My head is burning.

Are you even listening?

I stop talking, pull the bedcover up around me and sit very still, trying to hear anything that hints at a presence in the room. Silence reverberates back.

I picture a breathing flickering fire with the people I love around it, and then another thought enters my mind.

Hey, Daniel, I was just thinking that maybe, once someone has that 'sensation of home', they can take it with them—a living coal close to the soul—wherever they go. Perhaps I'm talking about something spiritual. The coal is the living spirit in us. I'm not talking about god, well not in the traditional sense. I don't believe my hole is god-shaped; I think it's always been people-shaped. Who knows, perhaps it's both? Most human beings need other people to help feed the coal, to keep it lit. We are social creatures; we are meant to be in a tribe, even if tribes are different now.

I already have a curious tribe of wonderful people around me and I think it's going to get easier to find more. I have, too, this overwhelming ache to feel my family's presence around my hearth. I miss them. I have always missed them.

I miss you, too. Somehow you still breathe life into my flickering coal.

Te amo, duérmete bien, *sleep well.*

Fourteen

Eddie, my wandering spirit little brother, arrives a month later for a visit. It's unexpected, and a last minute change of plans after a trip to the US. Over the last ten years we have seen each other only a handful of times; both of us have been crossing the globe, often in opposite directions. I will have him close for a few weeks. It's a chance to strengthen ties.

At the airport I'm jittery, expectant. I wonder if we will find the old thread or whether it will be forced and stiff. Then I see him. He looks different, more grown up, his face now roughed up with five-day growth. When people see us side by side they always say, 'you guys look identical'. We have the same face. His is the boy version and ten years younger, but no one misses that we are made from the same clay. He has always been the one I relate more easily to, but we have seen so little of each other over the years, I fear both of us may have changed too much.

As he gets closer I see the cheeky spark in his intelligent brown eyes, but there is a new maturity there, too, as well as a tiredness in the faint lines around them. The last year has been hard. I know he will have things to say.

'Sis.'

'Eddie.' We hug. It's a little stiff, but warm. 'So, welcome to Buenos Aires. You're going to love it here.'

Happiness fills me as we walk towards the taxi. My feet want to jig.

Our first foray onto the streets of Palermo later that day is a dangerous affair. A bus almost plasters him into the pavement when he looks the wrong way. Distracted, already infatuated with the city's female inhabitants, he's unable to take his eyes off the gorgeous girl-parade. I can see his neck straining as he whips his head around, trying not to miss anyone—girl walking towards us, girl on bike, girl on bus going in the opposite direction.

'Stop it, you'll do yourself a serious injury,' I berate him, sounding eerily like our grandmother.

'God, they are so cute,' he says, eyes glazed.

'Don't kill yourself over them.'

Later than night, sitting on the balcony watching the moviescape moment as the sun sets over the city from our sixteenth-floor perch, we try to fill in years' worth of gaps.

We chat about the incredible view, the cosy flat, my lovely flatmates. I tell him I miss the greenness of home. I'm so excited to have him here but somehow I can't quite believe he is. We sit quietly for a long moment, perhaps scared to start talking about serious stuff, to expose ourselves. I know from his emails that things between him and Mum have reached a boil over point. I hope he feels he can open up more, now we are face to face. There are things we both need to say.

When our mother got cancer she stopped being a lawyer and left our hometown to open a small shop in Auckland selling cushions. Each beautiful and intricately designed piece was made with her own hands. It started as a kind of therapy, a way to tolerate the chemotherapy, and the uncertainty. I have a picture of her, taken just after she shaved off her hair. She is sitting on a sofa, alone, her head rasped and strangely white, surrounded by her amazing cushions. The first time I saw it, I was extremely sad to see her putting on a brave smile for the camera. I wasn't there for her. I should have been, but I was wrapped up in Daniel and his troubles, and my life across the Tasman Sea. I did go home to visit her later, and we went on a family holiday in an attempt to heal more than just bodily wounds, but none of us seemed to be able to close the gaps and support her. The opportunity for healing wasn't used as it could have been. And now that she has been free from cancer for more than five years, it feels like the distant past. The chance to move in close has been lost.

The cushions attracted attention, and so did she. She made her own clothes for working in the shop, and after receiving many wildly positive comments, decided one day, as only our mother could, to become a fashion designer. In record time she broke into the fashion world and her label started to do well in both local and Australian markets. Eddie took on the role of business and marketing manager, while finishing his MBA. The job, and working together, had taken its toll. Both of them have strong personalities and fixed ideas on how things should be. It isn't difficult for me to imagine the clashes.

The silence on the balcony is getting heavy. I can almost detect the racing thoughts, doing laps, in Eddie's head. I ask the question that has been hovering between us. 'So, how's it going with Mum?'

I see his jaw stiffen. His gaze remains fixed ahead as he says, 'Bad, I don't know how much longer I can stand it.'

'What's going on now?'

'She's totally stressed all the time. It's unbearable. The other day she lost the lid off a container of buttons and then totally flipped her lid.'

I nod, picturing the scene he's describing. 'Her stress does tend to suck the air out of a room. But hey, you've made a pretty good effort, lasting this long.'

'Because it was going so well. Shit, she is amazing.'

'I know. Only she could do it. I wish I had half her talent. Imagine having just ten percent of her energy!'

'That's the thing, though; you need more than talent and energy. She's such a perfectionist, it takes forever to finish things. We pay New Zealand dressmakers by the hour, it's insane. It's getting impossible to compete.'

I can see his hands tensing, his eyes wide.

'What are you going to do?'

'I think I have to go. I'll try to find a replacement… then, just go.'

'Well, you're here now. Try to relax and enjoy it.'

He breathes out one long noisy breath, and shakes himself.

'I can see why you stay away,' he says, looking at me.

'I never really planned to, but it's like there's this invisible barrier around New Zealand. I just can't bring myself to go back.'

'I get that. I want to get far away, too.'

'What's wrong with us?' I say, though I don't expect an answer.

'Don't know.'

Eddie dives full-heartedly into all that the Buenos Aires day and night have to offer. He comes alive and fills up. Our time together goes too fast, but he swears he will come back for longer next time. It makes me happy to hear *next time*.

On the night of his final *fiesta*, I ask what he'd like to do.

'Something over the top.'

'I have just the place.'

It's Thursday, and every Thursday a huge Palermo nightclub transforms itself into a cousin of the Parisian Moulin Rouge; it shimmers with sexy dancers in glittering lingerie, *travestis* with feather boas and piled on makeup, lean muscular breakdancers and an ample dose of sexual over-flow to titillate the wide-eyed crowd. It's called Club 69 and it's a Buenos Aires phenomenon.

I'm curious about seeing the *travestis* up close as I haven't quite worked out how to place them. They are not transvestites, though they are men who dress up as women, nor are they transsexuals, even though most have implants and other surgeries. From my discussions with some students I gather they are mostly passive homosexual men who want to look like women in order to be more attractive to straight men. I'm thoroughly confused.

It's not hard to persuade Bree to come with us. While Eddie makes us some strong gin and tonics, Bree and I parade around the living room in our outfits. We aim for subtle glam. Bree does a twirl in my very short suede skirt and a red spangled top, while I do a slow turn in my slightly longer tight black skirt and a blue and gold Japanese-inspired top that Laura has lent me. Eddie is happy in his T-shirt and jeans.

The second we walk in, my brother is wrapped, practically smothered, with a pink feather boa and lovingly manhandled by two enormous and very striking *travestis*. It's a small taste of the night to come.

'Wow.'

'I know, cool huh?'

'Perfect. Right up my alley.'

'Eddie!' I call out, alarmed when he starts to entwine a reluctant Bree in pink feathers.

Eddie has always been the clown who pushed just a bit too far. He's the whirl in the middle of a party. He plays jokes on people; he pushes their buttons, perhaps to test if they will still love him. They do, but sometimes they also develop a strong desire to strangle him. It makes me laugh when I remember that his nickname as a small child was Button.

'Enough,' Bree shouts as she escapes.

'Eddie, be cool.'

Despite the dense humidity of bodies squashed in too close and the thick cigarette smoke irritating my eyes, I feel extremely happy, strangely light.

Around the middle of the night, Eddie decides to have some fun with two extremely tall identical twins with curls and goatees. 'What's the weather like up there,' he asks, as he attempts to physically climb them. They think he's hilarious (at first). We end up hovering around them, their cousin and a small group of their friends. I don't really pay much attention to anyone. I hang close, only so Eddie can be removed if he goes too far.

The music is mesmerising; it shivers through my feet, up my spine and beats through the wall of my chest and out my fingertips. The DJ, a woman, knows sensual sounds. I dance and dance, in my own hazy world. My eyes are almost closed; hands in front of me massaging the vibrations of sound. It's magical. I feel enclosed in my skin but somehow connected to everyone around me.

Suddenly, two warm hands reach out and hold mine, gently but firmly.

What? Who's that?

Without pulling away, I lift my eyes and scan slowly up a strong, firm male body. I pause, apprehensive, at the limit of the subtly bulging chest muscles that run into a soft-skinned neck. I take a tiny step in; he smells so good. One movement more and then my eyes meet warm brown ones, set in a lovely handsome face. It's the cousin of the giant basketball players. He's tall too, strikingly Spanish looking, floppy dark hair, masculine but elegant features, a slightly brooding stare.

'*Hola, soy Diego,*' he says.

'*Soy Jessica.*'

'Jessica.' He pauses, as if taking it in. '*¿Estás disfrutando del club?*'

I nod. '*Sí, mucho.*' How could you not enjoy this, the sense of fun and the fantastic music? I smile at him.

'*Estás muy linda,*' he says, smiling back.

'*Gracias,*' I say. It's lovely to be told that I'm pretty by this gorgeous guy, but a thought streaks through my head: here we go… another sweet-talker, for sure.

Later, when he tells me he's thirty, I think he's lying as he looks younger. Then he tells me he's a lawyer. '*Chamuyero,*' I tease, only half in play.

He throws his head back as his face opens into a smile. I can tell he's laughing at my accent and fake bravado. '*Chamuyero*, very good. No, I tell truth.' he says, in English as thick as winter soup.

I give in to the moment and decide to relax in his gentleness. Diego doesn't try to kiss me but with every moment, my hands are being encircled tighter in his. I could remove them, but I don't. He moves slowly, confidently, teasingly closer and then he draws back. It's enchanting, a waltz of energy.

Eddie appears next to us. 'Diego,' he says loudly. Then he attempts to get us to kiss by forcing our heads together.

'*Basta*, Eddie, enough, please.' I shove him away; it's mostly playful.

'*¿Tu hermano, no?* Diego says.

I confirm my wayward brother's identity as I glare a warning at him.

'We met,' Diego says, his face already showing signs of weariness regarding Eddie's antics.

'He's hot,' says Eddie, in a loud whisper. Then he bounces away in search of the tall twins. I notice Bree has very sensibly hidden herself from him in another room.

'Have to go *al baño*. Stay here, *por favor*,' I say to Diego. I can't wait any longer.

'No, I come with you,' he says quickly. I sense he feels an escape coming on, though nothing could be further from my intentions. He parts the crowd for me, making an easy path, and then he stands vigil outside the hallway to the restrooms.

My body is shaky. I think I look alive and fearful when I stand in front of in the mirror to wipe away some smudged mascara. I take a deep breath.

When I stride back out, I see him standing there, leaning slightly against the wall. He spots me and smiles. Something leaps inside me. I walk over, push him back into the wall and kiss him.

His face tightens in surprise and then he falls into the kiss. His lips are softer than I'd imagined. We ride waves of intensity and then the rhythm softens to gentle, playful and warm. It's immensely intimate. We spend the rest of the night enveloped in each other, pressed together, hands and lips tingling.

Bree breezes by us a few times, floating on gin fumes. Her face gives radiant signs of approval. I can't help but notice that my special suede skirt, which she borrowed for the night, looks like it has been tumbled around in a rubbish bin.

When the music stops, Diego and I look at each other as the lights start blinking on. 'Come home with me,' he says.

I look at his face. I want to, but I know not to. 'It's Eddie's last night. I can't, but let's see each other again,' I say in Spanish.

'*Sí, seguro*,' he says, disappointment showing.

I give him my contact details.

He tells me he's going away the following day with friends, for two weeks. I wonder if it's a ploy to persuade me out of my good behaviour.

'When you get back, call me,' I say.

He kisses me and says, 'I ring you, *te lo prometo*. I promise.'

I believe him.

There's a torrent darkening the sky outside. A thick cascade of rain bounces off the street in a fireworks display of water, the drops catching the orange and white glow of taxi head and tail lights. It's beautiful. The heavy resonant clatter of rain hitting pavement hums in my ears.

Standing at the entrance, Diego puts on his dark blue wool jumper. I see tight abdominals as his T-shirt rises about his belt. Electricity runs through me. We kiss again. Then he wraps me in two strong arms and hugs me. It's tender and heartfelt. I don't want it to end.

In the taxi, jammed in between an inebriated Bree and inanely chatty Eddie, I lose myself in the memory of damp wool mingled with his scent. I shiver. I felt so safe with my face pressed up against him, held tight.

I wasn't even looking.

Bree sheepishly admits she tried to breakdance—on the filthy alcohol-soaked floor.

'Oh, so that's what happened to my skirt,' I say.

She gives me a 'naughty puppy' expression and I press my head into her shoulder, happy.

Eddie's advice for me the following day is, 'Don't be needy, don't chase him, be chilled.' He knows me too well.

Then he says, 'I'll be back.'

'When?'

'Soon as I can.'

'Cute girls, eh?' I tease him. 'The city got you fast.'

'Sure did.'

At the airport we hug like we have never hugged before. There's no stiffness, no early pulling away.

I feel calmer than usual, but I have words with myself anyway: *it was one lovely night; maybe he'll contact me, maybe he won't.* I obey Eddie and push back any thoughts that might lead me to do, say or text silly things.

When my mobile rings on Saturday two weeks later, I jump nervously. For two days I haven't let it out of my sight.

'*Hola, ¿Jessica?*' The voice is strong and clear.

'*Sí, yo soy,*' I answer.

'*Soy Diego.*'

'*Sí, sí, yo sé,* I know.'

Then my stomach pinches as I wonder how we are going to understand each other past *hello*. Fast-talking phone Spanish sounds to me like chipmunks chattering and my brain fuzzes over almost instantly. I need to be able to watch people's faces in order to detect the meaning of the message.

We struggle for two eternal but comical minutes, trying to arrange to meet that night for dinner.

'I pick up you, 9.00p.m. *¿Dónde vivís?*' he asks.

The thought of trying to give him my address makes my brain go blank. I can't remember our street number. It's two thousand and something. The big numbers still catch me out. 'Um, I'll text you the address, okay?'

'Perfect. See you later,' he says.

'*Chau.*'

I can't resist dancing solo round the living room.

That night I pull on tight jeans, a fern-green T-shirt with a pretty girl's face printed on it and black knee-high boots. I allow my hair to be wild and free. I wait, sitting on the precarious balcony, watching the lights in the boxes blink on. Nine o'clock passes. I'm okay. Argentines are notoriously tardy. 10.00p.m. passes. I start to twitch. At 10.30 he rings, says he's sorry, and asks if he can pick me up later as he's with some friends at a bar. 'How about midnight?'

Not again.

Disappointment stabs through me. I agree to the change in plans because I don't know what else to do and the words in my head seem stuck in transit. I don't want to wait restlessly in the apartment, so I tell him I'll meet him later at the bar.

'Okay. We're in Jacko's,' he tells me, and then spells out the address slowly.

I think, *jackass.* I hang up, miffed and confused. Then I ring Bree, who's now working in another Irish pub not far from our flat. 'Do I go or do I just forget it? This feels like the start of more games. I'm just not up for it.'

'Be cool, Juicy,' she says, gently. 'Come here. Let's talk.'

I sit at the long wooden bar with a huge glass of red wine in hand. Thank god for Bree. And for Malbec. 'These glasses are like fishbowls.'

'We're not meant to fill them that high, but for you, Juicy, in your hour of need…'

Bree makes her way over to me whenever she's free. Her dancing Irish tone calms me.

'Just go, what do you have to lose?' she says. 'He's being Argentine; they always meet late. He probably doesn't even realise this is bad form. And maybe he's scared about a dinner, with the language stuff.'

'I know, it's just…'

'You met him once. Relax. See how you feel when you get there.'

I am so grateful to Bree, for her care, for her common sense. I know she's right. But I can feel my cool slipping. 'There was something… I don't know; I really liked him.'

'I really liked him, too. Nice energy. Super cute! This will probably all be fine.'

Another gigantic red wine later, I feel a little like I'm swimming but I'm determined to go. When I jump down from my perch at the bar, I almost lose my balance. I blow a kiss to Bree and head off.

Outside Jacko's, I take a moment or two to float back into my shoes and then I push through the door and into the crowd. I see him, his form jumping out from the masses. He's encircled by a group of tall, sturdy, pleasant-looking characters. His smile is wide and welcoming.

In two long strides he's in front of me. 'Jessy, I'm sorry. Next time, dinner, okay? Come meet my friends.'

He places his hand across my back and moves me towards them. I look up at his face. It shines.

He attends to me like a personal butler. I'm never without a drink in my hand, never left alone. Drinks flow, feet and hands move, lips press together and bodies crush into curves.

Suddenly I feel faint, the room spins and I drop my heavy head onto his chest. A wave of regret about those huge glasses of consolation wine passes over me.

'*¿Estás bien?*' he asks.

'Outside, please,' I say. So stupid, I think. I learned my limit many years ago. This is an old sensation I thought I'd never feel again. I don't want to lose control.

The fresh air helps. He sits next to me, stroking my hair and neck, but nausea starts to rise. He looks at my face. '*A casa,*' he says. I nod. It's all I can do.

He helps me to a taxi and takes me home with him. When we arrive, he gives me a Paracetamol, a large crisp glass of water and then he removes my boots and tucks me into bed, with my clothes on. The last thing I feel is a sweet kiss.

I wake up to smiling eyes and more tender kisses.

'*¿Estás mejor?*'

'*Sí, mejor*. Better.'

I smile.

He smiles.

Both of us close our eyes and fall together. Layers of clothes are slipped off. Skin is caressed in long soft strokes. I shiver as his fingers leave warm sensitised trails behind them. Two bodies press into each other, hands find sensitive places. My mind floats away as I allow myself to fall deeper. Hard kisses and heavy stroking movements along the lengths of backs raise heartbeats and send almost painful jolts along spines. When skins are hot and damp our bodies' arc together in a strong, powerful movement that takes us to another place.

When our breathing returns to normal, he starts to stroke my face softly, as if he wants to know each curve, each line. I see happiness reflected in his eyes.

I realise I allowed him touch more than my skin.

Later, over a coffee and succulent *medialunas*, we unwrap more layers. Our desire to understand each other, along with gesture, slowly enunciated words, touch and smiles enables us to pull in closer. I'm surprised at how much intimacy we gain with so little shared language. Hope uncurls like a new spring leaf.

Diego tells me he was born and raised in Pergamino, a medium-sized city three hours from Buenos Aires, but has been living in the capital for the last seven years. When he talks about his brother and sister, both doctors, I see pride in his eyes. Then they sparkle like coals when he imparts, leaning in close, the gossip about his friends from the night before; an intriguing bunch of larrikins by all accounts. It's true that he is a lawyer and thirty. I make him show me his ID.

'You still think I'm a *chamuyero*,' he says in Spanish, laughing.

'No,' I say, cheeks heating up. 'Lots of guys here are.'

He nods. 'Now, I show you my city.'

'That sounds great.' I can't untie my tongue to say more. I want to show how happy I am to be with him, but I'm tight with nerves.

We take the subway to the Palermo parks. He pays for the tickets, and while we stand, rocking with the movements of the underground train, he keeps a steady hand on my upper back. Keeping me firm footed. I feel protected. Perhaps it's a claim of sorts, too.

After circumnavigating one of the manmade lakes, we find ourselves kissing passionately in the centre of a white wooden pergola-style bridge. Flowering vines weave around the wood, their buds near bloom. Swans drift across the water under us, leaving trails of smooth ripples.

I have a sensation of taking leave of my body for a moment, floating above us, watching. It seems surreal: too bright, too perfect. I get scared. I get scared of the hope I'm feeling.

I'm bursting with it.

Fifteen

Dear Biba,

I've changed my flight back from London so I can see you. I arrive there next week. I will be there for your birthday, my Darling. You will be thirty-four! I can't believe it. Can you arrange an apartment for me? I don't want to go to a hotel.

See you soon.

Mum

I READ THE EMAIL several times, trying to work out what her desire to visit means. I want to see her, but it scares me. I haven't seen her in over three years, and my last visit home was rushed and full of unspoken tension. Two family visits in less than three months, I should be happy.

I didn't even know she was in London and I sense something is wrong. I wonder if she was there to escape some emotional pain. I know from our infrequent contact that she has recently ended, finally, a long and damaging relationship with a very charming but unavailable man. For many years this man had kept her in a secret gilded box, to which only he held the key. He would unlock it once every few months to woo her and love her, before returning her to her place to wait for the next time. It has been devastating to watch the way it sucked the power right out of her, leaving only a shell behind.

I go to meet her at the airport. When I see her coming towards me, I notice that her arm, pulling a large suitcase, is extremely thin.

'Mum, let me take that,' I say, taking it from her.

We stand there, facing each other.

'Ah, how…' I start. We fall into a clumsy hug. 'How was the trip?'

'Terrible, I couldn't sleep. I'm so tired.'

I nod. She seems nervous, stressed. I feel my own nerves straining. 'I've arranged a place in Palermo, close to me. I think you'll like it.'

In the taxi, I can still feel the impression of her bones marking the flesh of my—now strong—arms. Mum has always been tiny, but never frail. She's the opposite of me: petite, dark eyed and olive skinned. She could pass as Spanish, or Argentine. This person sitting next to me—gripping tight to the edge of her seat—is not the mother I know. This is a shadow of the person who always had ten times more energy than any normal human being, who was always doing things, creating things, being passionate, moving. It's the first time in a long time I've seen her look beaten by life. Not even cancer did that to her.

I hope that a good night's sleep will dissipate her unhappiness, but it doesn't. A terrible, consuming darkness clings to her as we try to explore the city. She's unable to enjoy anything. She hates the smeared dog droppings everywhere and the broken pavements, the cash machines that attempt to eat her cards, the food, and even the people.

'They aren't *that* attractive. The women are horsy looking and the men have terrible haircuts,' she says as we walk around Palermo, which is as reliably stuffed with beautiful people as ever.

Nothing pleases her. I can't help her. I can't tell her how happy and hopeful I am about Diego and being near to her sadness drains some of that hope from me.

Midway through her week-long stay, I try to create space for her to talk, to let me in.

We are sitting in the living room of her flat. After a long, winding discussion about 'the man', his loss, and the hole where he was, she says, casually, 'I've been thinking of doing a Sylvia Plath.'

'Mum—'

'But I thought it would be too mean for you. You know, having to organise for my body to be shipped back home.'

'It's that bad?'

'Yes, some days. But I've been here before. I think I can...' She fades out.

'Please don't.'

I start to cry desperate tears.

'Oh, Biba. Don't cry. I'll be okay.'

'Will you?'

'I just really hoped I could be with him. That he would love me. It's been a long ending. I'm tired, that's all.'

There is a long pause. As the light fades outside, the air darkens around us.

'Another tea?' I ask, unable to think of anything meaningful to say.

'Yes, less milk this time.'

I feel paralysed, useless. I'm not a good enough daughter to help her. I'm not a good enough psychologist, either.

Later, in the moment right before sleep, I have terrible thoughts of life without her. If she weren't around anymore, would some of my angst go, too? Would it be, in some sense, a relief? Would I be released? Would I be able to grieve the loss I have always felt for her? Thoughts that make me sick. How can I think these things about my own mother? I'm wishing her gone.

No, no, I can't lose anyone else in that way, I yell in my head; it's too violent for those left behind. I understand when the mind is stuck on one track, heading for the cliff, there's no possibility of thinking about others. But it's like saying *none of you are worth staying around for*, which is a terrible thing to leave behind you.

I don't know what to do.

The following day we go out to dinner for my thirty-fourth birthday with Bree and Laura and some Argentine girlfriends. I invite Diego to come because I feel it's polite, but it's too soon for him. We've only been on a handful of real dates, so it's too soon for me too, really. And I realise that I want to keep him and Mum apart, not risk contaminating one with the other.

My mother looks beautiful that night; she's wrapped in one of her own stunning creations: an earthy, dark grey dress with one buckled shoulder strap. Even now, when she's brittle, crushed, it's still possible to see the woman who devastated men with one look, one witty comment or one shimmy of her hips. She has a pile of destroyed hearts accumulated at her feet.

I watch her quietly all night as she bravely charms the room.

'Your mum is amazing and so talented,' says Laura, almost gushing.

'She's very trendy and cool,' says Bree, eyes wide.

'I know, I know,' is all I can say; and it's true.

I'm happy that this evening is a tonic for her. A familiar niggle asserts itself, though. I've always felt like a somewhat frumpy caterpillar next to her, the ever-fluttering butterfly. I'm proud of her and what she can do, but I've always wanted more of her.

Diego invites me to his place for dinner the following night. I can see he's made a genuine effort to make it special. The table is set with a white tablecloth, there's a vase in the middle with one red rose standing tall, petals barely open. A steaming plate of homemade chicken, tomato and basil pasta takes centre stage. He looks goofy in his pride as he waves a hand over the table.

'*Feliz cumpleaños*, happy birthday, Jessy,' he says, smiling, eyes turned down. I can tell the overt display doesn't come easily to him.

'*Gracias*,' I say, hugging him. I want to stay like that, not moving, head resting against him.

'What's that necklace you're wearing?' he asks.

'It's a *pounamu*, a special necklace made by Māori people,' I say, showing him my long, beautiful New Zealand greenstone pendant.

'*Pounamu*,' he mouths slowly.

'Yes, *pounamu*,' I say, letting the word slip smoothly off my tongue. Nostalgia for home mists my eyes.

'It's very cool.'

'I know. It's very special to me. Mum gave it to me for my thirtieth birthday,' I say, touching it. It warms under fingers.

'How is your mum? You haven't said much.'

'She's fine. She had a good time last night, with the girls.'

I lie. I can't tell him the truth, not yet; it's just too soon in our relationship. Even if I could, I don't have the words in English, let alone in Spanish.

After dinner, he disappears. When he returns it is with a gift-wrapped present.

'*Para vos*,' he says, almost dropping it into my lap. His face is expectant, slightly pink.

I open it to find a trendy black T-shirt. I turn it over and see intricate silver wings printed on the back.

It takes all my force not to cry.

'*Gracias, es perfecto*.'

My mother and I decide to have a lovely lunch on our last day together. It's our final chance to try to talk about all the stuff floating around, the stuff that's making even the air heavy. I choose a cute little place in Palermo that seems to have interesting food that Mum will enjoy. We sit in white wooden chairs, each of us contemplating the things we need to say. We play the old game of avoidance. We make comments on the décor; she likes the high ceilings and I'm fond of the wooden shelving, adorned with old glass bottles. When the food arrives, we both focus intently on it.

'Oh… shit,' she says, her hand flying to her mouth.

'Mum, what's wrong?'

'I've badly burnt my mouth. Stupid people,' she says, her face twisted and her hands a flurry.

'Are you alright? I mean, can you keep eating? What should we do?'

'No, I'm *not* alright. I'm sure they just heated it up in the microwave. Can you talk to that waitress? They can't serve food that hot.'

The pressure of her stare bores into me.

'Okay, okay,' I say, frustrated, reluctant.

I wave over the waitress and in my disintegrating Spanish I explain that the food has burnt my mother's mouth, and that they should be more careful.

She shrugs and offers a weak apology. Then she walks away.

The incident shuts down any attempts to communicate. We speak the same language, but no words can be found to express, in the right way, what's going on in each of us. Perhaps we are also scared of the harm that could be caused if we get it wrong.

A burnt tongue. Symbolic.

What's left at the table as we quietly finish eating is a tangle of emotions—disappointment, sadness and perhaps some rage.

We walk back to her apartment in silence. Then I help her get her things and hail her a taxi to the airport. A hugely overweight sweating man pulls up, so fat his belly swallows half the steering wheel and threatens to spill out into the car. Mum looks at me, her face saying, *you would send me away with that*! She's defeated. Normally she would refuse to get in and he would be sent on his way with a flick of the hand, a new taxi demanded.

I messed up everything.

She gets in and is gone.

I walk home in tears, wondering if we can ever fix the brokenness between us. I wanted so badly to have her close, to feel connected to her. But it's been a disaster, and we were disastrous in our attempts—nothing new.

Over the next weeks I email back and forth with my brothers, especially Eddie. I ask him to watch out for her, to push her to seek help. I know the situation is too much for him; he's already tired of being strong. But what's my other option, to go home myself? I consider this. I cannot do it. I am starting to feel that I have a new life here, and Mum's visit proved to me that I am not the one to help her. Neither is Eddie, I know. I have to accept that I, we, are powerless, but still, I can't bear to give up on the idea that she and I might understand one another better.

I write a long emotional email and ask Eddie to print it for her. I can't talk on the phone. I write to try and get it right; I need to edit to get it right. Perhaps I need the distance to be more honest. The long letter she writes back releases me from some guilt as I can detect between the words the old, stronger her. She's angry with her ex-lover, and she's using her anger to propel herself forwards.

I am still terribly worried about her, but I believe that she is past the point of wanting to die. And the truth is, I feel helpless in the face of this desire. I have spent years confronting it in many of the people closest to me and it has left me numb, convinced of my own impotence. I don't know what to do. I stay because I cannot go.

My body is strong, but in my mind little cracks are forming. I want to take refuge in my new relationship with Diego. Part of me wants to lose myself in him, but I know that would be dangerous. And besides, we seem to be strictly following the rules. Friday night is his night with the boys; Saturday is normally ours, and Sunday too, until late. During the week some casual texts are sometimes sent. I desire more but I'm scared I'll ruin it, that I'll grab too tight and he will flee.

My English conversation classes with Andrés have been almost entirely transformed into tutorials on Argentine dating etiquette. I go over in detail the events of the week with Diego. Andrés contemplates, illuminates a few things and then tells me I must be level-headed and not chase. I argue with him. I tell him I don't like this 'girl waiting for her man' stuff. I tell him it feels childish. If we like each other, why play all the games and follow rules?

'*Es lo que hay,*' he says, shrugging.

'I hate that expression!' I tell Andrés, who shrugs again. Roughly translated, it means 'It is what it is,' or 'that's just the way things are.' Right now, it's not what I want to hear.

'Look, he seems to like you,' says Andrés. 'You just have to let him come to you.'

I do my best to follow Andrés's advice but the next couple of months are challenging, not least because my emotional energy is split between fretting about progress with Diego and worrying about Mum. Eddie writes and updates me. It seems she has found her strength and is powering forward with new projects. I hope it is more than her blocking out how she feels with activity. But then, that's the way she has always coped. Things appear to be back to 'our normal'.

I feel fragile. It takes constant effort not to push for more from Diego. I am mostly successful, but I suspect that I can only claim part of the credit. One afternoon Bree and I are drinking coffee on our balcony when I make a confession.

'You know, when it comes to relationships there's a wonderful positive side effect of not knowing a language very well. It's much harder to be clingy, and to fight. I just don't have the vocabulary to be hysterical.'

Bree laughs one of her deep belly laughs.

'It's true,' I say.

'But you aren't hysterical.'

'I can be when it comes to men.'

'We all can sometimes, especially here. You really like him.'

'Yeah, I do. And I really would stuff it up for sure if I could construct a better sentence.'

'Juicy,' she says, in a tone that warns me not to be too hard on myself.

'I haven't seen him or heard a peep from him in almost two weeks. I'm going a little crazy.'

'I thought you'd been home more.'

'Yesterday I wrote out a whole spiel about it. You know, "what is this between us? Are we going somewhere, or is this casual fun?" Then I translated it into Spanish. By the time it was finished, I was laughing at myself. I ripped it up.'

'Good for you.'

'He must think I'm super chilled out because I haven't pestered him with calls. It would be nice to know, though, one way or the other.'

'I've seen the way he looks at you. This isn't over. Be patient. It's still early days.'

'I know, you're right. I also wonder whether maybe he's a little scared.'

'What do you mean?'

'Scared of opening up. He told me he'd had two long-term relationships but he's been dating for five years since then, I think he's a bit jaded. He seems kind of shut off, like he's holding back.'

My talk with Bree makes me feel better but when the weekend arrives and I still haven't heard from Diego, my mind starts to try to adjust to the idea that maybe it's over. On Saturday I spend time with the girls, visit the cats in the cat garden and cook an early dinner of Thai curry for the three of us. After dinner I pull on my capoeira pants and then knot the thick green rope around my waist, hard. I can feel the strength in my arms. I take a bus to the capoeira headquarters to join the *ronda*. I need to kick.

My mood lifts as I enter the door. It's crowded. Faces are smiling; attractive people, proud of their firm bodies, are pacing and chatting and practising moves. Loud clanging Brazilian music moves feet and hips and I feel I can ride the waves of positivity vibrating through the room. Hours whip by and I am absorbed in the sounds and the sights of strong legs cutting through the air, inches from heads.

When the *ronda* finishes around 10.30p.m., I go and get my bag. I click open my phone and see three texts and two missed calls from Diego.

Text One: Jess, are you doing anything tonight?
Text Two: Did you get my text? Let's go out.
Text Three: Great dance party tonight. Come with me.
Phone call One, message: I really want to see you. Please ring.
Phone call Two, message: Please ring me when you get this.

Okay. I ring him. The relief is palpable in his voice.

Things change after that night. There are no more disappearing acts, and when we are together more of him is there with me.

I decide to cook for him, something spicy, something he hasn't tried before. I pick Southeast Asian, one of my great food loves. Argentines are not known for seeking out new flavours and most have an aversion to spicy food. Diego eats a typically Argentine diet of pizza, pasta, empanadas, meat and *milanesas*. Perhaps I'm testing him to see how he reacts. It's important to me that we share an appreciation of food from all over the world.

I spend hours in his kitchen one night, trying to make Vietnamese rice paper rolls. Ah, damn, I say, as another one rips apart. I try dipping them in the water for less time. Better. My fingers find the way and neater rolls start to appear. It's totally weird food for him. I am nervous about what he will think of these strange creations.

I hear him coming towards the kitchen and cover my work with my hands. 'Go away, it's not ready yet.'

'What's that smell?' he asks, his nose wrinkling.

'Thai curry.'

'Oh,' he says and retreats.

I finish the rolls and stack them in a perfect pile, with cilantro leaves and chillies for garnish. I tip some sweet chilli sauce into a white teacup, as there are no small bowls or dishes in the house. I pour my homemade spicy peanut dipping sauce into another cup. I check the rice and turn the curry down.

When I place the rolls and sauces in front of him he looks at them and then me with a totally baffled expression. I explain in my best Spanish where they come from and how they are made.

'You don't fry them,' he says.

'No, they're not spring rolls, not like the Chinese ones.'

He carefully picks one up, hovers over the two sauces and then picks the sweet chilli.

I watch.

He takes a bite, screws up his face, chews and then nods his head. 'So… The sauce is tasty.' He sees my face drop. 'They're nice. Interesting. Crunchy.'

When he samples my curry his eyes bulge and then he opens his mouth, fish-like. 'Wow, hot.'

'Too hot?'

'I'm just not used to it,' he says, bravely taking another mouthful.

I make the curry milder the next time, and then two times after that he begs me to make it hotter. I can't help but smile.

Is any of this enough, though? Can we make it when our communication is still so disjointed? Can we go deep enough without more shared language? There are things I want to say, connections, understandings I need, but it's complicated. Moments pass without being fully caught. What we do have is a soft rhythm, a quiet intimate speaking without language. We read each other's expressions well and some things are just known, no words needed. I still wonder, in the hard moments, when he shakes his head while trying to understand me, *am I grabbing again, to stop myself from floating away?*

I gravitate to Laura. Her presence is calming. I often find myself pressed into the tiny kitchen alongside her, while she cooks. One night, a month or so after Diego's first curry, she's preparing tom yum soup. Its chilli, garlic, ginger fumes reach up and tickle my hunger. I tell her about my worries.

'I really care about him but it's hard to talk. Our conversations are missing something.'

'That will change over time. Your Spanish is getting better, Jess.'

'I don't know if it's fast enough.'

'Just enjoy things with Diego.'

'You're lucky with Julio. He speaks English so well and your Spanish is great. I'm a little jealous of that.'

'It doesn't stop us having miscommunications, though.'

'Really?' I'm surprised. I think of them as such a happy couple. 'Like what?'

'His jealousy is getting in the way,' she says, chopping noticeably faster. 'I'm getting tired of him stalking me with calls and texts. I just want him to trust me.'

'He's an idiot not to. There does seem to be a tendency to the green-eyed monster here, though.'

Laura nods. 'I know. And his last girlfriend was unfaithful, so there is some context for his anxiety.'

'That makes more sense, but even so: it's horrible for you.'

'I'm being patient, but for how long?'

Something in her tone makes me think she is running out of patience not just with Julio but with Argentina. I realise how much I would miss her if she left. 'Do you want to stay here? Or does that depend on whether you can work things out with Julio?' I ask

'I love it here, but truthfully, someday I want to go home,' she says. 'What about you?'

My heart sinks a little. 'I think this could be home for me. I haven't ever really felt at home, before.'

'Not in New Zealand, or Melbourne?'

'No. The problem was me, not the places. I think this whole "being a foreigner" thing feels consistent, somehow. It's like my inner world and the outer one are in alignment. I've felt kind of foreign all my life, now I truly am.'

'That's a bit sad, Jess.'

'No, it's okay. I don't feel sad anymore, just a bit confused.'

Later that week I'm in class with another favourite student, a fellow psychologist and my Argentine replacement for Dave. I love going to his office. It's like a mini-sanctuary; I feel looked after in his presence. His bright eyes always light up when he sees me. His round face gets rounder and his neatly trimmed beard twitches.

The conditional tense occupies us for half an hour but then he suddenly asks, 'Are you okay?'

'Yes, why?'

'You have a sad face today.'

Before I can stop myself, I tell him about my fears and hopes and the uncertainness of my place here.

'Jessy, relax; take a breath. Things will become clear over time.'

I'm grateful to him for his kindness, for this reassurance.

My phone beeps. I ignore it. When the lesson is over I receive a warm hug, which almost makes me cry. After class, as I'm marching fast along the uneven pavement towards the bus stop, I remember the text. I open the phone, scroll down. It's from Diego.

Te amo, Jess.

I close my eyes. The clearly etched letters flash onto the dark inner wall of my eyelids. I float to my next class. My poor student keeps saying, 'Jess', with an increasingly frustrated tone. I can't keep my focus in the room. I'm thinking about what these words mean. Maybe I've found him, or he's found me. Do I feel the same way? Yes, it feels like love: not the intense and desperate love I felt for Daniel; not the mad, needy love I had for Paco, but something warm, sane, real.

Is this it? Is he the one I've been looking for? Was the psychic right?

Really?

When I see him that night, he looks bashful. 'Thanks for the text,' I say, and then bite my bottom lip.

'Oh, sure, okay.' He looks ready to jump out of his skin.

'*Te amo, también,*' I tell him.

He goes red. I reach out and take his hands in mine, and then look up at him. Something feels different. 'Wow,' he says, as his face opens in surprise.

'You feel it too?' I ask.

'Yes.'

A flow of energy passes through our hands. It's as if a switch has been turned on and the current can now flow freely.

That night there is a different energy in the bedroom. We move slower, kiss slower, while breathing each other in. I feel warm inside out, outside in.

It all starts to become real, concrete. Possible.

Sixteen

'I'm going home,' says Bree one evening as we sit drinking coffee on the balcony.

I look at her. She's staring at the little boxes of lights flickering on. I knew it was coming; I'd seen her losing energy for the game of BA life. I want her to be happy, of course I do, but it stings. My eyes well up. I look away over the city as I don't want her to see.

'When?'

'Mum's helping with the ticket. I think in a month.'

'Oh.'

She slaps me softly on the back.

'That's great, Bree, I mean, if it's what you want.' I pause. 'I just don't know what I'm going to do without you.' I choke the words out of a dry mouth.

She turns to face me. 'Juicy, don't worry. You'll be fine. You have Diego, other friends.'

'I know, but you and Laura; I…'

'You'll be fine,' she says firmly. 'And I'm not gone yet.'

I get an email from Eddie the same week.

> Hey sis,
> Did you get the present mum sent you? Was a late birthday gift.
> She sent it at the end of September, about a month ago. I didn't
> hear from you so… well, let me know.
> Kiss, Eddie

'Never trust the Argentine post,' a long-term BA resident warned me when I first arrived. She told me things simply don't get delivered; they just disappear into the twisted bowels of the Argentine postal monster. Even if they do miraculously arrive and you receive a card notifying you of this event, you are required to drag yourself down to the crumbling warehouse-like customs office near the port and queue for your life to retrieve your package. If the attending staff detect you are foreign or *really* want what's in your parcel, suddenly all kinds of special taxes appear. I assumed it couldn't possibly be that bad and maybe she'd just had some rotten luck.

By mid-November I realise the present has gone forever and I am a believer in the monster. Seems it likes to eat precious things.

Eddie outlines 'the losses' by email. I'm sad about the tins of Wattie's baked beans, the pineapple lumps, Vegemite and Black-Knight liquorice. I'm gutted about the amazing skirt Mum made for my birthday. But I just can't bear to imagine 'the opener' of the package throwing away the twenty one-off family photos I had asked for, and discarding the letter from my mother.

I spend many nights wondering about the letter's contents. Strangely, just imagining what it may have said makes a difference. Any attempt to connect, to clear a path through the rubble between us, is a precious thing. It's a thin fishing line cast out over a wide sea.

As my connection to Diego grows stronger, Laura and Julio's is stretching to breaking point. A nasty green vine is twisting tighter around the base of their bond, and it's suffocating their love. On some level Julio seems to know Laura is loyal, but once the power of the jealousy grasps him, nothing is logical anymore.

On a girl's night out one weekend, Julio first sends texts and then makes lengthy calls. Bree and I watch, powerless, as Laura's evening is destroyed and her hope for their future is wounded once more. Not long after midnight (very early by Argentine standards) he suddenly appears at the bar. They argue. I see Laura snap as she gives in and they leave together. Bree and I sit at the bar, wordless.

The next day he promises to calm his jealousy, but it doesn't last long. His expensive psychotherapist and all of Laura's love and patience can't help him sever the vicious vine.

Laura's heart leaves Buenos Aires and she too books a flight. 'I want to be home for Christmas. It's time,' she says.

Bree leaves first. Our last hug sends a sharp ache through my heart. I break into sobs.

'Juicy, stop it.'

'Can't.'

'You'll be fine.'

'I know.'

She has been a witness to it all: to the me I was in Cusco, the Paco adventure, the new start and a new love. She has always been the wonderful distraction that pulled me from my cave and dragged me into the light outside.

'I will see you again,' I say.

'One day, for sure,' she says, in her sweet, singsong accent.

For days after she leaves, I keep seeing her smile and the naughty shine in her vivid blue eyes. I hear echoes of her outrageous jokes and unflinchingly witty comments. As a memorial to her time in Buenos Aires, every day for a week I buy a sweet, sticky, *dulce de leche* and chocolate-laden *alfajor*. She used to eat one every afternoon, always cut into eight perfect tiny sections, which she would savour one at a time.

I realise something when she's gone. I know so little about her past. She talked about her mother, sister and brother but I don't even know if her father is alive. I sense he is 'away'. I always felt there was sadness and hardship there, through the door, in the attic of her mind. When I scratch back to our conversations about family, I can remember only me talking. When I tried to get behind some of her words she would whip the tale away, swiftly turning to another topic, any topic. I think perhaps she joked away the pain. I knew her well in the moments we shared, but the door to her past was always closed tight. Now I wonder if the anesthetising power of red wine keeps her from walking up the attic stairs and opening the door. Or does it numb her to the glimpses she sees through it? Am I reading too much into it? When I try to settle in her shoes it's still all me in there: the me that thinks you must venture into the attic and poke through the boxes. Perhaps she just doesn't need to.

When Bree moves out, Matt, a jovial London lad, moves in. He has come to live thousands of kilometres from his home after falling in love with an Argentine girl. I introduce him to Paco and they become firm friends: Paco's visits to our flat get more frequent. It's good to have him around.

We have both been busy with new loves. It took bumping into him at a party a couple of months before Bree's departure for us to reconnect. I was there with Diego and he was with his new girlfriend, a laidback girl with un-Argentine short hair and groovy glasses. I liked her a lot. Paco and Diego clicked instantly. It was a relief to see the two of them getting on, a confirmation, somehow, of how far I'd come.

Paco may be much happier than I've seen him in a while but his moods are still mercurial. One day we are sitting as usual on the balcony, he with a coffee, me with a tea in hand. 'I can never get enough of this view,' he says, looking, almost mournfully, out over his city. A city he both loves and loathes, depending on his mood, or the day's frustrations.

'It is amazing. I'm not sure we're going to be able to stay in this flat, though.'

'Why not?'

'Laura's leaving soon and in a few months we have to pay six months' rent in advance again. I don't have that kind of money anymore.'

'No guarantee,' says Paco, nodding.

'Nope.' Real estate agents in Buenos Aires require a third party's guarantee that they will pay the rent, in case the tenant defaults. And the person offering the guarantee has to own property themselves, in the city. It means that if you're a foreigner, without family connections, you are excluded from renting in most of the market. Your choices are limited to paying up front, expensive short-term lets for visitors or favours from friends of friends.

There's a long pause.

'I could move in. I have a guarantee.'

'Whoa…what?'

'I love this apartment. Why not?'

'Right, it's just…' I trail off. It's a pragmatic solution and I certainly don't want to leave, but what will Diego think of me living with another guy? The whole thing is complicated by the fact that we have never discussed the fact that Paco and I were together.

'*Vamos*, Jessy.' He shakes my arm, rattling me out of my head.

'Matt will be keen.'

'Are you keen?'

'Yes, of course,' I say, though I really don't know for sure.

On the walk over to Diego's apartment that night I run through what I'm going to say ten different ways, each translated and edited and discarded. None seem quite right. How much do I tell? Is this a terrible idea? Perhaps it's just all too much trouble.

I stand for a long time outside the door of the building. I keep reaching to dial his number. People in the street, seeing me loitering, start to give me suspicious looks. I push the buzzer.

'Diego, Jess.'

'Come up.'

The door buzzes open.

I kiss him hello, and then launch right in before we have even sat down.

'Diego, Paco came round to visit today. You remember him?' I say, trying to keep my Spanish steady, calm.

'*El pelado.*'

'Yeah, the bald guy. I met him in Cusco, remember?'

'Yes, and so...'

'Well, when Laura goes, he wants to move in.'

Diego looks at me, suddenly paying more attention.

'We need someone with a guarantee for the apartment, otherwise we have to pay six months in advance. I can't...' I lose track, watching his face.

'Fine, why are you asking me?'

'Well, it's just Argentines seem funny about girls and guys living together.'

'You're already living with that English guy.'

'Oh, right, yes.'

I take a deep breath and decide the moment has come to spell it out a little clearer.

'We're good friends now, that's all. But we travelled a lot together in Peru and then in Ecuador. We had a fling,' I say tentatively, leaving room for questions I'm not sure I know how to answer.

'It's fine, Jessy. No problem.'

'He has a girlfriend, you met her at the party, too. Cute girl, short hair, Maria,' I add.

'Jessy, it's cool.'

'Oh, okay.'

His reaction is so unexpected that I wander around, dumbfounded, for days. After seeing Julio and Laura's troubles and having many long conversations with Argentine friends and students, I had discovered that it is almost impossible for them to accept that the opposite sexes can be friends. They appear to believe, wholeheartedly, that men and women cannot be close without sexual desire taking them over like some temporary psychosis. I have seen my students shaking their heads and saying, 'it's impossible, and *dangerous.*' And if the friend is an ex-lover, then, *well no way in hell* could they be just friends. It was different in my other homes. As a student in New Zealand and then in Melbourne, I had lived with lots of male friends over the years.

Diego's lack of jealousy and dramatics impresses me. I see him in a new light, with all my cultural perceptions stripped away. He is just Diego, he is himself. He has this central calmness, this sureness, that gives him solidity. I feel steady too, in his presence. He seems to trust that if I love him then there is nothing to worry about. I do love him. He's right.

Paco makes arrangements to move in.

Laura leaves a couple of weeks before Christmas. I'm there on the street, hanging back, as she and Julio say their final goodbye. His face is pale and touched with regret, hers streaked with tears but numb with resignation.

The next morning, in that misty state of almost awake, I dream of them. They are standing back on the pavement where they met, only this time, both see their future far out in front of them. After an incredibly beautiful meeting of eyes and souls, they head off on their own paths again, in opposite directions. I mourn the loss of her, and I mourn for their loss, too.

When Paco moves in a couple of days later, I scrabble around in my head, analysing my motives. Was this really all about pragmatics? Am I sure it wasn't some kind of test I've set up for Diego, and for myself?

The first time I see Paco leave the bathroom in just a skimpy towel, torso still glistening with vaporising water, nothing leaps inside, nothing tingles. He looks comical rushing to his room, hand tightly holding onto the towel.

I'm going to be okay. I think Diego and I are going to be okay, too.

Seventeen

Christmas is here again, like the prize at the end of the steeplechase. Everyone looks exhausted but happy they made it alive, though it's possible to detect in subtle gestures who won and who limped to the line. I can see that most people treasure Christmas, the time with family and the summer beach holidays that typically come afterwards.

This will be my second Christmas in Argentina. I'm not sure where I'll be. The last one was spent with all the foreign strays I knew; we made a lovely hodgepodge family for the day. It was fun, the turkey was huge and the stuffing had just enough herbs to make it delightful.

Andrés tells me in our last class for the year that I should forget about having a romantic holiday away with Diego this year. I would have to wait a whole other year before that happened: six months is too soon.

'Really?' I respond.

'Yes.'

'The rules?'

'*Es lo que hay.*'

'Stop saying that. You know how much I hate it.'

He laughs. 'I'm telling you for own good, Jessy.'

I take a few days to build myself up to ask about holiday plans and Christmas. I try to mentally prepare for any outcome, but my hope, or perhaps my desire, is winning out.

'Diego, what's the plan for Christmas?' I ask lightly one night, over pizza.

'I'll be going home,' he says, looking uncomfortable.

'Family dinner, right?'

I can't help calculating when I was last home for Christmas. Four years, or is it more?

'Yes.'

'Oh, great and…' I let the question dangle. There is silence.

'Sorry, Jess, it's too soon.'

I put my piece of pizza down, appetite gone, and say, 'Too soon to meet your family?'

'A little, yes.' His eyes are averted. He puts his pizza down, too.

'It's been six months. And I don't have anyone left here to celebrate with,' I say, in a voice that's too high, and doesn't sound like mine.

'I know, sorry. Next year, I promise,' he says, in a reassuring tone, while giving me a shoulder squeeze.

I can't help thinking that maybe he doesn't think I'll be around then.

He sees my face and says, 'You'd feel very uncomfortable there. My family's big. Everyone would check you out.'

'Okay,' I say, quietly. Something pinches in my chest. I don't ask about a summer holiday together.

Matt will be having Christmas dinner with his girlfriend's family, Laura and Bree have gone. All the strays from last year have gone home, too. Argentine friends will be with their families.

So, what now?

The following day I wander around my flat in a daze. It makes me feel a little sick to think of being alone on Christmas Day. I'm used to having Christmas away from New Zealand with random collections of friends, or housemates in Melbourne who also live far from home, but I've never had only me for company.

Paco bursts in the door, loaded up with bags and cameras from his new job in a film production company. It's hot out and beads of sweat are breaking across his forehead.

I unburden him.

He shakes his shoulders in relief.

'Cold drink?'

'*Por favor*,' he says, slumping down on the sofa.

When he finishes the last drop of water I've just handed him, he looks at me. 'Are you okay?' he says, his eyes screwing up in concern.

My face is so easily read.

'Diego's going home for Christmas. He thinks it's too soon for me to meet his family. Maybe he's right.'

'Come home with me, then,' he says.

I see he means it. 'Are you sure it's okay?'

'Of course, Jessy, you know my parents practically think of you as family! Anyway, you won't be the only extra. Billy's coming, too.'

Billy is an American friend of Paco's who is making Buenos Aires home, with the strong motivating factor of a stunning tango-star girlfriend.

'So he's not invited to his girlfriend's for Christmas dinner either?'

'Guess not. Pepe and Mum will be delighted to see you.'

I wonder why I hadn't thought of this option. Was I so sure Diego would ask me?

'Me too, it's been too long since I saw them.'

'*Listo*, done.'

'Thank you, Paco.' Once again, he has provided me with the sense of home I needed. I feel relief flooding through me.

'*De nada.*' He grins.

Later, in Diego's apartment, I tell him the news. 'All's good. I have somewhere to go for Christmas,' I say, tone upbeat.

'That's great, Jess. Where?'

'Paco invited me to have dinner with his family. Do you remember, I told you about Pepe and his mum, the artist.'

'Oh good,' he says, sounding nonplussed. 'I didn't want you to be alone.'

I'm not sure if I'm relieved or annoyed by his reaction.

'Next year, I promise you,' he says, hugging me.

I give in to it, a little stiff, ice at the edges of the hug.

Over the next few days I make my peace with our separate plans, and then I find myself getting excited about dinner on the night of Christmas Eve, *Noche Buena*, when Argentines celebrate Christmas. My heart swells at the thought of seeing Pepe and Monica again, and I can almost smell the *asado* sizzling. It's an aroma that's now infused with something more than the pleasure of eating good simple food. It's become the smell of family, of loud and passionate talking and of smiling faces.

The welcome I imagine as I'm sitting on the subway, chatting with Paco and Billy on our way over to Paco's grandmother's house, is given with gusto.

'Jessssy,' says Pepe, as he bowls over to the door and scoops me up in a hug.

'Pepeee,' I return. I can't reach around his back. My head rests on his shoulder.

Then Monica kisses me and hugs me tight, and then Paco gives me a spontaneous hug, as does Billy.

'This is *mi Abu*,' says Paco, helping his grandmother over.

She's frail, at ninety, but I see a bright light in her face and sharp awareness in her eyes. I hug her carefully; she squeezes me tight. Billy gets the same treatment from everyone. I have to bite my lip to stop the waterfall of tears.

We are six in total: Pepe, Monica, Pepe's mother, Paco, Billy and me. It's a tight fit in the small living room of his grandmother's house, but big enough for six human spirits to interlace around a pile of steaming crusty red meat, salad and bread, with plenty of Malbec to wash it down.

Later, soft tears trickle down my face while we watch Paco's *Abu* play haunting tunes on her old piano—her tears give mine freedom to be. It's mesmerising to see her weathered hands move with such grace over the keys, as if they had minds of their own and memories to share. She sings a little too, in a voice ragged with age but honey sweet. I can't catch all the words, but they are mournful and intense. Tango, for her tango-loving guest. Billy is thrilled.

'I feel this might be my last Christmas,' she confides in me later that night.

I lean in close and softly squeeze her hand. Her skin is almost translucent but flecked with sunspots. It's softer than I imagined it would be. I watch her as she looks around the room, taking in her family, as if recording a mental film of them to take with her.

My mobile rings at midnight.

'*Hola, mi amor*,' Diego says warmly, a whiff of guilt at the edges of the tone.

'*Hola*,' I return.

'Is everything alright there?'

'Yes, we're having a lovely time. Paco's grandmother has been playing the piano. We had an *asado*, of course,' I say in a steady voice.

'Oh, okay.'

'And you, your family?'

'Great, great…' He fades out.

'Diego?'

'Yes. Cookie, I wish I had invited you. I feel so stupid.' The words gush out, running into each other.

'It's fine—'

He cuts me off. 'They really want to meet you and I want them to meet you, too. I love you and I want you to come home with me for New Year's Eve.'

'What? Slow down.'

'I want you to meet them for New Year's dinner. Please come.'

'Yes, of course I'll come.'

I'm bewildered by his release of emotion, by so many words; usually he maintains such calm control. Then I become elated, and then terrified. I wanted this, but now I will actually have to meet them all. It's daunting.

'Okay, great. Then I want to take you to the beach. Just us. What do you think?'

'I'd love to.' My heart leaps.

'*Te amo*, Jess,' he says, the words swelled with emotion.

'*Te amo, también*,' I say. My voice sounds husky.

I am distracted by my thoughts for the rest of the night. I can't help wondering if I'm ready. I'm going to be laid bare to scrutiny and judgment by all the people who love Diego. What will they make of this strange foreign girl, some years older than him, who can't speak Spanish properly? I'm sure they must already be asking themselves: what is she doing here?

I force myself back to the moment and smile at Paco's grandmother, at Pepe. Then I remind myself that this is what I wanted. I have to be brave.

A week later we drive to Diego's childhood hometown, Pergamino. It takes three hours and requires some hair-raising passing of slow-moving trucks, lined up tailgate to bumper. There are no passing lanes.

When we arrive, his parents are waiting just inside the front door to welcome us. They look shell-shocked when they see me. I feel them survey me up and down, down and up, their gaze eventually settling on my face.

'This is Jessica,' says Diego, pressing me forward with a hand in the centre of my back.

I lean in for a kiss and a hug. I receive a handshake from his father and a light cheek peck from his mother, whose arms stay by her side.

They don't like me.

Fears rises and constricts my throat. '*Hola*,' comes out choked.

'Welcome, welcome,' they say, ushering us inside.

In the privacy of Diego's childhood room, filled with basketball trophies, magazines and the odd teddy bear, my anxiety surges as I fight with my wild mop of hair, trying vainly to tame it. If I can get it right, somehow everything will be okay.

Diego takes me in his arms and says, 'They will love you, just be yourself.'

'They didn't hug me.' I feel pathetic once the words have slipped out.

'Oh, Jess. That doesn't mean anything. People outside of Buenos Aires are a little cooler when they first meet someone. Give it time. You will get hugged, don't worry.'

His mum seems shy; her eyes flick up and then away when she talks softly to me. Later I hear her talking with Diego and she breaks into a schoolgirl giggle. It makes me smile. She's the recently retired headmistress of a small primary school, but I can't see it: my images of headmistresses are of tough, stiff women and she doesn't fit. As I watch her make preparations for the evening ahead, something about her reminds me of my grandmother. She's always on the move, quietly attending people and making sure everyone is comfortable, but she's busy in a calm way. Unlike my own mother, whose caring activity is always more whirlwind than soft breeze. I can see straight away that Diego inherited his steady, thoughtful core from her.

His father is different. I sense clusters of thoughts competing with each other behind his pale blue eyes. He wanders around, slightly on the fringes, almost always with a *mate* gourd for drinking the ubiquitous hot beverage in his hand, as if it's a protective goblet against all the badness in the world.

When we arrive at Diego's aunt's weekend house, where the family dinner is taking place, I see two long tables joined together. There are people and kids everywhere. When they spot me, they stop, look over, pause and then come over en masse to welcome me.

My back is crushed by two enormous hugs from the giant basketball-playing twins, Diego's cousins whom I met the same night I met him, in Club 69. Then I receive about twenty more warm and curious welcomes from his mother's four sisters and their families, Diego's sister and her boyfriend, and his brother.

As with every family, there are some crazy-beautiful characters. I find myself drawn to his artist uncle—father of the twins—who paints all night and sleeps all day. He seems to be revelling in each moment, while grinning like a naughty boy. He looks like a giant chipmunk: narrow forehead, huge flushed cheeks and big intense eyes.

'I'm writing a book,' he tells me.

'Great, what's it about?' I say, practicing my tipsy Spanish; the words sticking on my lips.

'It's a mystery fiction.' He leans in to me and whispers, 'But some of these guys are in it.'

Diego tells me later that night that, over the years he's been writing the book, his uncle has been killing off his *characters* in some pretty bizarre and blood-curdling ways. It has become a family joke to try to guess who will be next and how they'll go out. Once I know this, I think I can see Uncle Jorge eyeing me up, wriggling me into the tale. I wonder if I will be around long enough to kill off.

The table keeps being topped up with bread, salad, wine, soft drinks and meat, the biggest pile I have ever seen. If there was suddenly a shortage of cows, I'm not sure Argentines would know what to do for a family gathering. It seems almost sacrilegious to eat anything other than perfectly grilled steak.

I notice I'm the only younger woman eating red meat. Diego's cousins and sister avoid it, picking instead at small pieces of chicken and mounds of salty salad. It seems dieting is a year-round affair for some, without any days off for good behaviour.

When my stomach can take no more, my plate is piled high with criss-crossed bones, glistening with fat. The guys are impressed. 'Wow, she can eat, that girl,' says one uncle.

'And drink, too,' I overhear his cousin say to Diego. I look around. I do seem to be the only woman drinking and I've drunk a little more wine than I intended to, trying to smother my nerves. Damn. They must think I'm a glutton and a drunk. I push the thought away and concentrate on the warmth I can feel all around me. As we all watch the fireworks, spraying out over the city, at midnight, I am as happy as I've been in years.

When, the following day, back in Buenos Aires, Diego shows me the photos of the dinner, I fill up with hope. I'm smiling a big expressive smile with my whole heart in it. Is it possible the other people in the photo already feel like family? Or am I romanticising? There is, of course, a yearning for my people, too. I miss them, and what I wish we could be but fear we might never manage.

On New Year's Day I get short, warm emails from Jonny and Henry, responding to my short-story length one. Dad rings but the line is bad and it cuts out before I can tell him how happy I am, and how I wish we could see each other soon. Eddie writes that he's coming to visit again in a month. It's a great present for the New Year. Even better is the surprise at the end of his rambling mail, where I find some heartfelt words from Mum that set the seal on my happiness.

> Dearest Biba,
> I'm sad about the special parcel. Everything always seems to go to "custard" with us. The clothes were special, but the worse thing was losing those special photos. I wrote a very long letter and I can't start again here. I just wanted you to know how much I love and admire you for the incredible qualities you have. I wish I could turn back the clock on a lot of things and your childhood had been happy. Neither of us were parents who made you feel secure and good about yourself.
> The last years have been hard. I hope things improve and I am so happy for you knowing you have someone who loves you and can show you that.
> Hug to you and Diego.
> Love, Mum xxx

A few days after the New Year's Eve party, Diego and I arrive at the coast, some four hours away from Buenos Aires. We spend the afternoon in the famous and extremely overcrowded city of Mar del Plata. It's nearly impossible to claim even a square metre of sand to sit on or cold Atlantic sea to swim in.

'It's insanely crowded. Why are there so many people here?' I ask, exasperated and trying not to dwell on all the great stretches of nearly empty sand and sea that I have grown up with.

'Nearly everyone takes their holidays either in the first two weeks or the second two weeks of January.'

'Why would they want to do that?'

'It's just the custom, and they want to go where the action is. I have to take holidays in January because my job expects me to go now.'

'I don't get it. People complain all year long about queuing and too many people in the city, and then they all go to the beach at the same time, to queues and too many people.'

'They like it,' he says simply.

'What about December, March?'

'Yes, some people go then, and it's cheaper.'

I shake my head.

'We're crazy,' he says, shrugging.

At sunset we drive down narrow streets of sand and packed-dirt into a small beachside village called Mar Azul, nestled among pine trees and sand dunes. Outside, it's quiet. I hear a faint wind through pine needles, but no voices.

'This is better.'

'I thought this would be more your thing.'

He picks me up and swings me around. 'Our first holiday together,' he says, smiling widely.

I grin back at him. 'Where are we staying?'

'There it is,' he says, pointing, his face bashful.

I look round and spot the tiniest log house I have ever seen. It measures about three metres by three and a half metres, has a small wooden door and one tiny window. It's a perfect doll-like construction, dwarfed by the tall pines that reach up like spines on a hedgehog.

'Sorry, I booked late. This is all I could find.'

'I love it.'

The built-in *parrilla* on a small deck is almost as big as the house (Argentine priorities—so long as you can grill enough meat for twenty, all's right with the world).

While I unpack, Diego drives to the store to buy supplies. He returns with a massive grin, arms weighed down with bulging plastic bags.

'I'm cooking tonight,' he says, while extracting a large chicken from one bag. He slams it down on the small wooden bench and starts enthusiastically raining salt and lemon juice on it. I open the wine, find the plastic cups we brought and fill two. With the chicken vigorously *condimented*, he attacks the task of lighting the *parrilla*. The wood, pine cones and coals are damp, but he patiently persists, in an almost trance-like state, distracted by nothing.

I stand and watch as he turns into that man that men become, in the presence of fire. His eyes glaze over, wild, fixated on the bursts of flame. It's both sexy and scary. He becomes territorial. 'Get away, Jess, you'll ruin it,' he says, shooing me off when I move in to help.

Just as the chicken starts to sizzle and scent the air with fat, cold sharp drops of rain begin to fall from the now pitch-black sky. Instead of panicking, Diego calmly goes in search of a way to save our meal. He drags something from under the house. I see he has a square of sheet metal held carefully in his hands. Its sharp edges are begging to maim fingers. He constructs a roof with it to protect the chicken and live coals. Exactly half a minute after he finishes, the sky opens and spills its load on us. We huddle together inside our pixie house, soaked, but grinning happily about our rescued meal.

Squashed together around a thin wooden bench on two stools made from tree trunks, we devour our dinner with wordless enjoyment. It's the best barbecued chicken I have ever tasted, grilled to perfection and lightly steamed for tenderness.

As we're picking over the remains I say quietly, 'I'm lucky I found you.'

'What?' he asks, chicken grease shining at his lips.

'Nothing. Thank you.'

I look at him. *Is he the one?* Have I finally found him, having waited for what felt like such a long time, and travelled half-way across the globe? Was the psychic right, all those years ago? Love at thirty-two, thirty-three, she said. I was thirty-three when we met.

Later that night, as we lie quietly in spoons, there is no sensation of a limit of skin, of two bodies—of him and me. In its place is a buzzing emotion; a pure moment of melting into each other, content and secure. We breathe in time and our moist breath mingles together in the air around us.

I think, *this is what a calm spirit feels like.*

As I drift into dreams, I remember (from two years of high-school

Latin classes) that the word spirit comes from *spiritus*, which means breath, breathing, life. Breath, the inhaling of oxygen, feeds us, as it feeds fire. Breath is spirit and spirit is breath. It exists everywhere and in everything. I sleep so profoundly, even though dampness seeps up from the cabin floor, that no dreams, no fears, can reach me.

In February Eddie blows back into my life, all smiles and pure energy. He plans to stay for two months and start a small business exporting beautiful Argentine leather bags to New Zealand. He sleeps on the couch in the living room at first and then progressively claims my room as I spend more time at Diego's apartment. It seems that the more Diego and I are together, the less time we want to be apart. It's easy; we hardly ever fight, it's as if we instinctively know each other's dance. Our dances are different in many ways but they both work with the same music, they share a rhythm.

Eddie nicknames Diego 'Diggers', and seems to get extra enjoyment from finding and pushing his buttons. Diego mostly tolerates it, but sometimes he snaps. It's like watching a big, old dog growl at a restless, tail-biting puppy.

Their conversations consist of Diego teaching Eddie *lunfardo, Porteño* slang.

'*Che, boludo, que lindo culo.* Hey, idiot (affectionate), what a nice ass,' I hear Eddie say, while he gestures suggestively towards Diego's backside.

Diego shakes his head.

'Sorry,' I say to him.

'Really, it's okay. I'm getting used to it.'

I begin to suspect, judging by his reactions over the next week or so, that he actually enjoys the baiting and antics. Eddie can be very funny, and he's naturally appealing. It's hard not to love him. By the end of his stay they have become firm friends and it's lovely to see them and Paco and Maria laughing together in the small apartment, sixteen floors closer to the stars.

They are my family.

Eighteen

THREE MONTHS LATER Diego and I decide to move in to our own place. When Eddie left, Billy practically moved into my room, as I was hardly ever there. But Diego's small flat is getting crowded. His brother, Pedro, has an almost live-in girlfriend, too. It makes sense to have a fresh start together in a place of our own. We're in love, it's what you do: move forward together. Happily for us, it's now at the same pace.

After some weeks of increasingly restless looking we stumble upon a small, recently renovated second-floor apartment at the back of a seventy-year-old building in Palermo. The flat woos us with high ceilings, wooden sash windows, black and white tiles in the kitchen and fresh paint job.

'I love it,' I say, jumping up and down like a kid.

'Calm down. Don't look so keen. I want to bargain the rent down a little,' Diego whispers to me.

'Okay, okay, but it's so cute,' I say, trying to hold back the excitement.

Seduced, with glowing eyes, we sign the contract that day. They don't move on the rent.

'Our first home,' says Diego on the day we move in. Then he picks me up and swings me around near the entrance to the living room. One foot clips the wall, hard.

'Oh, shit,' I screech.

'Sorry, sorry.'

He laughs at me, hopping on one foot. I shoot him a nasty look before I break into laughter, too. Then I wonder if it's a bad sign.

On our first night in the new place, surrounded by boxes and piles of clothes and kitchen things, we celebrate, wildly and freely, our new home with a soggy pizza, a bottle of wine, three kinds of ice cream and a dance in the living room. Then we jump into our freshly made up bed and cuddle in close together, too exhausted to do anything else.

I drift off to sleep so content that no thoughts enter my head; it's the sleep of a person at peace, with herself, and the world.

We wake up to the sounds of hammering.

Ignoring the building under construction right next door wasn't a smart thing to do when we signed on the line.

It's not long before we discover that our new home has many other flaws. I blame myself for being blinded by its apparent sweetness and for refusing to really see the dank and grubby entrance hall to the building, the lack of light and the view of a concrete wall. Not even the million buses that grind and puff their way past the front door every minute made an impact on my momentum. Perhaps, basking in the initial glow, I had once again succumbed to over-reaching-hope syndrome. Diego had been less certain. I feel bad for dragging him into the false glow.

After a short period of valiantly glossing over the inconveniences, the noise starts to play twister with our nerves. We can never escape it. We wake to bone-rattling pounding, insistent tapping and neuron-searing drilling sounds every day, even Saturdays. With the noise come shaking fits, some so hard that gaping cracks zigzag their way across the ceiling and down the walls. When one wound is fixed (after complaints, inspections and wrangling with contractors and the landlord) another tears into our lives. Paint peels and flakes, then mould spots spring up like anxiety-induced eczema all over the house and flourish in the humidity of our closet, ruining clothes. It's almost funny, but not quite. I thought my days of surviving bad houses were over.

Then, just to make our life even more interesting, a *travesti* prostitute moves in right under us. The hours of the day are marked by the comings and goings of a steady trickle of shady or demure looking men. At night, strange computer beeps, ringing phones and odd noises intrigue us. We come to the conclusion he has his own live website.

It takes six months for the building next door to go up and the reverberating, clamouring noises to halt. Then our intriguing downstairs neighbour brings home a noisy Doberman puppy; and then the gas line cracks. Everything important is gas: the hot water, heating and the stove. Hot, red-skin hot, showers are a major passion of mine and I love to cook. It's pretty devastating news and my mind fills with painful imaginings of endless dinners of sandwiches and cleaning intimate parts with humid flannels.

'Diego, how long will it take to get the gas back on?'

'Probably a couple of weeks,' he answers, calm enough.

'A couple of weeks? Noooo,' I moan.

'*Qué sé yo, quizás más*. What do I know, maybe more,' he says, with a typically Argentine resigned shoulder shrug.

A week turns into a month. No one wants to pay for fixing the gas lines, which are rotten throughout the entire building. Half the inhabitants haven't been paying their building expenses and the other half are fighting with them as, understandably, they don't want to pay for the whole job. It's a *quilombo* of meetings and heated *Argy Bargies* that echo throughout the building on a regular basis. While the arguing continues, everyone just goes without. Passionate, stubborn and tight is a bad combination for getting things done.

Three whole months later, the gasman turns our gas back on.

I realise our little home is like a speck of Argentina in a Petri dish. The building is a reflection of the crumbling infrastructure, the confusion and avoidance of responsibility, the long arguments that often don't lead to a solution and the stress of just trying to live well enough. It's a test, and I wonder if I'm up for it.

Then something strikes me: perhaps it's these constant tests and crises that keep people together. Perhaps it's easier to drift apart if you don't have to be roped together to survive, if you don't have to share your pain and your small victories.

Living through those months without gas has brought Diego and me even closer together. His steadiness and my willingness to adapt have made the experience almost fun. We are grateful to the Argentine friends that offered kitchens and showers, and to the landlord who lent us an electric element so we could at least heat a pan. It is amazing what you can cook with one element and some imagination.

It's a crazy home but I accept it as it is, laugh and cry with those around me and live in the moment like there's no tomorrow, because a tomorrow like today is never certain in Argentina.

I'm proud of the way I've learned to be flexible, but I'm still a steady Kiwi at heart.

In January the following year, when we've been living together for seven months, I reach out for more stability.

Sitting on the couch with our limbs lazily intertwined one seemingly ordinary day, I start a conversation. I have practiced it and all its possible deviations, first in English and then in Spanish.

'Diego, um, I want to feel more secure here… so I think I need a DNI to work properly, to come and go from the country without problems.' (A DNI, *documento national de identidad*, is the Argentine national identity document.)

'Okay, that sounds fine.' He has no idea what's coming.

'I'm tired of going to Uruguay all the time.'

'It is a pain. So…?'

'I've researched it and the only way, well, the easiest way, is if we get married.' Watching his face carefully, I continue before he can speak. 'I mean, just the registry office. Just for the papers… I don't really believe in marriage.' I run out of stream and then I wonder if I have made a mistake.

'Ah, get married, wow. I don't know.' His eyes and mouth are open wide.

'We don't even have to tell anyone except close family. I don't need a party or anything, no church, just a quiet thing so I can feel more secure. So I can look for proper work. It's not to trap you or anything.' I feel a flush rise: sometimes words slip out.

I see him thinking through his answer.

I hold my breath.

'I love you very much, Jessy. And I want us to be together, to have a future—children one day. But marriage. I'm uncomfortable about marriage and weddings. I want to be with you but I don't need a piece of paper, or a big show.'

'I don't want a show either, but I do need a piece of paper. I'm so temporary here. I want to feel more permanent. This is not my country. I don't have a work visa, or a tax number.'

'You don't need those here,' he says, looking at me quizzically.

'I know no one really cares, but I do. I'm a Kiwi. I want to be legal and to do the right thing.'

He laughs at my earnest expression and then says, 'You're definitely in the wrong country.'

'I'm being serious. I love you and I want to stay here.'

He grabs both my arms and shakes me a little, while staring into my eyes. 'Okay, Cookie, let's do it.'

That night I'm ecstatic but being as I am incapable of evading self-doubt for long, the following day I start to worry about my motivations for the proposal. I need to discuss them with Dave. I email him, outlining in great detail all the reasons for wanting a DNI. I tell him it would give me more options and security, explain that I had recently lost the opportunity to work in an international school teaching psychology, because of my visa situation. Was it valid to ask Diego, though? Are my reasons just superficial excuses covering up a deeper need? Do I want to hold him tighter, make it harder for him to leave? Is this insecurity, dangerous grabbing? Dave, some advice please.

He writes back.

Oh Jessica, Jessica.

Yes the reasons are valid enough, but perhaps the timing is a little fast. Less than two years, right? But it's done now. And yes, perhaps there is some insecurity there. Sometimes we can't escape the underlying motives for our actions. From all you have said about him, I doubt he would sign up for something he really didn't want.

Are you sure you want to be with him? That's my question.

Dave

Yes, more than anything.

Once the ball is in motion, there is no stopping it. We book an appointment at the *registro civil* in March and tell our bewildered families and some select friends about our plans. At first we both attempt to downplay the significance of the event, but that just confuses the people close to us, who in turn don't know how to react.

'Is it real, or is it like a green card thing?' asks my dad.

'Um, real, but… it's for the DNI, so I can work and stay here, but yes it's real. We love each other very much. We plan to be together, have kids one day.'

'Oh. So should we come over?'

'No, no, that's not necessary. We'll do something in New Zealand at some point. I'll let you know.'

'Well, okay. So you're staying there, then?'

'Yeah, I guess I am.'

I feel flushed, confused. What are we doing? What does it mean?

I have never dreamed of a white wedding; in fact as a young girl I had nightmares about the big dress, the high heels and everyone staring at me. I didn't understand the other girls who chatted on and on about what their dress would look like and the ring and the perfect man. Living with a group of vegetarian feminists at university pushed me even further away from the idea. Some of the relationships I most admired and aspired to have been the unmarried ones. A wise friend and colleague from Melbourne once said to me about his relationship of many years, 'We choose to be together every day. We work hard to keep loving each other. We don't need to be married.' His words stayed with me.

In the end, though, despite the fact that I'm not religious and I don't believe love needs a contract, I do believe in a lifelong bond, and in having a firm base for a family. Marriage is one way to provide those things. I also realise, to my surprise, that I do have dreams for my wedding day: dreams of an uncomplicated ceremony, surrounded by closest friends and family, a ceremony that declares mine and Diego's love to those we love. Simple, connected somehow to nature, perhaps barefoot on a beach, or standing on a green hill, with wind blowing out wisps of hair. There would be heartfelt poetry and a passionate kiss, many hugs, and the joining of two families.

The ten-minute meeting with a registrar, a simple *tramite* (the Argentine word for an admin task that typically revolves around endless paperwork) is very different from that dream.

'So, basically it's going to be a *tramite*?' says Paco when I tell him.

'Well, kind of,' I say.

'But you are getting married?'

'Yes.'

'Good for you. You seem very happy with Diggers.'

'I am. Don't tell anyone else, we're kind of keeping it quiet.'

'Why?'

'Because we don't want to make a big deal of it. Most of Diego's family don't know.'

'Oh.' I can see that he is a bit baffled. Increasingly, so am I.

As the date pushes closer we realise that getting married means a great deal more to both of us than simply signing some paperwork so I can get my legal status sorted. We start to embrace the significance more fully. Diego surprises me one night with an exotic thick silver ring, full of little randomly cut pieces of a dark-green semi-precious stone, neatly fitted together like a puzzle. It's a perfect match with my earthy Kiwi-girl no-fuss style (plus I had told him I didn't want or need a gold ring or diamonds, or anything expensive). I find it hidden in a sushi roll. Not an overly demonstrative display of love, but I have learned that isn't his way. I am moved to tears as I suck off the rice grains and slip it on.

'I love you, Jess,' he says simply. His eyes shine.

'I love you, too. Are you sure about this, though? We can wait,' I say, looking into his eyes.

He holds my gaze. 'I've told my family now. Anyway, I want to.'

Me too. The light I see in his eyes and the glow I feel in mine brings me *home*.

Our wedding day may be turning into something much more than a *tramite* for us, but there's still plenty of paperwork to be done. Before the marriage ceremony, the parties involved are obligated to have a blood test.

At 6.00 in the morning, ten days or so before our date with the registrar, we find ourselves waiting in a massive queue of other couples with long faces, in the corridors of the indicated public hospital of our administrative zone. The public hospital is in a sad state; grubby water-marked walls give an impression of decay, the rows of seats are spilling their foam through tears and there are pieces of paper Sellotaped haphazardly to the doors and walls with handwritten information on where to go and what room is behind the door. It's full to bursting even at this hour. Some of the mothers holding infants and small children look as if they have been waiting all night to be seen, their faces set in resignation while their hands grasp *mates* and their downturned mouths rhythmically sip the strong brew to help the minutes go by. It's not a place I would want to be if my children were sick. Nausea rises and then mixes with relief. I'm immensely thankful I now have private medical insurance. Most of the time, I reside in a whole other world to these women.

After what feels like an interminable wait those of us queuing to do the blood test are separated into two lines, male and female. When it's my turn, an extremely sour-faced rotund nurse ushers me into a cubicle, whips the ragged blue curtain across, grabs my arm and then punctures it with a needle. She sucks out a vial of blood, roughly plasters a cotton patch onto my arm and then directs me out the door with a brisk wave. (A nasty blue, green and yellow bruise marks my arm for the next two weeks.)

'Why do they take our blood?' I ask Diego afterwards.

'I don't know. It's a regulation.'

'What are they testing for?'

'Not sure.'

'Don't you care? What do they do with the results?'

'I guess they tell us if it's all okay.'

'That's totally crazy. We don't have to have a blood test to get married in New Zealand. I've never heard of it before.'

'It's done now. What does it matter?'

It matters to me. I search the web for information. I can't find any. I ask my students. No one seems to know why it's a legal requirement to have a blood test before you can marry in Argentina, and even more disturbing, they don't seem to care. Someone tells me it's a test to determine whether there might be problems of incompatibility if the couple have children. Another tells me it a test for transmittable diseases—okay, like what? I'm sorry, I want to say, but the government is sampling your blood, testing it, recording the results, and you don't even wonder why? In any case, I know what the answer would be: we have other things to worry about. Argentines are passionate people, they fight for their rights, but sometimes they just shrug things off that in other countries would never slip by without being at least questioned. It both amuses and baffles me: a sensation I'm beginning to know well.

The results came a week later. There's no specific information as to what was or wasn't found but we passed. We can get married.

Barbaro, great.

The date is coming up fast and I can't find anything I want to wear; everything is too small, too prissy or too normal. Then Mum comes to my rescue. I see a lovely cream dress on her website and ring her to ask if I can have it.

'Of course, darling.' I can hear the smile in her voice.

'Thanks, Mum. It's so beautiful and it will mean a lot to wear one of your wonderful creations.'

'How do I get it to you? I couldn't bear a repeat of the last package.'

'No, me neither.' I shudder at the memory. 'I have a new Kiwi friend, Emily, who's over there now and can bring it with her when she comes back.'

'Oh, nice to have a fellow Kiwi around.'

'She's great. I met her a few months ago at an afternoon tea organised by the New Zealand ambassador. You would love her. Very elegant, smart. I told her about your clothes.'

'Which one, Emily or the ambassador?'

'Oh, Lucy, the ambassador, but Emily is cool, too: no messing around, from Taranaki. She's only twenty-six but she's practically running a company here.'

'Wow.'

'I know. Gotta go, Mum. Thank you for the dress.'

'My pleasure. Will it get there in time?'

'Yep, with two days to spare. It looks as if it should fit, don't you think?'

'It's a loose cut, so yes, I'm sure it will.' She pauses and I wait. 'You'll look so beautiful.'

When I hang up I am full to bursting with joy.

Two weeks later when Emily pulls out a neatly wrapped package from her suitcase I am like a little girl. The urge to rip it open conflicts with a desire to carefully savour its contents. I manage something in between. I hold the dress out in front of me and it unravels in a cascade of raw silk and creamy pure cotton. It's an earthy, whimsical, pinafore-shaped cotton dress, with big mother of pearl buttons down the front and a large pouch for treasures hanging from a strap off the hip. A silk underskirt peeps out cheekily from underneath, in asymmetrical waves. A lump forms in my throat.

I'm so grateful, in a way that feels very real.

I've always had trouble feeling as grateful as I know I should, especially when it comes to my mother. Over the years she has made some grand gestures but I've always felt numbed by them. They didn't make me happy, even when I wanted them to. I think that perhaps I didn't feel it because I was like a kid who gets given an extravagant flashy toy but would much prefer to play with the box it came in, to make it into a play house with a window and a door, and serve tea to mum and dad. I think I was resentful of the big presents because I always wanted a hundred tiny moments in their place.

'There are some other things,' says Emily, pulling out two boxes from another bag.

I open the first one. It contains a thick bracelet of fine woven silver metal with a large flat green stone enmeshed in it.

'Wow, it's stunning,' I gasp.

'Your mum has good taste.'

'Always.'

It's a perfect match to my ring.

Then I open the other box. Inside, nested in tissue, is a simple *pounamu*, a *Toki*-shaped pendant. I had asked Eddie to buy it for me, as a gift for Diego. The *Toki* design represents power and good character. When given and received with love, the Māori people believe the pendant takes on part of the spirit of those who handle it and wear it, allowing it to become a spiritual link between people over time and distance (so Eddie becomes present, too). It's a perfect gift for a special day celebrating the joining of two people's lives. It's my ring to him.

When Diego opens the little box later that night, he shudders. I place the pendant around his neck and he reaches for it and holds it for a long minute, as if in prayer. He has seen how important my *pounamu* is to me, and he understands without words the significance of my gift.

I too get shaky, seeing it resting on his chest, warmed by the touch of his skin: a tiny piece of my land—*Aotearoa*, land of the long white cloud—and of me, close to him.

The night before the big day, Emily and some Argentine and foreign girlfriends organise a small party. There is pink champagne, nibbles of thin sliced steak, sundried tomatoes and rocket on toast, marinated fish treats and tiny fruit desserts. I spend the night at Emily's apartment, snugly wrapped in thousand-or-so thread Egyptian cotton sheets.

In the morning she wakes me with Colombian coffee and French toast.

'Hurry, I have a treat for you before your nuptials,' she says, smiling.

After a brisk drive, she marches me into the beauty salon of a spunky gay friend of hers.

'Oh, so this is what you have in store for me...' I try to sound sceptical, but actually, I'm touched.

'It's a special day. You have to have professional hair and make-up. Plus, have you seen your nails lately?'

I peer down at my hands. She may have a point.

When the whirlwind of activity terminates, my lion's hair has been tamed into silky tresses, my face smoothed and features lined subtly but beautifully, and my nails have been French manicured into neat, white-tipped marvels. Something new for them and me.

So this is the day I get married, 30 March. It has a nice ring to it.

I see Diego already waiting outside the registry office when we pull up. We eye each other nervously as if it's a second date and we're terrified and excited about the possibilities. Rain is tumbling from the sky. The gutters have become a stream with a regatta of discarded wrapper-boats floating by. Everyone is smiling despite being drenched from head to foot—baptised by the universe. Once safely out of the rain, we huddle in our intimate group, waiting our turn. We are nine: Diego's mother, father, brother, sister and her partner. I have my token Kiwi, Emily, as one witness and Diego brings his friend Gabriel as the other.

As we enter the room, the celebrant stands up from behind her wooden desk. She asks Diego and me to stand in front of her. We move to do so and I try to reach Diego's hand but he's looking nervously in front of him, hands pressed into his side. She commences a short official speech. I only hear a few words as I'm floating a few inches out of my skin. Diego still looks petrified. I reach for his hand again; it's wet and cold from the rain. He looks at me, and we both relax.

'Would anyone like to say something?' asks the celebrant when she finishes.

I look neurotically around, wondering if this is the moment when someone says, 'Stop this is a charade!'

Diego's father stands up.

Diego grips my hand harder.

'I'm very happy to be here today to witness this ceremony. You both look very happy and it's the start of a whole new stage in your lives,' he says, and then he looks right at me and continues with visible emotion.

'Jessica, I consider you to be another daughter of mine. I'm proud of you.'

My legs lose energy and my head swims. His words set forth a flurry of emotions—pride, happiness, surprise and sadness, too. I have never heard words like those before.

Soft lips bring me back. Diego's kiss is warm, sweet and brief. I laugh at him as he goes pink, and looks sideways at his family.

Once the registry ledger and our bright red marriage booklet are signed, a series of arms squeeze me tight and welcome me officially into the family. As we make our way out the door, past the couple waiting to go in, a shower of rice and rain pummels us.

Later, in a popular restaurant in Palermo, we start the celebration with a few bottles of classic Malbec and empanadas. We order meat. I watch it cooking on the huge *parrillas* that line one side of the restaurant.

Fire, food and family, and perhaps a little faith, too.

As we laugh and eat and share stories, I start to miss the presence of my caustically funny brothers, and my parents. I wish I hadn't cast the whole event as mere paperwork. I'm sad they are missing around the table. I want them to see my wide smile and to meet this special person I hope to have around for a long time.

When I speak to Dad later, I promise to make it home soon. 'I missed having you guys here,' I say.

'Well, we did…'

'I know. I don't want to leave it too long before we celebrate in New Zealand.'

'Christmas?'

'Yes, if we can get there.'

'Let me know what you would like to do. I'm sure Cheryl could put something together. I'm no good with that stuff.'

'That would be great.'

'Christmas, then,' he says.

'Christmas. Love you.'

'Yeah, okay. Bye.'

After dinner, we go dancing with friends. In the flow of the night a joyful stream of people passes us, wishing us well. Paco slaps Diego on the back and then hugs him. I can't help smiling, watching the two of them together.

Some people ask how we met. When we tell them it was in Club 69, they laugh and shake their heads; they say 'how amazing that you found each other there.' I wonder if it really is such a strange place to meet your pair. I met all my loves that way. I saw Daniel's soul when he danced, alone, full of a sweet light, full of grace. It was the pure version of him, no construction, no care of the other; he was just being, moving, naked and honest. It was the same with Paco the night I saw him for the first him: his eyes closed, in his bliss. It wasn't sexual, it was a soul thing. Few people are brave enough to dance like that in a crowded room. It was different with Diego. With him it was me in my moment, in my skin—not trying, not acting but just dancing. It was him who saw the revealed me and then came to me. It took longer for me to see Diego's soul because it was wrapped in tight layers. Once stripped bare, he realised he didn't need the safety of the layers because the warmth came from inside him. Then I felt it, too. There is no bonfire with him, no blinding light, just a warm, strong fire.

Waking up married feels both the same and totally different. Despite my small lingering doubts about the validity of the ritual we performed, I do have a greater sense of sureness, of being somewhere firm.

Diego groans awake. He kisses me and then rolls back over to go to sleep again. We had fallen, exhausted, into bed at 7.00 in the morning, not at all unusual for an Argentine wedding. I have now been to two, real, church and party weddings and both finished when the sun came up, eight-year-olds and grandmothers alike valiantly lasting to the very end. Sweet *medialunas* and coffee or pizza and beer were served to the survivors at dawn, before they wandered home.

Argentines know how to have fun.

Nineteen

Now that I'm part of Diego's family, they don't gloss over things in front of this girl-from-another-land anymore. Argentina is my new home, so they want me to understand the good and the bad—the caresses and the grit flung in eyes. It becomes obvious quickly that Diego's father has been hurt by his country; the painful tapestry of recent Argentine history is reflected in his eyes and words. Various economic crises pilfered nearly everything from him when he was a young father with grand hopes for his children's futures. He was forced to change careers and pick himself up, again and again, in order to give his family the best possible opportunities. Diego's mother worked hard so that rural children could get the education they deserved. Together they raised three seriously good human beings, all of whom became excellent professionals.

Diego speaks with his parents almost daily on the phone, but we don't see them as often as we would like, perhaps every few months. When I'm in their home, I can't help but notice there is something in the way they move and talk that betrays the struggle and the disappointments.

Diego's father rages at the television news, eyes and hands dancing in anger and frustration. '*Ladrones*, thieves, *mentirosos*, liars,' he yells at the politicians as they weave their tales and shake their fists and swear to be doing everything 'for the people'.

He thinks his country is broken, unfixable. I wonder if that's why he is always fixing things. Everyone in the family goes to him with broken things: fans, sunglasses, light fittings, drawer handles. He patiently takes whatever is brought to him and mends it with glue and nails, and string and screws. He's the protector of us all, too. He's the checker of oil and water in the car, and the tester of air in tires and the safety of electrical fittings. He's the one who asks 'where are we going?' and 'how will we come home?' I see some of my grandfather in him. He doesn't say much about emotional things but he shows you his love, every day, in small ways.

Sometimes the fighting for rights, for fairness, for safety and the grind of everyday life in Argentina wears down even the strongest people. I hope that doesn't happen to Diego. To me. I hope the future will be better than the past.

Diego was a toddler when the last military dictatorship came to power in 1976. *El Proceso de Reorganizacion National* (or simply *el Proceso*, the 'Process') was an extremely dark period, amongst many, in Argentina's chequered history. During the 'Dirty War' armed forces raged, at times indiscriminately, through the population looking for left-wing 'subversives'. This dictatorship ground on like a massive killing machine until 1983. By then thousands of people (some estimates are up to 30,000) were dead or missing. Most of these people were tortured relentlessly and viciously in clandestine centres before being loaded into planes and flown over the Rio de la Plata to be dropped, still alive, drugged and chained together, into the vast river or the sea. The majority of the bodies were never recovered to be buried by loved ones. Argentines have a special word for these lost people, *los desaparecidos* (the 'disappeared ones').

One of the most horrific parts of the 'Process' was what happened to the children of these disappeared people. A number of pregnant women, caught up in the sweep, were kept alive in these ghastly detention centres until they gave birth. After they were killed their babies were adopted by people within the military government or those connected with them. Now in their thirties, these kidnapped babies are being reclaimed, one by one, by their real grandparents. I can't imagine the kind of emotional pain caused by finding out your 'parents', the people that helped you with your homework and kissed you goodnight, were connected to a regime that *murdered* your real parents. How can you ever make sense of that?

This history has left a wound on the psyche of the Argentine people that remains visible, and is raw when touched.

After hearing a shocking story from a student of mine I ask Diego about the dictatorship. 'Do you know any disappeared people?'

He looks at me as if he wonders why I want to know about such painful things.

'Do you not want to talk about it?'

'No, it's fine, and no, I don't personally know any. The worst of it happened in Buenos Aires. My family and their friends escaped it, being in Pergamino.'

I nod, relieved for him and the family. 'One of my students told me today he almost got disappeared.'

'Really, what happened?'

'He's a psychiatrist. He said it wasn't safe to work as one.'

'No, the *militares* didn't trust them, thought they were subversives.'

'So he was working as a photographer instead, and one day he bought a new camera lens and was on his balcony, testing it. Problem was, his balcony overlooked one of the military headquarters.'

Diego is shaking his head.

'I know, bad mistake. He said he was so happy with the new lens that he forgot for a second, and then he ran back inside.'

'Too late?'

'Three minutes later his door was smashed open. They tore the house apart and found one old rifle in a closet.'

'Oh, shit.'

'It was his grandfather's and hadn't been used in years. There were no bullets in the house, and his camera didn't have film in it, but they dragged him away anyway.'

'But he survived?'

'Obviously,' I say, laughing nervously. 'He was jailed for over a week at the local police station, without even one phone call. His family thought he was dead.'

'God.'

'Two thugs came by one day, and he knew he was going to be taken away, with no return. But then something really amazing happened. The police chief of the station intercepted them and argued that my student was innocent. It was a very risky thing for him to do. They said, "We'll be back for you." Then they left.'

'He was released?'

'Yes, a few days later.'

'Lucky.'

'He knows it.'

'A lot of people weren't so lucky.'

A cloud I know well darkens Diego's face. I feel bad for recounting this tale of his country's terrible past. 'I'm sorry.'

'No, no, it's okay. It's just hard to believe it really happened.'

I reach over and hug him. He leans into me.

The next time I see Diego's dad I catch him in a moment of contemplation that reminds me even more clearly of my grandfather. His face has the same look as the one Granddad wore when Jonny and I naively asked him if he had killed anyone in the war. He didn't answer directly, and we were old enough to know not to push.

My stoic, quiet grandfather never recovered from his experiences during the Second World War. It took his two best friends from him and scarred his soul. But he fought a war against 'the enemy'. Here, I'm starting to realise, the enemy lurks within the borders; the main fight is against your own. It's Argentine against Argentine: rich versus poor; political faction versus other political factions; one power bloc versus another and the interior versus the capital city. It has been like this from the beginning and continues to tear the country apart.

'We had such a bright future,' Diego's father says, when I dare to ask questions. 'A hundred years ago Argentina was one of the ten richest countries in the world. It was up there with England and the US, Australia.'

He looks up at me and then quickly glances away.

'What happened?' I ask.

'We happened. We ruined it, with corruption, lying, cheating and stealing the country's amazing resources.'

'That's what I don't understand. Argentina has so much natural wealth. It's a gigantic and fertile farm compared to small New Zealand and dry Australia. It should have…' I trail off, aware that I know too little.

'Yes, it should have. But we have always given our leaders too much power and they use it destructively while making themselves very rich. No one looks to the future.'

'But why do Argentines keep voting in people like that?'

He shakes his head in disbelief. 'We suffer from a child-like need to have a leader save us; an all-powerful *caudillo*.'

'What's a *caudillo*?'

He tries to find the right words. Then he huffs and says, 'A *caudillo* is a charismatic, power-hungry person who presides over the masses while crushing the opposition.' He makes a crushing movement with his fist on the table.

'Like Mussolini?' I ask.

'Yes, and Fidel Castro and Hugo Chavez. Or General Perón,' he says, spitting out the last name.

'Lots of people still talk about him.'

'That's when it all started going rotten.'

'I've heard a lot of people say they're Peronists.'

'Yes, but even they don't really know what it means anymore.'

'A student of mine said "Peronism is a feeling",' I say, helpfully, holding my hands to my chest, as my student did.

'Ha ha. A *feeling*. It's populist short-sighted crap, that's what it is.'

His face is getting red. I thank him and make my exit before he explodes.

The pictures I've seen of Buenos Aires—*Fair Winds*—taken one hundred years ago, show an elegant city, a wealthy hub of activity and a place brimming with hope. While Australia has fulfilled its promise over the last century, Argentina has dismally failed to deliver on hers. I think it's the loss of this dream that is painfully visible in the eyes of many Argentine people. They are grieving, stuck between denial, anger, bargaining, depression and acceptance. Some are unable to stop ruminating about the past, *the what if's and what could have been's* of the other, now lost, pathways. Their anger and bitterness is spurred on by every protest and each corrupt act. Others are more depressed. They feel powerless, hopeless; they trot out my least favourite expression: *es lo qué hay, qué vas a hacer*? It's just the way it is, what are you going to do? Then there are those who swing violently from anger to depression and back again. I hear bargainers, too. They say, eyes glowing with hope: if we get new, better, more honest leaders, everything will be okay. If we can just get it together, everything will be fine.

I'm reminded of the 'store behind the store' that Elle and I visited in Peru, and the devious selling of national treasures and antiquities. In Argentina there are many rooms behind rooms. On the other side of the thick grey curtain, people sit and scheme and rob the riches and future of this incredible country. I hope the dirty curtain is ripped away and they are blinded by light. Thankfully there are brave people trying to make this happen, but can they turn back the tide?

Diego and his friends sometimes dwell in the angry, depressed, hopeless stages, but then there's an acceptance, too. This is what we have to work with, let's try to move forward. A good number still believe the pathway can be changed and a new direction forged. They have hope. I hope they are right. Pessimism is catching.

Periodically the fallout from the *Cromañón* nightclub tragedy in which nearly 200 people were killed appears on the news. More than two years after the event that devastated the whole nation and nothing has been resolved yet; the families are still yelling for *justicia*. It feels like an ongoing reminder of everything that is wrong in Argentina.

I have been thinking a lot about my steadfastly honest and fair grandfather lately and I can't help but think that if he lived here he would be hurt, too, just like so many Argentines. In fact most Kiwis would find the confusion and mess intolerable. They live in a country where being honest is valued, giving everyone a 'fair go' is right, and where people understand that following *just* rules is what holds a country together. New Zealand politicians get in trouble for having a free lunch; here they buy private planes and condos in Miami.

'Why do you stay here?' my students ask me often.

It is hard to explain. Part of it is pragmatic. Diego's job doesn't translate to New Zealand. The legal system is totally different there, and there's the small issue of his level of English. But it's more than that. I can't imagine returning to work as a psychologist. It drained what little energy I had, so I'm scared to go back. If we moved to New Zealand or Australia we would both have to start again, and I'm not sure either of us is willing to do that. But these are facts, why I stay is about a feeling—an intangible *something* that warms my heart.

Argentines feel it, too. When you ask them if they would ever live somewhere else, the grand majority say, 'Absolutely no way.'

Why not?

I can hear the answer echoing, one voice over the other. 'My family and friends are here.'

After a long and painful search I found that *something* here. Perhaps I would have found it elsewhere; perhaps, now that I'm different, I would be able to find it in my other homes, too. But in the end I found it here.

The reaction to the crying baby in the café still resonates vividly in my mind. I want to have my family here.

'*¿Diego, podemos buscar un bebe?*' I ask one evening, near the end of the year.

Buscar un bebe literally means to 'look for', 'search for' a baby. I have always loved the phrase. It's as if they believe the baby is already out there and just has *to be found*.

He almost chokes on his spaghetti.

'Oh, yes, sure, but not right now,' he says, looking up at me, chin smeared with red sauce.

'It's just, I'm getting older and I'm worried it won't happen.'

'You'll be fine, Cookie,' he says, clearly attempting to soften me with nicknames.

'I'm already thirty-six. It gets very hard after thirty-five.'

'Jess. Don't worry so much. It will happen. I'm sure.'

'What makes you so sure?'

'I have super sperm.' His face is perfectly expressionless.

'What? Diego!' I say, screwing up my face. Why do men have to make important things so base?

'Another year, and then we will start. I promise.'

He reaches over and holds my face in his two lovely, strong hands, kisses me fully and hard on the lips.

'One year, no more,' I say firmly, pushing him back.

Twenty

Sitting beside Diego on a flight bound for New Zealand on 23 December, I let out a gleeful, muffled shout. 'Yay.'

'You're going home.'

'I'm going home. You can see where I grew up. Meet everyone.'

'I can't wait,' says Diego. His hands are gripping the seat and his face is pensive as the plane starts to lift off the tarmac.

When the flight levels off, he says, 'I'm worried about my English.'

'It's okay; I told you, they're not big talkers. I'll translate. And you have Eddie!'

He rolls his eyes.

'You love him.'

'Yes, I do, but...'

'I know. I'll tell him to be on his best behaviour.'

'Still, I should have learned more English. You should have helped me,' he says, eyes narrowing.

'Hey, I tried, and you always said, "Let's do it later, I'm too tired".'

He mumbles something.

'Look, don't worry, honestly. They will be so happy to meet you. And to see me.'

'Five years is a long time. How are you feeling?'

'I'm good. It's been way too long, though,' I say.

'I couldn't do it. Are you sure you're okay?' he says, looking into my eyes.

'I just want to see them.'

During the long transpolar flight I keep looking over at Diego. It feels like forever since I sat next to someone on a plane. It's nice not to fly alone.

As the plane slowly inches towards '*the land of the long white cloud*', I can't help feeling excited and nervous about our plan, which is to stay ten days with Mum in Auckland and then a week in New Plymouth (my home town) with Dad before flying to Australia for another ten days. We have a stopover of two days back in Auckland before returning to Argentina.

Eddie picks us up at the airport. His eyes are blurry and his hair is standing on end. I feel guilty for waking the owl so early in the morning. It's not even light yet.

His first words are, '*Che, puto, ¿cómo estás?*' Hey, fag. How are you? Then he falls on Diego, arms outstretched and hugs him hard.

I roll my eyes but Diego smiles.

'I have a surprise for you,' says Eddie.

He drives us up a winding road to the car park on Mount Eden (a large centrally located hill and the site of an old Māori *Pa*, fortress). We walk the steep path to its flat summit in the first muted rays of daylight, then sit close together and watch the sun rise over Auckland. Light floods over the cityscape in miniature, sparkles off the ripples in the sea and flashes up the sides of tall buildings and the elegant Sky Tower. We all sit like that for a long time, pressed close together to combat the morning chill. It's a beautiful sight. A sting of homesickness stirs up memories. I do miss it here: the calmer life, green hills, wild beaches, kind-hearted people and riding a horse freely over lands where few people are seen.

'Thanks, Eddie,' I say, leaning into him. A watery veil blurs my vision.

'I thought you would like it. It's a special welcome to *Kiwilandia* for Diego.' He looks away but I see that his eyes are glowing, too.

'What did he say?' asks Diego, already lost in translating our words.

'*Eso es un regalo de Eddie*,' I translate, '*un bienvenido a* New Zealand *para vos*.' This is a present from Eddie, a welcome, for you.

'Oh, thank you. Very nice,' he says in thick English.

'*No problema, puto*,' says Eddie.

'Eddie, stop it.'

Diego reaches over me and cuffs Eddie's head.

'Ouch.'

I'm squashed tight between them. It's nice.

Once the sun is up, we set off for Mum's, which I know only from photos. At the end of a curved driveway the unusual old brick building comes into view. Thick lush green vines cover its square double-storied exterior, giving the impression of an old farmhouse or barn, somehow incongruous with its inner-city home.

As we enter, the smell of eggs Benedict and browned toast assaults our senses. When my mother sees us she nervously wipes her hands and then fixes her hair by running fingers through it. Tight dark jeans accentuate her skinny form but she looks more filled out than the last time I saw her. Her collarbones no longer protrude. Relief drops my already tense shoulders.

I see loneliness in her. I know there's no one new to hold her.

We hug longer than either of us is used to. I can feel the whirling inside her.

When we break apart Diego surprises her with an all-enveloping embrace, practically lifting her off the ground.

It obvious she's chuffed by the gesture. I watch her as she scans him head to foot and back again, resting her gaze on his face. She tilts and nods her head slightly. I take it she approves of the man in the flesh.

Diego's eyes widen as he takes in the interior of the house, which is also part shop. The entire downstairs area has been given over to her fashion label. There are elegantly dressed mannequins and beautiful wooden racks of clothes. The polished concrete floors and large modern art paintings blend with some simple antique furniture, creating a warm balance and a chic appeal. The building started its life as a bakery and it feels right that we arrive with the scent of baked bread lingering in the air. I remember seeing pictures of the building before my mother claimed it. Her hands have transformed it into something special. It's what she does. She makes wonderful-looking nests.

I spent my childhood in houses that were being beautified. Mum loved to buy derelict old farmhouses and transform them—with frustration, tears and blood—into spectacular stately homes. (Often there was actual blood, as she carried out most of the renovating herself and was prone to accidents. Even a nail jammed right through her hand didn't slow her down very much.) It took years of painstaking work because not one detail could be missed. When complete our homes looked like they belonged in House & Garden Magazine. We could finally invite friends over to stay—without worrying they would fall through the floor.

The frantic construction of nests never satisfied her. She was never able to rest when they were complete. Perhaps it mirrored her relationship with Dad: a damaged house that could never be properly renovated no matter how much beautifying work was done—too many unopened and unexplored boxes in its attic. These never-ending projects were her drug of choice and her way to survive her pain.

It took three years to complete the building of our final family home. I remember feeling happy, thinking this brand new house would mark the end of the moving. I was partly wrong.

During the design phase an architect friend of hers had shown her a drawing for what he called 'The Ruin'. The name was apt: it looked like an archaeological site, strangely deconstructed, with long windows and bits of broken off pieces forming various separate living spaces. She rejected the design at the time but then, less than a year after the house was finished, she started to seriously consider demolishing it and putting up 'The Ruin' in its place. We all said no. She gave up on the idea and then couldn't stay anymore. In reality she had been slowly leaving for years.

I don't remember the day she left; it's a blank page. I just remember her being gone, with my two younger brothers. Jonny ran to our grandparents and I stayed with an empty father in a house that echoed. Her leaving left us scattered and in ruins. But I knew that in less than two years, I could run away to university. That goal kept me going when the voice in my head told me to jump into nothing.

Now, arm around Diego and watching my mother give us her rapid-fire tour of this latest beautiful house, I wonder if this will be her final home. I think it's unlikely. She has been running all her life: from shadows in her past and ghosts in her present. Always running towards some vague glinting mirage she sees on the other side of the desert. When she stopped for a minute and looked around her, at us, at me, it was amazing, as if the shutters had been flung open for the day to let the sun shine in. Then she would turn her face away and run again, the dust of activity flying around her. I think she has always felt alone in the world, disappointed by people, by love. I want to say to her, 'We have always been here.' We wait for a place next to her; we each have a space beside us for her.

My youngest brother, Henry, appears suddenly from the spare

bedroom of the bread factory.

'Heni,' I say, sweeping him up in a hug.

'Sis,' he says, squeezing me back.

I step away and look at him. He seems taller, thin as a poplar tree, stiff like a professor in an English boarding school.

'Oh, sorry.' I forgot Diego for a minute. 'Diego, this is Henry, Henry, Diego.'

'*Hola, bienvenido,*' says Henry, practising his school-learned Spanish.

'*Gracias,*' says Diego, pulling him into a hug.

Henry's face shows alarm, and then bewildered joy.

My mother has made a temporary home for Diego and me in a partitioned off section in the large studio space on the second floor. I can't stop smiling when she opens the sheet-curtain and I see our bed-nest: a comfortable thick mattress on the floor, with intricately patterned and tasselled cushions arranged on top to give it colour and warmth and a lamp on top of some thick art books.

'Thanks, Mum, I love it,' I say, seeing her embarrassment about the tent-like structure.

Diego wakes with a shout the next morning, pulling me abruptly from my travel-weary sleep.

'What?' I say, with a hand on his back. He is sitting upright, his face pallid, as if he has seen a ghost. '*Gato, gato negro,*' he splutters, pointing.

I see Mum's pitch-black cat, Puss, skulking nearby. Her green slit eyes are boring into us as she slowly licks her mouth.

'I woke up and she was right there, staring into my eyes like she wanted to eat them,' Diego says, glaring fixedly at her.

From then on we have to block off the door to the upper storey to prevent her from venturing in and doing her worst to him. Furry creatures with sharp teeth and claws don't sit well with Diego—he's a city boy at heart.

We spend the day before Christmas exploring Auckland city and the harbour, with its cafés and bars and impeccably cared-for yachts that rock gently in the light winds, giving the impression of a forest of pale-barked, leafless trees reaching into the blue sky.

'It's very beautiful here. I think I'm in love,' says Diego. His arm tightens around my waist. I feel proud of my country, happy to be showing it to him.

'It's very peaceful down here today,' I say. I had expected to see more bustle and people.

'The pavements and streets are so clean and even, no holes. The houses and gardens are…' I see him drift off. His face is set in amazement.

'Well looked after?'

'Yes, I guess that's it.'

I look around. I had almost forgotten how neat it is here, how pristine. In some ways I feel as if I'm looking at the city, the country, for the first time. The houses, buildings, streets and even the cars look smaller. Everything seems shiny and surreal. I feel bigger; gone is the feeling of being towered over. I see blue sky everywhere. Perhaps I have become so used to the broken pavements, grubbiness, dog droppings, cigarette butts and the crunched up wrappers texturing and colouring the streets of BA, that I don't notice them anymore. Have I become accustomed to the mess?

'No rubbish either,' I say making a sweep with my hand.

'I know,' he says, an expression of disbelief making his face look sweet, innocent.

I suddenly remember my childhood lessons on littering. I once had to walk a kilometre down a country road because I threw a banana peel out the car window. I argued it was organic. Dad still made me get out and search the side of the road for it.

'Yep. Even the air seems so clean,' I say, breathing in.

'It's like a fairy tale,' he says.

I laugh. 'Yes, almost perfect.'

'You're crazy not to want to live here.'

I have been sort of expecting this moment. 'It's not that I don't want to live here. It's an amazing country. Half the world would love to live in a country like this.'

'Then what is it? You seem to be very against the idea of returning.'

'It's hard to explain. Everything functions here. If you work hard you can have a decent life. But it's not as luxurious as people in Argentina think. Even upper-middle class Kiwis don't eat out all the time, like the same kind of people in Argentina. They don't have full-time maids either!

And they don't have expensive holidays. We never went overseas or hired an apartment by the sea, we went to campsites in Nana and Granddad's tiny caravan, and once Jonny and I went camping in a tent with Mum. Most people spend their lives working to pay off the mortgage on their house and send their kids to university, if they can.'

'I could handle having a bit less in order to avoid the chaos,' he says, looking confused.

'Let's sit over there,' I say, pointing to a park. I feel I need to sit down to explain the difficult part.

We cross the road and settle under a tree out of the midday sun.

'Okay. It's more of an emotional thing for me. I never felt at home here. Mostly that's to do with my family and childhood, but I think there's more to it than that. When I lived here I felt that lots of people had difficulty expressing emotions and talking about important things, especially psychological problems.' I pause.

'Like, they were closed? Cold?'

'No, not cold. Kiwis are kind, caring, but perhaps "less open" is one way of describing it. They're friendly, but it's harder to get right in close. They're proud of being tough; I think too tough. But I don't know, I haven't lived here for a long time, maybe it's different now. I do know for sure that they don't see psychologists as much as in BA, and if they do they would never ever talk proudly about it.'

'We totally overdo that! Okay, I see what you're saying, but…'

'I don't know, it sounds silly but I guess I love all the kissing and hugging and expressiveness, it makes me feel part of something bigger than me. I need it, somehow. I would miss it. That's why I want to stay in Argentina.'

I see him frowning. 'Diego! I stay for you too, of course.' I put my arm around his neck and kiss him.

'I know.'

'The openness, all that warm touching, it's what attracted me to South America even before I knew it was something I was missing.' My heart is racing. I feel as if I'm somehow betraying my other homes. I also worry that I can't make him understand.

'Okay, *tranquila*, calm down,' he says, seeing my struggle.

He grabs me up in a hug and I sink into it.

The walk home is subdued, but my hand is held firmly all the way.

There is no physical litter to deal with here, but I worry that emotional litter might ruin Christmas. We haven't been together as a family in more than ten years. There was always one or more of us missing: Jonny in London, me in Australia, Eddie in the US or Japan.

'That's just wrong,' says Diego, when I try to calculate how long it's been on my fingers.

'I know.'

'That would never happen in Argentina.'

It's just Mum, my three brothers and us for Christmas dinner. Mum prepares a huge turkey, roast parsnips and potatoes, fresh green beans and baby carrots, succulent herb-infused stuffing and rich gravy.

A happy silence hovers as the tender pale meat disintegrates over tongues, its thin crispy skin rich and savoury. The vegetables are perfectly cooked, still bright, with crunch.

'*Muchos penes para vos,*' says Eddie, smirking and waving thin beans and stubby carrots in Diego's bewildered face. His mouth snaps open in shock. Henry understands and laughs. I don't know whether to laugh or give my brother a slap.

'What did he say?' Mum cuts in.

'Lots of little penises for you,' I translate.

'Eddie!' she remonstrates with him, but by now both she and I are starting to giggle.

'Just breaking the silence. You were the one who cooked all the little phalluses!'

'Eddie, enough,' I say, with tears running from my eyes.

I can see Mum's chest shaking as she swallows her laughter.

'I used to him now,' says Diego in stuttering English. He attempts a smile while biting his lip.

During the evening I find myself watching Jonny. He's a tender, thoughtful person who has always had a heaviness hovering around him. His eyes hang with sadness even when he's telling a joke or a story; and he is a wonderful storyteller. Sometimes he looks tired just being awake, but tonight I see moments when his eyes shine, and the laugh is full. It's a wonderful sight.

Mum looks tiny surrounded by my brothers but she's smiling, too. She reminds me of a mother hen (a very sleek one) fluffing her feathers, proud of her flock.

Later, poor Santa gets it, with jokes about his alcohol problems (the red nose and flushed cheeks), his proclivity for overly friendly relations with his reindeer and his enormous bottom getting stuck in chimneys. Nothing is sacred. My three brothers on a humorous sarcasm roll is something to see, and we all laugh till we leak tears.

I reach out to Diego as I can see he is missing it all.

'Are you okay?' I ask, my stomach constricted with the giggles.

'Yes, I just miss the jokes. It looks funny though,' he says, with a brave face on.

I try to translate but I'm not fast enough.

I feel sorry that Diego's pleasure is second-hand; he can only react to our reactions. I know how frustrating this is, having sat through a hundred dinners feeling lost, trying to stick my head into the storytelling ring.

At the end of the night our plates are littered with turkey bones but emotional litter never made it to the table.

Over the next few days I try to make a bridge between my mother and Diego by translating their words to one another. It feels stiff and forced. In each other's presence they are transformed into ten-year-olds in the seconds before giving a school speech: wide-eyed, nerves on edge.

We see little of Mum during the day as she works long hours in the shop or studio, but when each day ends, she reaches out to us with food. We dine on corned beef dripping with mustard sauce, roast lamb topped with mint sauce, roast pork with crispy glistening crackling and apple sauce; the tastes of a New Zealand childhood. I try to help her with the meals but she waves me away and continues to flutter around the kitchen, doing ten things at once. She disappears into another place when she's focused on a task. Her eyes glaze over and she finds peace there.

I watch her, impressed with how her tiny body has survived some violent attacks in the last few years: cancer, a broken bone in her neck, and a level of activity that would bring most people to a shuddering halt. Not to mention many lost loves and the death of her parents just a week apart. I feel proud of her.

I'm happy she's not gone.

I wonder if all the activity is a way to avoid talking, avoid the rehashing of our last terrible encounter. I keep saying to myself, tomorrow we will talk. We don't. I think we are both still too fearful of ripping into the boxes in the attic and making a bigger mess. I put Diego between us, she puts her work in the shop.

We do manage a single brief moment, one evening after dinner. She finds the words to shrink the space between us.

'Diego seems like a very warm person. You're lucky to have found him.'

'He's lovely. I feel loved and safe with him.'

'I'm really happy about that. You deserve it,' she says, twirling the stem of her wine glass in her fingers.

'So do you,' I say.

She avoids my eyes.

Diego bursts into the kitchen and the moment passes. '*Vamos*, let's go,' he says. 'Eddie's here.'

Eddie whisks us away.

'Where are we going?' I ask, once we're in the car.

'You'll see.'

He drives onto *Karangahape* Road, or K'road as it is affectionately known. Despite some recent gentrification, the word still brings up images of prostitutes, drug users and danger. It's also the place to go and see alternative bands, find experimental culture; it's the edge of things. In fact one of the interpretations of its Māori name is, 'winding ridge of human activity'.

Eddie ushers us down a flight of stairs and into a cave-like underground nightclub. It feels claustrophobic and stuffy; faint smells of stale beer and old sweat tickle our senses. I glance over at Diego. He's looking around like a lost child, hands in pockets, body puffed up but vulnerable.

'This is very Kiwi, well, alternative Kiwi,' I say, leaning close to his ear as the thumping grinding music is loud and echoes menacingly in the tight space.

'I can see that,' he returns. He looks nervous. I feel nervous that we've brought him to the wrong place.

'Hey, I see some friends, be back soon,' says Eddie, disappearing into the crowd of swaying bodies.

We get drinks and sit on stools at a high table, facing the band. Our backs rest against a large column, my head on his shoulder.

I try to see the crowd from Diego's perspective. It must seem wild to him, the melting-pot of faces, the styles of clothes and hair and all the shapes and sizes of the people crammed into the small space. I spot a tiny, doll-like Asian girl in a tight pink top, blue and pink schoolgirl kilt, perfectly straight fringe and enormously high-soled platform boots. A few paces away a huge Polynesian man stands, legs apart, muscled biceps tattooed with traditional patterns. His physicality surrounds him and invades the room, but his face is set in an amicable grin. The contrast makes me smile.

'What?' asks Diego.

'I'd forgotten how different the people are here.'

'I've never seen so many distinct kinds of people in one room,' he says, looking around, mouth ajar.

'I love that about New Zealand. The mix, and the freedom the dress as you like and be who you want to be.'

'We are more conservative, I see that now.'

My pride melts away a little as the night progresses and bellies become swollen with beer and whiskey, rum, gin. More than a few people start to stumble; they look seasick, as if the room has become the bowels of a ship, buffeted by a wrathful sea. The mood goes from joyful to cantankerous as the night drags on.

'You guys drink a lot,' Diego states, looking nervously at some faces around him.

'Yes, I know,' I say. I revert to worrying that this night was a bad choice, that his impression will be tainted.

The possibility of violence ripples in the air, and I'm reminded that in all the years I've lived in Buenos Aires, I've never seen a fight in a bar, a club, or on the street outside one. I have witnessed some male posturing, some shouting, a shove or two, but no fists pounding, no blood. I have dozens of fights etched in my memories of my youth in New Zealand, and my years in Melbourne, and there was blood.

'Can we go home?' says Diego, squeezing my knee.

My heart sinks but I don't want to stay either. 'Yes, sure.' I get up.

'What about Eddie?'

'Oh, yes, Eddie. We have to find him.'

I see him across the room in an animated conversation. I hope extraction won't be hard. He leaves with us, reluctantly.

Diego seems tired by the night. I ask in the taxi, 'Did you enjoy it?'

'Yes, it was different.'

I am not convinced, but I leave it be.

We spend New Year's Eve camped on a wild, virgin beach on the magical Waiheke Island: a small, lightly populated island contained within the curves of Auckland's main bay. A misty rain falls gently, leaving tiny translucent bubbles on clothes and hair, and a shine on faces. Electronic beats filter through the air from two generator-operated speakers. We are sitting on logs around a scorching hot bonfire with Eddie and a large group of his friends. The soft rolling and crashing sounds of the sea are like natural backing tracks to the music, the cracks and sizzles of the living fire add top notes. It is pitch black behind us but all the faces around the fire are highlighted beautifully by the flames. I feel at home; connected to the universe and the warm bodies around us.

'Do you like it here?' I whisper to Diego.

'It's perfect,' he says, squeezing tighter into me.

I can see the reflection of the fire flickering in his dark eyes. His jersey is damp, I can smell the wool. It takes me back to our first night. I never imagined… but here I am.

'See you later, Mum,' I say, as we set off to drive down the coast to see my father and old friends. Eddie is designated chauffeur.

'I've taken a few days off, so on your way back we will have time,' she says.

I think, *time to talk.*

'Don't forget to give Dad his present.'

'I won't, and thank you. Such a beautiful idea.'

'Hope he thinks so.'

'He will. Thanks, Mum. See you in a week.' I give her a hug. Then Diego grabs her, too.

As we drive away I look back at her standing there; she has a smile on, but her eyes are serious.

We arrive at my last childhood home, New Plymouth, down New Zealand's wild, west coast, five hours later. When the house appears at the bottom of winding tree-sheltered driveway, my nerves and happiness clash together.

I see my father come out the front door. He looks trimmer; the beer belly is almost gone. His hair is white and receding off his head. He looks both older and younger. I see a spark in his stride as he walks towards us.

I hug him.

He stiffens and then pats me on the back.

Diego shakes his hand.

'So, Eddie got you here okay?'

'Yep, for a crazy boy he's actually a very good driver,' I say.

Cheryl comes out to meet us, looking flustered, as if she's just polished the entire house, which she probably has. She welcomes us warmly, directs Dad to pick up my bag and leads us all inside.

It feels familiar, but different, as if its frame is the same but its contents have changed. There is nothing left of my mother in the colours of the walls, the furniture or the gardens, except rows of painstakingly made rock walls. She has been largely erased.

Then I see a bottle of Baileys on the table.

'Thanks, Dad.'

'No problem. Just don't drink it all at once,' he says.

Upstairs I laugh when I see that a touch of me remains.

When we were younger, Jonny and I decorated our bedroom doors with tributes to our favourite music and best friends. Then we had a war. He would write mean things alongside my friends' names, or scribble they suck next to my bands. I would retaliate. The doors ended up a mess but they told our story. Surprisingly, they haven't been painted over.

'So… you were a bit of a Goth or a punk, when you were young,' says Diego with a smile as he reads my door: The Cure, Sisters of Mercy, Depeche Mode, The Clash, The Sex Pistols.

'Yep, I did the dyed spiked hair, white face, black makeup and clothes, meeting in cemeteries at night to drink red wine… all of it.'

'Thank god you grew up.'

I open my pack and pull out the present for my father.

'There's something I have to do.'

'Okay.'

Dad's in the kitchen. 'Here, this is for you,' I say, handing it to him.

'What's this?'

'A gift from us kids.'

He flicks quickly through some pages and says, 'Thanks, it's nice.' Then he makes a rapid exit. 'I'll guard it in my room,' he adds over his shoulder.

The gift is a photo album filled with childhood photos of him with us. It was tenderly put together one long Sunday afternoon when Mum found herself with a spare moment and decided to attack the old army chest that contained hundreds of photos rattling around loose, dusty but not forgotten. The monumental and emotional effort produced an album for each of us kids and one for him. I think it was her attempt to weave a thread closer to us and perhaps to him, too. Although she didn't appear in his album, he would know she was behind it.

He's overwhelmed, I say to myself. That's why he ran.

Later that day when I pass by his open door I see it on his dresser sitting in among his odd, disordered collection of favourite things: twenty or so assorted pig figurines he keeps getting as presents, some ancient medical instruments, some small notebooks and a couple of hunting knifes with antler handles. I imagine him poring over the photos in his own time and space. It makes me happy.

There is a new photo in the house. Alongside some other family shots, I see a small framed photo of Diego and me on our wedding day, looking damp and aglow. I feel present again in my childhood home, not forgotten.

I think the photos in the album were looked at, each and every one, because something changes in Dad after that day.

One afternoon Eddie takes Diego down to the river on the four-wheeler motorbike. Cheryl is out buying food for the party that she and Dad are hosting for us the following day, so Dad and I are alone together in the small family room off the kitchen. He's sitting on the sofa, and I'm perched on an old stool, looking through the window at the green hills of the neighbouring farm. It's a view I've seen a million times; a view that always calms me. I love the colours of that hill, brown after harsh days of summer, fresh green in spring, dotted with big cows and small ones, blurred by sheets of fierce rains and golden in the afternoon sun. Its shades and forms are always in flux, but never its lines: they are always the same.

I try to animate the space between us. 'Lola is so cute,' I remark. Lola is Cheryl's two-year-old granddaughter.

'Yes, she is.'

'I was watching her earlier collecting stones and stuffing her pockets with them. She's so curious and calm. And that mop of blonde curls is fantastic.'

Silence. I watch him as he slowly turns his hands around each other. Do I ask? Is this the moment? I wait, my heart beating faster. I move my weight, ready to leave.

'I don't really remember you as a child.'

'I don't remember me, either.' As soon as I say it, I want to take it back.

'I see little Lola and how much love she receives, and how much attention she needs...'

'Yes, they need a lot.'

A heavy pause hangs.

'Dad, what was I like as a child?'

'You were very sweet, so quiet. Then you stopped talking for a while.'

'What do you mean?'

'We sent you away to Ireland with your nanny. A couple of weeks, that's all.' He laughs nervously, and then continues. 'When she brought you back you had stopped talking. You hid under the table at day care and wouldn't come out.'

'What happened?' I'm scared to change my tone, in case he stops.

'I don't think it was anything serious. I think you were just confused by being there, the accents, new people. You were very shy. She told us you hid under a tree in the yard most of the time you were over there.'

My mind blurs with conflicting thoughts. I don't know what to say.

'I know you think that stuff is important, being a psychologist...' His voice fades off.

'Those kinds of separations are hard on kids.' I try to stay curious, dispassionate. I feel sick inside.

'Well, much worse things happen to children.'

'I know, Dad. But it does have an effect. Those early years are the emotional base of everything that comes later.'

'We dumped you all over the place.'

Dumped, he said dumped. My mind jams on repeat. I look at him. He's still focused on his hands, as if he's absorbed in the lines of them. He looks old and sad.

'It's okay, Dad. Thank you for telling me. I know a lot was going on back then.'

'Yes... that nanny, I think her name was Margaret, she loved you, and you loved her. She went back to Ireland not long after you got back from that visit. We got you a new one. Irish, too. You liked her as well.'

Margaret, I say to myself. I fight with a veil that's draped over my memories. I know it's perhaps too long ago, but I sense something pulling at the edges of my mind. Soft white skin on her arms. I can't see her face. I wonder if that's why I feel so calm and happy in the presence of Irish people. I picture Bree's wry smile. I miss her.

'Then later Nana came over and took me and baby Jonny back to New Zealand, right?'

'Yes. You two were happy with Nana. So chubby and tanned by the time we saw you again.'

'I've seen the photos. She sure liked to fatten us up.'

'Ah, I've got to mow the lawns before the party; Cheryl will kill me.'

He springs up and darts past me, mumbling to himself. I can't help smiling.

'See you, Dad,' I say after his retreating back.

So few words, but some powerful glimpses into years of unsaid things. I am lost in thought, slightly stunned, happy that we've talked.

I find myself back in my old bedroom, in front of my childhood dressing table. It's made of golden oak with neat small drawers each side of the oval mirror. Large drawers give it a strong base below. I rummage through each drawer, my hiding places for precious things. I find shells, dulled by the years; little coloured stones, hair ribbons and clips, a few coins. Then some things from teen years: dark eye shadow, lipsticks borrowed from Mum. I'm surprised to find an empty packet of contraceptive pills. I wonder why the drawers have never been cleared out.

As I'm combing through the years I go over my father's words. I have more questions, but my need to ask them has faded away. His intent was clear, the illumination enough. I'm light with relief, content, as if the final piece of a complex puzzle had just been pushed carefully into place. I understand more fully the feeling that has been chasing me all my life. I can let go now.

Then I find a crumpled plastic bag. I open it and out into my hand slips a pony tail of my little-girl hair, rubber band still in place at the cut end. The sight hits me like a punch.

I sit on the bed, hair in my hands, and decide to try something I have never done before. It helped with Daniel, so maybe it will help with me, the little me.

Hi little Jess. It's me, grown up you. I want to talk to you about life. I want to help you feel less sad and lonely. I know you try very hard to behave well. I know you stay quiet so you won't bother people. That's okay, but you don't have to be good all the time. I want you to know you can be angry, too. Mum and Dad love you but they're distracted by lots of things and don't always show it. They haven't been there enough for you and you're allowed to get mad about that. If you don't let yourself feel all the different emotions you will get stuck. It will hurt your insides and make you sick. You feel what you feel and that tells you important things. Don't hide from it.

You are brave. I want you to stay curious and to open your eyes wide to the beautiful things in the world. You will find a lot of good people in your life. You just have to let them into your world. It's going to be hard growing up, but I'm here for you. You are not alone. Talk to me when you need to. I'm always here. Try not to let the sadness eat you up. Go and enjoy playing in the park when it's full of flowers. Get your little hands all messed up with pretty coloured paint. Play with your furry animal friends. Write your quirky stories and don't worry about the spelling.

And please, know you will have lots of love in your life and lots of hugs. Be patient. Ask for what you want and believe you are special, because you are. I'm hugging you right now. You are loved.

As I say the last words, a flood of emotions and memories rushes through me. I pull back my arms from the imaginary hug. After sitting dead still for a long time, a calm lightness begins to pour in. With each measured breath I feel clearer, braver.

I tell myself I'm not that child anymore. She's part of me, but now I can finally free myself from the patterns and thoughts that started in her mind and gained strength over the years that followed. I'm an adult now, who can construct every day a new truth for myself. It's time to look forward, to shake free from the past.

I hear Diego bounding up the stairs. I had forgotten about him. He opens the door, steps in and stops. He looks at my face, and then the hair in my hand. I slide my feet onto the floor, ready to rise. He grabs me in his arms and hugs the breath out of me. I give in to sobs—not sobs of grief, but of release.

'I'm okay, really I'm okay,' I say into his chest.

'I know. *Está bien. Está bien*,' he says, while pressing his face into my hair.

'Party today,' I say in the morning. I feel fresh and alive.

'Yes, party,' he replies in English.

'It will be fun. My friends are cool. You'll like them.'

'I wish I could talk to them.'

'Emily will be here. Great timing as always. She turns up just at the right moments. You can talk a little with Henry and Eddie, too.'

'I know. I'll be okay.'

I give him a big kiss. He doesn't close his eyes. I can see he's nervous.

By early afternoon we are in the middle of an intimate gathering of my lifelong friends. Some are visiting home for the holidays and a couple have recently returned to live in New Zealand after having long adventures away. Andrea, the one who dragged me to the psychic all those years ago, is here. It's heart-warming to see her; she's still so small but she wields a massive presence.

She gives me a long warm hug. Diego practically lifts her off her feet as he hugs her. I wonder whether people here do embrace each other more than I remember. *Did dark clouds block my vision?*

'I told you she was good,' Andrea says with a smile when she's heard my story. 'You thought she was mad and were so furious you would have to wait so long to find him.' She eyes Diego. 'Worth the wait I see.'

'Yes, more than worth it,' I say, slipping my arm around Diego's waist. He looks at me, with an expression of *I have no idea what anyone is saying and I give up*. 'She was right about South America, too. Who would have guessed that,' I say quietly.

Andrea nods as if she wants to say, *Of course she was right—she's psychic. You dummy.*

We spend the day in the sun, by the pool, fuelled by sparkling wines and some stunning bottles of crisp New Zealand Sauvignon Blanc. Four small kids run around our feet and a baby squawks periodically from deep within the house. There are shrimps and crayfish, various meats from Dad's hunting trips and tasty things to nibble on all day and well into the night.

The years apart snap into minutes as old roles and jokes take us back to our schooldays. Glimpses of lives between our last meetings are given. Everyone is more open than I expected. Perhaps I've been overestimating the differences between my homes.

I ask about a missing friend.

'Oh, now that's a story... You'll never guess where she ended up,' says Andrea.

'Last I heard she was living in Paris, working as a chaperone for the wives of the Sultan of Brunei,' I say.

'Well...' Andrea pauses for effect. 'She married his younger brother, Prince Jefri. He's a bit of a charmer by all accounts. She became wife number five.'

'What?' I say.

'Yep, she married a prince.'

'I always thought she would marry well,' says another friend, looking bemused.

'Me too, but I didn't think she would share a husband,' I say.

Those words set off an explosive conversation. We just can't see her, a girl from a good Catholic family, being someone's fifth wife. We come to the conclusion that, personally, not even a couple of billion dollars could make that arrangement appeal. But who knows? She has disappeared into a different world since her wedding, and no one has been able to contact her.

'Marrying a billionaire prince kind of trumps marrying an Argentine lawyer!' I say to Andrea later, fake pouting.

'Yours is still a good story. I always knew you would do something unusual with your life.'

'Just say it: crazy.'

'No, not crazy, just outside the norm. And you don't have to share your husband.'

'Ha, true.'

When the time comes to leave my childhood home I thank Cheryl for hosting a great party and looking after us all week. Our hug is awkward, but warm. Then I give my old man a big hug. He stays in it for a long few seconds. I wonder if he's been relieved of something by our talk. I know I feel kinder towards him. I also wonder whether feeling loved and safe in my relationship with Diego has allowed me to be more open to fixing the brokenness between us. Dad is almost retired and secure in his marriage, so perhaps he has had time to think, to look over his life and see more clearly his children, and the things that were missing for us all. It's as if the lines of us are filling in and our ghostly forms are taking on colour—for each other.

Diego and I fly to Sydney and then drive down the coast to Melbourne in a hire car (which Diego names *la nave*, the space ship). We stay for a week with Dave in his half-renovated, half-crumbling Victorian mansion in St Kilda. He approves of Diego. So does Elle, with her new musician lover in tow (at thirty-five he's much older than the previous ones). Friends and old workmates welcome me back with dinners and lunches and a lot of hugs. I feel genuinely missed.

Periodically I suffer attacks of nostalgia, mostly sparked by the great variety of food from around the world and the fabulous coffee, but I don't miss living in Melbourne. It's an incredible city and I still love it, but it's tainted by memories of unhappiness, which I can't seem to rub off it.

'I could easily live here,' Diego says, looking at me like I'm crazy.

'I'm sorry, but I don't think I could.'

'It's okay. I get it. I think.'

The stopover back in Auckland flies by so fast that there are no moments to be found to dig into the boxes in the attic. But something about this trip home, and especially my talk with Dad, has freed me. I don't have the same need to go back into past things with Mum.

When we are all packed up and ready to go, she gives me another special present, wrapped in soft tissue paper, to take away.

'Open it later,' she says.

'Thank you for everything,' I say, turning the gift over in my hands.

'Thank you very much,' says Diego in his best English. I know he wants to say more. I understand his frustration.

Standing at the international gate, Diego squishes my tiny mother in his big arms and then I hug her. I truly feel it, and I detect she does too. More tiny connective fibres continue their tentative, reaching journey between us. For the first time in a long time I believe we can weave those threads tighter and stronger. We need patience and the desire to make it happen. I think we have both.

When Diego is asleep on the plane, I carefully unwrap the tissue paper. Inside is a small book made of handmade paper. Its pages are filled with poems and important pieces of a life, my life. On the first page she has written a line by Marcel Proust. 'The real voyage of discovery consists not in seeking new landscapes but in having new eyes.'

'True,' I think. But then, I needed to fly into the wind to force open my eyes.

I flip carefully through the pages: there are clippings from old newspapers, including my birth notice; a tiny lock of my baby hair, some photos and some cards I wrote as a small child to Nana and Granddad, Mum and Dad. Attached to the last pages are some cartoons, stapled together, that Dad apparently sketched for me. I see flowers, a big sun, different animals and childhood characters like Tiger Tim. They are beautifully and carefully drawn. I had no idea he could draw or that these cartoons even existed. On the last page is a huge funny looking pig, with a rolling belly and a silly grin. I read the words at the bottom of the page: *For Jessica, from poor lonely old Dad.*

I would have been about three when he drew them. Opening them out and touching them as a big person makes me cry soulful tears from the core of my being.

He must have loved me.

Even stronger than that thought, I wonder about the sadness he felt back then. When I was growing up, I was told many times that my father was a sweet, kind and observant child. I ask myself when and why that little boy built such impenetrable walls around himself. I know his relationship with my mother had something to do with it but I think the walls were there well before. I wish I could have met that small child, and I know he still exists somewhere inside my old man. I'm sure the little me and that wee boy would have been firm friends. They would have understood each other.

Twenty-one

EXACTLY A YEAR LATER Diego and I move into an airy, fourth-floor apartment in the tree-lined neighbourhood of Belgrano. Our balcony looks out on the twisted branches of beautiful weeping trees, sprayed with bright yellow flowers, that drip light sap on you when you pass under them. The avenue below is one of the original roads of the stately old area. It's wide and cobbled, and lined with impressive homes and a couple of embassies, quite a different story from our previous haunts, and with very different neighbours, too.

I feel tired in the days after the move. Exhausted, but strangely content. I lost track of time with all the tasks of relocating but now I do some calculating. *Really, can it be?* I go into the bathroom and tidy my hair in the mirror. I look at my face. Pale. Some fine lines mark it now, but I don't mind. I silently ask the mirror, *is this a mother's face*? My heart is thumping.

I grab my keys and walk to the chemist, taking long steps, not wanting to run, but wanting to know. Packet in hand, I walk back, trying to keep hope afloat but not airborne. In the bathroom again, I sit, door closed, with the plastic stick in hand. I pee on it and then I wait. The very seconds are expanding in my head.

Two little pink lines form slowly, and then get brighter.

My world spins. I sit staring at the lines, thinking about just how much my life, our life, is going to change. I pace the house. Diego won't arrive home for hours. I make myself a cup of tea, with honey.

I reach for the phone. 'Hi love, guess what?' I say, voice high with emotion.

'What?'

'Guess?'

'I don't know. Is everything okay?' he says, sounding perplexed by my odd tone.

'You're going to be a dad.'

Silence and then a choking sound.

Oh shit.

'Jessy, wow, are you sure? Already? I'm eating pizza. Wow.' His voice cracks and fades out.

'Are you happy?' I ask, scared.

'Of course, *mi amor*, it's wonderful. I'm just shocked. Let's talk when I get home.'

Doubts swarm in. Does he really want this? Maybe he's not ready. I calm myself. Poor guy was eating pizza, not expecting a call like that.

I pace again, lost in the surreal world of new beginnings. I can't believe a real, tiny person has started growing inside me. One day, someone will call me mummy and want a hug after falling over and scraping their knee.

Diego walks in the door that night with a huge bunch of carnations, white, bright pink, soft yellow and rich blood red. He's smiling, eyes shining, arms out. Flowers and arms crush around me, petals and a pure sweet scent push into my wet face. When I pull back I see his face moist with tears. He can't speak. We stand there looking at each other, imagining.

We decide to wait three months before telling anyone, just in case. I wander around with a sensation of soft fluttering wings in my belly, tiny beats of hope and one real beating heart. Then sometimes, the buzzing worry in my head, like a million flies, drowns out the fluttering. I can't believe I've been this lucky. I ruminate on the worst things that could happen. If I think them, then I will be prepared for the pain.

It doesn't come. The little life inside keeps growing.

I'm grateful to the universe.

At the end of three months Diego and I sit down in front of the computer one night, with Skype open. We're going to call our parents.

'I'm nervous,' I say.

'Me too. But they're going to be so happy.'

'I know. Yours or mine?' I ask.

'Can we tell mine? I can't wait,' says Diego.

'Okay.' I feel relieved.

The sounds of Skype opening ring in our ears. I see the top of his mother's head.

'Mum, sit back, we can't see you.'

'Oh, okay.' She leans back. Diego's father comes into view. They squash in together, filling the screen.

'We have something to tell you.' I see recognition in their faces even before Diego says anything more. 'You are going to be grandparents!'

'Oh my god,' they say, their words melding together.

His mother cries and shakes. His father sits back, hard. I can see the blue of his eyes shine.

We all cry for some minutes and then we tell them we have to ring my parents. I hear his mother say again, 'I'm so happy,' as the line cuts.

My mind lights up with a thought: this child is going to be so loved.

'Your turn,' says Diego.

I ring Mum first.

'You're going to be a grandmother.'

'That's wonderful, darling,' she says. There's a pause. 'Can we think up another name for me, though? What's grandmother in Spanish?'

'*Abuela*,' I say.

'Oh,' she says, drawing out the sound.

I know that tone. 'You think of a name, then. There's plenty of time yet,' I say.

'Oh, yes dear, I will. I'm very happy for you both. It's fantastic news.'

I can't help smiling to myself. I know she's going to go away and look up exotic-sounding alternatives to grandmother.

The final call.

'Hey Dad, I've got amazing news; we're having a baby. You're going to be a granddad,' I say to him, when he finally works out how to turn the Skype video on.

'You're *preg*nant!' (He always emphasises the first syllable. It sounds as if he's describing an illness or a crime.) 'Oh, that's great.' And then, unable to filter out the inappropriate remark, even in important moments, he adds, 'I don't understand why people have kids; it's a real pain in the arse.'

'Dad, God, you had four of us.' I'm shocked, but not surprised.

Diego is hovering behind me. He's noticed the change in tone. He puts his hand on my shoulder.

'I didn't mean to,' my father says briskly.

I hear, *I didn't want to.* My heart drops off a ledge.

'No, no, it's great news,' he adds, in a rush. I sense he's realised he said the wrong thing. 'You've always wanted this. I'm very happy for you.'

After we log off, Diego asks, 'Is everything okay?'

'It's just Dad, he sometimes says the wrong things. I don't think he realises it hurts.'

'What did he say?'

'That he never really wanted kids.'

'What?'

'I know.'

'Sorry, Jess,' he says, hugging me.

I refuse to be unhappy and I know my father cares. And he is trying. Sometimes you must weave one thread at a time. I refuse to give up.

But now I'm even surer I want to have my child in Argentina.

In the final months of my pregnancy I start to dream in Spanish. It's as if my unconscious world is finally catching up with my conscious one. I ask myself, does this mean I truly feel at home here? The answer is: yes, for now.

Something about my state of being an almost-mother makes my friends and family ask more intently a series of questions. What's life really like for you? What are the people like? Do you plan on bringing up your little boy there?

One morning when I'm waddle-walking down our beautiful street, I'm suddenly taken over by a series of thoughts, a way of describing how I feel about my new country. She comes to me as a grain of an idea: a personification of Argentina and the people I know from the streets of Buenos Aires—the ones I walk beside every day. Looking both ways I cross the cobbled street. Excitement quickens my steps as words flash and ideas start to form into coherent threads.

What shall I call her?

'Argy,' I say out loud, with a smile; it's not very exotic, but it will do for now. I decide she is a she because, in Spanish, Argentina is feminine, and in any case countries and cities have always been she's to me.

In the lift on the way up to our flat I picture Argy as a not-quite-new friend who I'm trying to understand so I can make sense of our budding friendship and what the future holds for us. I drag my bulging body through the front door and collapse on the sofa. I close my eyes and try to imagine her as a real live person.

Argy is beautiful and affectionate. Also complicated. She loves to talk, and to argue. She lives for socializing, for the now, for the sharing of an *asado* with kin or a night out on the town with friends. The core of Argy's existence is family and she loves her children passionately. I see a vivid glimpse of her, at a wedding or party, with a horde of kids pulling at her skirt and laughing up at her.

Her moods fluctuate daily and I can never quite tell what to expect when I open the door to her. Sometimes she is light and joyful, at other times her spirit dives into a dark place and I feel myself trying to reach in and pull her out. She dresses carefully, to impress, to seduce. I know she spends a great deal of time stressing over her appearance and she can be self-delusional, believing the nips and tucks she has made won't be obvious to others.

She appears to be suffering from a pretty serious identity crisis. She doesn't know whether she's European like her great-grandfather, South American like her distant cousins, or Argentine. The truth is, she's incomparable and should be proud of that. She frustrates me sometimes with her attitudes towards people from different cultures and to her South American cousins and neighbours. At home, she and her siblings (from the provinces) often get caught up in passionate disputes that keep past emotional wounds raw. She loves and she fights in equal doses.

After a very brief period when she was the golden child, the rest of her life has been marked by insecurity, violence and unfulfilled promise. I think this causes her to keep searching desperately for a good father or mother figure that will set sensible rules and enforce them fairly. She wants to feel contained and safe but she chooses badly by putting her hopes in charismatic authoritarian figures that give her just enough of what she thinks she needs (at least in the beginning), before they lie to her and leave her disappointed and disillusioned again. Because of this past, and the grind of everyday hassles, she has lost her trust in the world and in anyone who's not bound to her by strong ties. Even though she knows that rules are necessary and that everyone should take responsibility for what they do and say, she doesn't think those rules actually apply to her—personally. She's become accustomed to avoiding them to get what she thinks she wants.

As her friend, my natural trustfulness has been challenged. Even though she's mostly loyal with her feelings, she's sometimes not faithful with her actions. But then, every few weeks she does something that shows me her true heart. I know if I fell sick she would be the first person to bring me chicken soup and give me a long lingering hug.

Argy can be disorganised and obsessive but I understand why she holds onto her old rituals (an *asado* for every social event, the same holiday every year and her grandmother's recipes). They make her feel everything is okay. They calm the ever-present anxiety that swirls around her, giving her a sense of some control in a place that can make you feel crazy. These rituals of Argentine life are vital to her; they fuel her strong sense of belonging and keep the bonds tight between her and loved ones.

She has developed a tough skin but inside she is sensitive, and I know my characterisation of her may hurt. I don't expect her to be perfect—no one is—but I do sometimes wish she would experiment with new things, tastes and ways of being. I sense she is stuck, stuck in the way I was before I jumped on the plane and flew.

She intrigues me—so full of contradictions and hidden places to explore. I don't think I will ever really know her and it maddens me that just when I start to get a feeling for who she is, she completely surprises me (about half the time in a good way).

There are times when I want to run from her but there's something in her, and inside me, that sustains our friendship. I'm caught by her. She's infuriating but she makes me feel so alive. I hope we can be friends for life, though nothing is certain with us. One day I might want to return to my simpler easier friends, even though I know it won't always be as much fun, and I might struggle to survive without so many daily hugs and kisses.

I'm not sure whether I can help Argy. I don't know the answers to her problems. Maybe she needs better figures to guide her, or perhaps she just needs to take the reins of her life despite having complicated parents and a distressing life story. I do know she holds on too hard to pain and anger generated in her past, and isn't always honest with herself about who she really is and where she's living. I hope one day soon she finds a way to move forward. Her children need her to.

Despite the insanity-producing winds that gust around her, I'm grateful to her for helping me find home. It was with her that I finally felt home.

I love her, but it's never going to be an easy love.

And maybe that's okay.

Twenty days before his due date, at 3.00 in the morning, the baby makes a wild movement that squashes the breath out of me. Then, suddenly, an incredible burst of liquid soaks my old granddaddy-style pyjamas and the bed.

Ah, he's coming.

I wade to the phone, leaving a trail of ammonia-smelling water behind me. Diego has gone out with friends to celebrate his last days before fatherhood. I try his phone. It rings and rings and then goes to voice mail. I try again: voice mail. I leave a message. 'Get home now, he's coming. Please ring me.' I leave increasingly desperate messages. The echo of *please leave a message* in Spanish sounds in my head.

Some thirty minutes later, he calls.

'Jessy.' He sounds way too calm. 'Sorry, *mi amor*, I didn't hear my phone. What happened?'

'My waters broke. He's coming. Come home NOW,' I blurt out, nerves prickling.

'Are you sure?' he asks.

'Yes, I'm very sure. Get back here.'

'Okay, okay I'm coming.'

When he bursts in the door he takes one look at me, crouched on the floor, and steps back as if pushed by an invisible force. He rights himself, runs over and kisses me hard on the forehead; his arm presses across my shoulders.

'Sorry I wasn't here. What can I do?'

'Get the bag. I think we have to go.'

As soon as we arrive at the hospital I'm hooked up to a drip, and a monitor is strapped to my belly. I feel like a fish in a net. Racked by contractions, I refuse the suggestion to lie down; instead I position myself on all fours on the bed, with two pillows under my arms.

A few hours later the door opens and an exhausted-looking woman is wheeled into the room.

I look over at Diego.

'We have to share the room,' he says.

I try to say okay, but my voice is sucked away by a contraction.

The woman's husband strides in, looking tired but elated. He squints into the morning light coming in the window. I can see he is Orthodox Jewish. Long curls of hair hang by his ears, wool fringes from his waist. He tells Diego they just had a boy. Diego pats him hard on the back. He almost keels over. I see his hands tighten on his Tanakh and then he leaves the room, trying not to look at me.

I'm in too much pain to feel embarrassed about being perched on my bed, bare bottom peeping through the light blue hospital gown. It's his wife I feel for; she has to listen to my loud moaning when she clearly needs to rest. I see her form curled under white sheets, her hair is spread out on the pillow. She gazes into space, her face set in an expression of supreme calmness. I wonder where the baby is.

My pain quickly becomes all-consuming. I fold in on myself and vanish into my own world, coming out only for seconds between the spasms of clamping muscles. I remember nothing from pre-natal classes. Measured breathing is replaced by long guttural groans. Between them I'm vaguely aware of Diego alternating between standing, looking lost, near the door and pacing the room, while running his hand through his hair. He seems scared of me, for a second I wonder why.

Before long he is happily distracted by a series of tasks. As it is a Saturday my roommate's husband and family are unable to do anything. Diego valiantly moves bags, switches on lights, elevates her bed. Between contractions, I watch him being husband for two. He finds a rhythm in the chores and relief shows on his face. Then his mother turns up in the early hours and her presence calms him.

After seven hours of feeling horribly and vividly each and every violent contraction, my resolve to have a 'natural' birth begins to wither under the constant pressure from everyone to get an epidural. They don't want me to suffer, and I'm sure they would also like a reprieve from the incessant moaning.

'They say you will feel better,' says Diego gently.

'It stops all the pain,' my roommate weighs in.

I look over at her and she nods firmly.

I give in.

I'm wheeled away to a sterile room. As soon as the liquid seeps into my spine, a warm relief washes over me—no more sharp stabs and powerful aches. No more anything. I start to feel detached from the whole experience. I have no control. The feeling is made worse when my paralysed legs are shoved like limp and heavy lumps of clay into the leather straps. I can't fight it. The bed under me is a flat, cold, metal contraption. Anger swells in me. I can't even sit semi-upright. *This isn't happening the way I want. I'm strapped down, tubes and monitors everywhere. No one is talking to me... this is horrible.*

Just before I start to cry, I'm distracted by the stunning sight of Diego. He's standing in the doorway—half in the room, half out. He looks as if he wants to run away. He's dressed in green hospital scrubs, his bare chest framed by the long V of the shirt. I can see his *pounamu* necklace hanging over his breastbone. He's hyper with nerves, his face alive with fear.

God he's so handsome, I think. I can't stop staring at him. He looks as if he's in pain. I start laughing and crying. He looks over, and his jaw drops. I laugh more, and then shake it away. I reach out a hand. He sees it and grasps it tight.

'It's okay,' I say.

He nods.

At 10.40 on a bright Buenos Aires Saturday morning, a brand new person makes his way into the world.

'Is that it?' I say loudly, totally surprised. Did I miss out on something by not pushing through the pain to get to the other side? Perhaps I miss feeling grateful for the relief, the gift at the end of the agony.

As the rapid succession of odd thoughts subsides, our little boy finally comes into sight. He's lit by delivery room floodlights, held up by his wee armpits: a tiny purple creature with a squashed in nose, large wrinkled hands and a cone head. Is that what they're supposed to look like? I think, a little frightened and perplexed by the sight of this strange wriggling thing.

Diego's eyes widen and darken. 'Is he okay?' he asks one of the neonatal doctors, a touch panicked.

'Yes, he's perfect, no worries,' the doctor returns. Then they whip him away. They don't even let me hold him—it was on my carefully written birth plan. I'm lost. I want to call out, *please bring him back to me.*

Back in my shared room, Tomás is placed gently in my arms—looking a lot more like a human baby now. His face is screwed up in a way that suggests he wants to open his eyes but is too exhausted from his journey. When I look down at him, overwhelming feelings of love, fear, pride and connection merge and rise up. I look over at Diego and see the same expression mirrored there.

'I can't believe we made a whole human being,' I say.

As if to make it real, he reaches down and cups Tomi's head in his oversized hand. Soft tears run in rivulets down our faces. It's so surreal. This little baby is a part of me, and part of his father. I'm his mother—finally, a mother.

Diego's sister arrives from being on call all night in another hospital. She helps me try to feed Tomi but he's too tired to get the hang of it yet.

Baby Tomás sleeps soundly, snug on my chest, for most of the day. His perfect little ear is placed between my heart and his food source, his tiny frog-legs are curled up under him. His wrinkly fingers never release their firm grasp of my finger; it's as if he never wants to let go. The following morning his intense, musky, milky baby smell envelops me, and I feel touched by something inexplicable—bliss, perhaps.

Diego has spent the night jammed uncomfortably into an armchair next to us. Now he snuffles, prises his eyes open, looks over and smiles.

'*Los amo, los amo tanto,*' he says, as his eyes tear up.

'*Te amamos también,*' I say. We love you, too.

He stretches out his legs and arms, like a cat awakening from a long nap, and then he comes over. He kisses us both and then gently runs his finger over the soft curves of our baby's sleeping face, his own face an expression of happy surprise. He hops up onto the thin bed, squishing in close.

A warm wave of happiness washes over me. The edges of the ghost hole shudder and start to close in on the remaining void. I know now the edges are semi-permeable; I just have to allow the love to seep in, and out.

The next day, expatriate friends visit with gifts and tiny home-baked chocolate cupcakes. There is a whirl of love around me. I feel at the edge of tears, of happiness, of exhaustion. The room is filled with expectation of something new, a new life.

Later, when the rush of visits has subsided, I look at my saggy, still pregnant-looking belly. I prod at it. Then I'm struck by the poetic nature of pregnancy. You spend nine months literally and emotionally gazing at your navel, and then there's a snap and your eyes find another resting place. Once your child is born you are unable to stop staring at this incredible little person, who makes snuffling sounds and mews like a kitten. It's an instant cure for excessive self-ponderings, a gift that causes you to look around and focus on another, very vulnerable, human being. You have to grow up instantly. You have to take the reins.

We take Tomi home.

I send a brief email to my parents with some photos attached. There is one photo that moves me so profoundly that my body caves in around an indescribable and sublime ache. In this photo he's wrapped in a light blue woollen cardigan and pressed tight into my chest. My shoulders are curved around him, instinctively protective; my lips are gently touching his light wisps of hair. There is no need to send many words.

Dad writes back: *Congratulations. He's a very lucky boy.*

Mum writes: *He's gorgeous, just like you were. My little Biba; you were so curious. You had these big wide-open eyes that looked around, fascinated by the world. I fell in love the instant I saw you. I can see in the photo you are feeling the same. Isn't it wonderful?*

Tomi spends one solo night in his bassinet, and then I make him a comfy, secure nest inside the curved breastfeeding cushion in the middle of our bed. Seeing him, cocooned in a blanket, just his head peeping out, reminds me…

Daniel,

I had a baby. We named him Tomás Ariki. I wanted him to have something precious from home, so I gave him a strong Māori name as his middle name. It means chief. I love the way it sounds, like a call from a special place that's not quite earthly.

You will be pleased: I finally made a nest. I brought some twigs from other places and carried them here, and then I added new ones to make a home. I wove them into something strong around me.

Did you ever watch a bird make a nest? They look intensely focused, alive, and so contentedly busy when they flit about searching for sticks and feathers and coloured bits of stuff to weave in. They are patient in their building. That's how I feel now.

I think about you still. I have a warm hug in me that I want to give you. Maybe one day, hopefully many years from now, I will.
Que duermas bien. *Sleep well. Jessica.*

A week after coming home from the hospital, I get a buzz from the front door of the apartment building. I pick up the intercom. '*Hola, ¿quién es?*' I ask.

'Jessy, it's me, Paco.'

I'm delighted and a little shell-shocked. Why doesn't he ever ring before he drops round? I buzz him in. I have four floors of time to prepare for an unexpected visitor, so I sprint to the bathroom to attempt some damage control. Nothing can be done about the knotted nests of hair forming at the back of my head, so I pull my hair up into a pony-tail. I wash my face. I stare at the dark circles under my eyes. Then I remember that new mums are supposed to look like this. I'm happy that at least the baby is sleeping, the musty smelling milk-stained top has been changed and the worst of the living-room chaos has been cleared away.

The elevator clicks to a stop. I open the door. He looks bashful. I see he's brought a gift with him. He hugs me with one arm as the other one awkwardly holds the base of a bougainvillea plant. It's covered with barely open buds.

'Here, this is for you,' he says as he hands it to me. 'I know it's not a normal gift for a baby. It's for you really,' he adds.

'*Gracias*, the flowers are beautiful,' I say.

While I'm admiring them a memory comes floating back. Its buds are exactly the same vermillion red as the ones that were climbing above us in the small café in Ecuador, some five years before, when Paco told me that he didn't want to be with me. It was that flash of colour that marked in my mind a very sad day and a painful change in direction.

Paco catches my whimsical expression. 'What? Don't you like it?' he asks, the worry showing.

'No… no, I love it, bougainvilleas are my favourite flowers,' I say, smiling. I keep the memory to myself. He has absolutely no idea what the flowers mean to me.

He sits heavily on the couch and then hooks his arm around one knee. I smile at him sitting there, so at home. He smiles back.

'How's Pepe? I miss him.'

'He's great, same as always. You have to come visit with Tomi.'

'I will, soon, when I get used to all this mummy business.'

'I still can't believe you have a baby,' he says.

'Me neither.'

We talk for a long time. When Tomi wakes, I bring him out and then pass him over to Paco to hold. He cradles him comically, like you would a large egg. He looks petrified but when I offer to take the squirming bundle back, he says, 'Give me a minute more.'

When Paco leaves, I sit, baby in arms, looking at the flowering plant. I feel a smile forming. The kind of smile I love, one that weaves its way right through the body, settling in every cell. Life is strange, and it is mystical too, if we let it be. Here they are again, the very same flowers, marking another huge and incredible life change.

I drift, my mind an explosion of memories. A thread unravels and I take a ride down the long memory rope of how I got here, to this physical and emotional place. As I journey along it I find myself stopping briefly at knotted points along the way. If I had taken the other path then, where would I be? What if I hadn't grabbed Paco's hand and travelled with him, or impulsively, deliriously, flown back to South America, leaving everything behind? What if I had returned to Australia instead of grabbing hope's tail and travelling to Argentina? What if I hadn't had a sweet revelation after seeing the crying baby girl in the café? What if I hadn't allowed my heart to open and let Diego in?

Where would I be?

Each pause lasts mere milliseconds as I continue to navigate the taken path. At the end of it all, I am where I am, and that's just fine. The heavy grief coat, the numbness, the being ripped apart and the piecing back together were all needed to arrive here, at this moment. It was painful, but I'm thankful for all of it.

I feel a stirring in my arms. Suddenly I become acutely aware that my tiny baby's warm skin is gently touching the etched hummingbird— whose essence, while still hovering, is content now to bear witness to a different kind of adventure.

A deft kick connects with my rib as he wakes from another mini-*siesta*. His milky blue eyes unscrew, open wider, and then he looks right at me. I know his sight is blurry, but I feel as if he is seeing me. It's as if he's saying, *who are you?*

'Hi there, I'm Jessica, your mum,' I say to him.

He blinks and keeps staring.

Two tiny hands grab at the air. I give him my finger again and he grasps it tightly with one pruned up hand. I am fascinated by his surprisingly long, almost transparent fingernails. His lips purse, goldfish-like, and then he jams one whole hand deep into his mouth.

Hungry again.

Acknowledgements

Thank you to all my friends and family, who have supported me in so many ways throughout this journey. A special thanks to those of you who read the first (rambling, poorly written, massively long) draft and gave sensitive assessments and a lot of encouragement. Many thanks to all the self-published authors out there who paved the way and gave me the strength to believe my story was worth telling and I could do it on my terms. Thank you to my two wonderful editors (and hand-holders) Claire Scobie and Helen Coyle, who helped me find my voice, while being both firm and encouraging. I am eternally grateful to Fern Petrie, the incredible Kiwi artist who created the stunning cover art for me. *Gracias* Osvaldo Plaza Torrado for your graphic design skills and patience! Thanks Jo Bayliss for your lovely author photo and 'Kiwi girls in Buenos Aires' chat sessions. Thank you to all the people who gave me the go-ahead to tell parts of their journey within this story. And I'm extremely grateful to my family who allowed me to share this despite it bringing up some difficult memories for everyone. I'm so happy the threads that connect us are stronger now than they have even been. Thank you to my wonderful husband, who put up with more than three years of my doubts and fears and highs and lows. And thank you to my precious little boy who was patient with Mummy when she 'lost' herself in the words. Finally, thank you to the universe that provides me, time and time again, with incredible serendipitous moments that keep me brave.

www.ingramcontent.com/pod-product-compliance
Lightning Source LLC
Chambersburg PA
CBHW070001180726
48002CB00019B/1792